THE STANDARDS-BASED ADMINISTRATIVE INTERNSHIP

Putting the ISLLC Standards into Practice

Donald G. Hackmann
Donna M. Schmitt-Oliver
Jaclynn C. Tracy

A SCARECROWEDUCATION BOOK

The Scarecrow Press, Inc.
Lanham, Maryland, and London
2002

A SCARECROWEDUCATION BOOK

Published in the United States of America
by Scarecrow Press, Inc.
A Member of the Rowman & Littlefield Publishing Group
4720 Boston Way, Lanham, Maryland 20706
www.scarecrowpress.com

4 Pleydell Gardens, Folkestone
Kent CT20 2DN, England

British Library Cataloguing in Publication Information Available

Library of Congress Cataloging-in-Publication Data

Hackmann, Donald G., 1955–
   The standards-based administrative internship : putting the ISLLC
standards into practice/Donald G. Hackmann, Donna M. Schmitt-Oliver, Jaclynn
C. Tracy.   p. cm.
"A ScarecrowEducation book."
Includes bibliographical references and index.
ISBN 0-8108-4426-5 (hardback : alk. paper)—ISBN 0-8108-4235-1 (pbk. : alk.
paper)
   1. School administrators—Training of—United States. 2. School
administrators—United States—Standards. 3. School management and
organizaion—Study and teaching (Internship)—United States. 4. Interns
(Education)—United States. 5. Internship programs—United States. 6.
Educational leadership—United States. I. Schmitt-Oliver, Donna M., 1942– II.
Tracy, Jaclynn C. III. Title.
   LB1738.5 .H33 2002
371.2'0071'5—dc21   2002005855

♾™ The paper used in this publication meets the minimum requirements of
American National Standard for Information Sciences—Permanence of Paper
for Printed Library Materials, ANSI/NISO Z39.48-1992.
Manufactured in the United States of America.

This book is dedicated to our spouses:
Tamara Hackmann, Gordon Oliver, and Steven Tracy.

CONTENTS

INTRODUCTION

Providing guidance to individuals who are involved in the clinical preparation of aspiring principals and superintendents—be they administrative interns, mentor administrators, or university supervisors—is essential. Over the past few decades, the educational reform movement has reinforced the central purpose of preservice training in effectively preparing aspiring administrators to be instructional leaders and change agents. One cannot fully learn effective leadership skills by sitting in a university classroom, no matter how engaging the course activities. As an applied field, educational administration must be learned through experiencing its myriad tasks and challenges. Clinical experiences, also called field experiences or internships, are vital to establishing connections between theory learned in the classroom and real-world experiences in the schools.

Internship activities must prepare aspiring administrators to lead schools of the future. The responsibility of designing these activities is too significant to be taken lightly; a poorly designed internship can be more harmful than helpful for someone who is striving to learn exemplary leadership skills. In this text, the authors argue for a *high-quality experience*, with carefully structured clinical activities that are authentic, engaging, and integrated throughout the student's entire preparation program. *Standards for School Leaders,* developed by the Interstate School Leaders Licensure Consortium (ISLLC) (Council of Chief State School Officers, 1996), provide a research-based framework that is invaluable in formulating a high-quality clinical experience.

This book is primarily designed to assist aspiring administrators and their university supervisors with structuring field-based learning experiences around the ISLLC framework. Mentor administrators may be unfamiliar with these standards because many completed their administrative training before the creation of the six standards and the 182 accompanying knowledge, dispositions, and performance indicators. This book can also be an excellent tool in introducing and explaining the ISLLC standards to mentors who have not been exposed to them. It will help mentors to understand their vital roles in ensuring a high-quality learning experience.

Chapter 1 is dedicated to planning an effective internship experience. Included in this chapter is a brief introduction to the six ISLLC standards, an explanation of the benefits of the clinical component for all parties, and a discussion of the roles and responsibilities of each partner—the university supervisor, administrative mentor(s), and administrative intern. Chapters 2 through 7 provide a more detailed description of the more significant administrative responsibilities inherent in each standard. Each chapter ends with suggested discussion topics, questions, and internship activities that are related to each standard. These are intended to help structure the clinical experience. In addition, suggested readings and Web sites are listed at the conclusion of each standard as additional resources. Appendix A consists of a complete listing of the ISLLC standards and accompanying knowledge, dispositions, and performances related to each standard. To assist the aspiring administrator in designing a high-quality internship experience, Appendix B includes an ISLLC self-assessment. Finally, Appendix C contains a sampling of forms that can be used to structure the field experiences.

❶

PLANNING AN EFFECTIVE INTERNSHIP EXPERIENCE

The educational reform movement that began with the release of *A Nation at Risk* (National Commission on Excellence in Education, 1983) has now been sustained for two decades. One significant outcome of this movement has been the increased attention on the essential role of school leaders in ensuring school accountability, raising academic standards, and promoting student success. Simply functioning as managers and maintaining the organizational status quo is no longer accepted practice, as school principals and superintendents are called upon to be leaders of their organizations, capable of establishing shared visions and becoming change agents (National Staff Development Council [NSDC], 2000). "The guidance and direction of instructional improvement" (Elmore, 2000, p. 13) has emerged as the educational leader's essential role. With instructional leadership as the central focus, principals and superintendents must guide their faculties through the process of restructuring schools that effectively ensure success for every student. Excellent schools will not happen without exemplary leadership.

As the school reform movement gained momentum, it prompted policymakers, professors, and practitioners to closely examine the relevance and efficacy of the nation's administrator preparation programs (Griffiths, Stout, & Forsyth, 1988a). In 1989 the National Policy Board for Educational Administration (NPBEA) decried the decline in the quality of administrator preparation programs over the past few decades, with programs increasingly characterized more by their weaknesses than their strengths. Instead of training administrator candidates simply to manage school organizations, programs must arm them with the knowledge and skills to effectively lead organizations, manage dilemmas, and resolve problems (Cuban, 1996). The NPBEA report offered nine recommendations for improving program quality, including strengthening curriculum content to keep teaching and learning at the forefront of school improvement and enhancing clinical activities for administrator candidates.

Many preparation programs have been criticized for being excessively steeped in theory, while lacking in practical applications for the practitioner. If aspiring educational leaders are to be prepared to fully confront the challenges of guiding tomorrow's schools, it is imperative that programs must deliver learning opportunities that integrate classroom theory with real-world applications (Clark & Clark, 1996; Griffiths, Stout, & Forsyth, 1988b; NPBEA, 1989). The university classroom can provide a wealth of learning activities that promote future administrators' acquisition of leadership skills through such activities as discussions, reflective analysis, problem-based learning, and case studies. These activities, however, are at best only simulations of real schools. Leadership theories and skills presented in the classroom have enriched meaning and relevance when students can practice their skills in real schools, learning leadership as it actually is practiced (Leithwood, Jantzi, Coffin, & Wilson, 1996).

With this aim in mind, in 1993 the NPBEA developed a knowledge and skill base for the principalship, which was intended to overcome "the inadequacies of traditional preparation programs, including weak theory/practice connections" (p. xiii). This report categorized these essential functions into 21 domains, called "a typology or convenient classification system" (NPBEA, 1993, p. xiii). Over the next few years, these domains served as a template for many educational administration faculties as they restructured and strengthened their programs for preparing future principals.

Cognizant of the reform movement embracing national standards in other educational arenas, in 1994 the Council of Chief State School Officers (CCSSO) created the Interstate School Leaders Licensure Consortium (ISLLC), whose charge was to fill this void in the area of educational leadership. In contrast to the NPBEA task force, which only focused on the principalship, the ISLLC team created a set of six research-based standards (see Figure 1.1) that were intended to encompass nearly all formal leadership positions at both the building and school district levels. Acknowledging the continually evolving roles of school leaders, the standards, which were announced in 1996, were consciously designed to focus "on matters of learning and teaching and the creation of powerful learning environments" (ISLLC, 1996, p. 8). Although these standards are deliberately broad, numerous indicators clarify the classifications of knowledge, dispositions, and performances. The complete listing, including the six standards and 182 accompanying indicators, is included in Appendix A.

At present, at least 35 states have adopted the ISLLC standards, either in their original form or with minor modifications. In addition, the National Council for Accreditation of Teacher Education (NCATE) also is utilizing a revised set of ISLLC guidelines for all educational administration programs that currently maintain or are seeking NCATE accreditation (NPBEA, 2001). Consequently, educational administration faculties throughout the nation once again are in the process of restructuring their principal and superintendent licensure programs to meet NCATE requirements, ISLLC standards, and/or state mandates based on ISLLC. By putting these standards into effect, it is hoped that the quality of administrator preparation programs will be improved and, in the process, the educational administration profession ultimately upgraded (ISLLC, 1996).

Standard 1
A school administrator is an educational leader who promotes the success of all students by facilitating the development, articulation, implementation, and stewardship of a vision of learning that is shared and supported by the school community.

Standard 2
A school administrator is an educational leader who promotes the success of all students by advocating, nurturing, and sustaining a school culture and instructional program conducive to student learning and staff professional growth.

Standard 3
A school administrator is an educational leader who promotes the success of all students by ensuring management of the organization, operations, and resources for a safe, efficient, and effective learning environment.

Standard 4
A school administrator is an educational leader who promotes the success of all students by collaborating with families and community members, responding to diverse community interests and needs, and mobilizing community resources.

Standard 5
A school administrator is an educational leader who promotes the success of all students by acting with integrity, fairness, and in an ethical manner.

Standard 6
A school administrator is an educational leader who promotes the success of all students by understanding, responding to, and influencing the larger political, social, economic, legal, and cultural context.

Figure 1.1   ISLLC Standards for School Leaders. *Source:* **Interstate School Leaders Licensure Consortium. (1996).** *Standards for school leaders.* **Washington, DC: Council of Chief State School Officers.**

THE ROLE OF CLINICAL EXPERIENCES IN LEADER PREPARATION

Clinical experiences historically have been an integral component of many professional preparation programs, most notably in the fields of medicine and law. Many national organizations dedicated to educational administration, including the National Commission on Excellence in Educational Administration (Griffiths et al., 1988a) and the NPBEA (1989), advocate that internships also are essential for administrator preparation programs. Milstein and Krueger (1997) note that internships "are unique, important, and irreplaceable aspects" (p. 107) of administrator training, to ensure that aspiring leaders have ample opportunities to apply skills learned in the classroom and to practice their craft within the local school context.

The University Council for Educational Administration (UCEA), the most prestigious organization for institutions with educational administration programs, requires that UCEA-member preparation programs include "concentrated periods of full-time study and supervised clinical practice" (UCEA, 2001). The NCATE's draft revision of ISLLC considers the clinical component so critical to administrator preparation that they have created a seventh standard wholly devoted to the internship, which states:

> Candidates who complete the program are educational leaders who promote the success of all students through substantial, sustained, standards-based experiences in real settings that are planned and guided cooperatively by university and school district personnel for graduate credit. (NPBEA, 2001)

Participating in these sustained, extended placements allows the intern an opportunity to engage in clinical activities throughout the academic year, see tasks through to completion, and gain a more systemic understanding of the organization (Hackmann, Russell, & Elliott, 1999).

Unfortunately, even though clinical experiences are highly valued as powerful learning opportunities by aspiring leaders (Krueger & Milstein, 1995), they have not been universally required in all preparation programs. For example, approximately one third of elementary principals report that they did not participate in internships during their preservice training (Doud & Keller, 1998). Furthermore, many

programs have implemented "notoriously weak" clinical requirements (Milstein, Bobroff, & Restine, 1991; Murphy, 1992), possibly
because approximately 95% of educational administration students
are enrolled on a part-time basis while retaining full-time employment (Griffiths et al., 1988b). Clinical experiences frequently are un-
coordinated and unplanned (Milstein, 1990), with exercises designed
around the working student's schedule—before school, after school,
and during teacher preparation periods.

If clinical activities are not structured properly, and interns and
mentors are not given appropriate training about their responsibilities, the consequence is unconnected and low-level activities, consisting primarily of shadowing administrators and observing meetings,
rather than being engaged in authentic, hands-on experiences (Hackmann et al., 1999). School leaders who agree to serve as mentors add
yet one more task to an ever-increasing list of responsibilities. The internship, although it admittedly provides a service to both the intern
and the university, should not be overly time-consuming for the mentor administrator. Sadly, a poorly structured internship—one that
does not clearly outline expectations for either the mentor or the intern—can be more of a hindrance than a benefit to both parties.

BENEFITS OF INTERNSHIPS

When field experiences are carefully conceptualized and well
structured, they provide numerous benefits for all parties involved:
the intern, the mentor, the school district, and the university (Milstein et al., 1991). These positive features for each party are listed
in the following paragraphs.

Benefits for the Intern

With the increased emphasis on school accountability, novice
school leaders no longer have the luxury of a honeymoon period to

acclimate to their new positions, as a form of on-the-job training. Rather, new administrators must be fully prepared to immediately assume their roles as change agents and instructional leaders. Therefore, the internship should help the student deepen her or his understanding of content and skills learned in the graduate coursework, through engaging in authentic leadership experiences while under the close supervision of the mentor and university field coordinator. By being immersed in the mentor's work setting, interns work alongside exemplary role models who can help them master skills that they can learn only within the unique educational setting. Furthermore, students who have completed high-quality internships will be better-prepared and more attractive candidates for school districts seeking to fill administrative vacancies.

Although the primary advantage is hands-on, practical experience, interns also accrue other benefits that are rarely mentioned in the literature. For example, even though they are enrolled in a preparation program, some students are not certain that they truly want to become administrators. Some students initially may lack confidence in their leadership skills or may be concerned about their ability to manage the stressors present in any administrative post. Clinical activities give students an opportunity to assimilate into the principalship or superintendency—experiencing both the joys and heartaches—without having to vacate their current positions. At the conclusion of their internships, they may leave with a new level of confidence and eagerness to seek an administrative post, or they may decide that they are not yet ready for school- or district-level leadership responsibilities.

When internship settings are carefully selected with diversity in mind, they can expose the intern to a wealth of new experiences. For example, individuals who only have worked in elementary schools should devote some clinical hours to the middle-level or secondary schools. A student whose only professional work experience has been with rural, primarily Caucasian students could be placed in an urban or suburban setting with high minority enrollments. An aspiring superintendent may want to spend part of the internship working in the state department of education to gain a better understanding of state policy and procedures, in addition to establishing professional connections with state officials. Regardless of one's academic or employment background, the internship should be viewed as an opportunity to broaden the intern's thinking, while exposing him or her to new settings.

Establishing a close relationship with a mentor offers yet another benefit: a reference who has direct knowledge of the intern's leadership skills and talents. When students assume their first administrative appointment, the mentor—who now is a colleague—can be consulted for advice, support, and encouragement during the initial years of the administrative career. The mentor also can help the intern establish a network that includes school leaders from neighboring districts and around the region.

Benefits for the Mentor

Certainly, mentors will be likely to feel immense personal satisfaction in seeing their charges grow into competent professionals. The benefits to mentors, however, should expand beyond the intangible altruistic sense of giving back to one's profession and furthering a colleague's career. Mentoring also can be a professional development activity for the veteran administrator, as she or he is exposed to the current academic content being learned by the intern. In addition, engaging in active reflection with the intern regarding their personal leadership style, experiences, and problems can assist the mentor in analyzing and improving his or her own performance (Milstein & Krueger, 1997). Seasoned practitioners may have internalized their decision-making processes to the point that they make many decisions routinely, with little analysis or deliberation. Explaining the underlying rationale behind decisions to the intern brings this process to the level of conscious thought. Consequently, these reflective discussions may stimulate mentors to reexamine and change their personal beliefs and practices.

School leaders who received their formal training prior to the implementation of the ISLLC standards have an opportunity to upgrade their skills, learning how the field of educational administration has been recast into one of standards-based preparation. The ISLLC standards and indicators can be used as an assessment tool for the seasoned administrator, serving to identify strengths and areas in which improvement is desired. For licensure renewal, some states are beginning to experiment with portfolio documentation of professional growth and continual learning, and participating in mentoring can help the veteran principal create a professional portfolio.

Finally, a well-structured internship should not add to the mentor's workload. As the intern gains confidence and develops skills, she or he becomes a fully contributing member of the organization throughout the duration of the clinical experience. Consequently, the intern should competently manage a portion of the mentor's work responsibilities, freeing the mentor to focus on other duties.

Benefits for the School District

Schools and school districts obviously will profit by having additional personnel in the organization who are acting in an administrative capacity. The ideal clinical experience, for both the organization and the novice, would be a year-long paid internship. The school system benefits by having a fully employed individual, acting in either the capacity of an assistant principal or an assistant superintendent, who is learning leadership skills at a reduced salary, thus resulting in a cost savings to the district. The intern is not forced to forego employment while fulfilling the clinical requirements and has the option of returning to her or his previous position after completing the internship.

Regardless of whether it is a paid position, school district personnel can personalize the internship within their unique organizational setting, training the aspiring leader in those skills areas that they believe are critical for a novice as the intern assists the school and district in completing administrative tasks. At the same time, school districts can closely observe the intern's progress and assess his or her potential with an eye toward eventual administrative employment within the system, prior to actually appointing them in the position (Milstein et al., 1991).

An additional benefit is to the educational administration profession as a whole. Providing quality clinical training to aspiring school leaders contributes to the pool of well-prepared candidates for school systems to consider when making hiring decisions. Employers prefer to hire novices who have engaged in extensive internships and whose successful performance has been observed and documented by mentors who are exemplary veteran school leaders, as opposed to candidates with little clinical training and whose performance is untested.

Benefits for University Preparation Programs

Clinical experiences are vital for educational administration programs to establish theory-to-practice connections and provide real-world training for aspiring administrators. Professors should provide a variety of learning activities that simulate the school environment, so students can practice and internalize skills within the safe and controlled confines of the classroom. However, as any veteran administrator will attest, the school setting is rarely controlled. Potential leaders need opportunities to practice their skills in real situations, so they can learn from both the intended and unintended consequences of their actions.

As the educational leader's role continues to evolve, emphasizing instructional leadership over building management, field experiences become even more critical. Aspiring leaders need to be in classrooms, observing effective teaching that leads to enhanced student learning, participating in school improvement activities, working side by side with veteran mentors who can teach them how to analyze data and make decisions that lead to students' success. Learning opportunities are maximized when skills are applied in the field.

Interns should be encouraged to share incidents that occurred during their field experiences with fellow students and instructors so that classroom discussions will become even more enriching and relevant (Cordeiro & Smith-Sloan, 1995). Instead of fashioning an artificial activity for students to dissect, professors benefit from having students present real-life issues that they have been struggling to solve. Students need these opportunities to engage in reflective practice, so they can increase self-awareness of their performance. Furthermore, interns sometimes may feel uncomfortable discussing a field-based problem with their mentor (especially if the mentor is contributing to the problem) but value advice and feedback from their university professors and classmates.

University supervisors, even those who have extensive practitioner experience, benefit in several ways from ongoing exposure to the field. First, by remaining connected to schools, they ensure that graduate coursework is relevant and programmatic improvements are made based upon trends that students observe in the field. Second, as state regulations become increasingly focused on performance-based documentation of skills as a condition for initial administrative licensure, university supervisors will need to provide evidence of students' successful completion of the clinical component before licenses are granted. Third, they can engage in field-based research that can improve practices in school systems. Fourth, through observing and identifying exemplary leaders in the field, they can ensure that interns are placed only with expert practitioners. Finally, through establishing close relationships with schools, they can work with school personnel to continue to collaboratively identify educators who would be outstanding candidates for administrator preparation programs.

DESIGNING SUCCESSFUL CLINICAL EXPERIENCES

In planning the clinical experience, all parties should keep in mind that the core purpose of the internship is "to assure the leadership required to support our schools. Internships can link intellectual competence with outstanding performance, if thoughtfully planned and conducted in stimulating settings" (Milstein et al., 1991, p. 6). So that they may be adequately prepared to be effective school leaders, when they are ready to assume the responsibilities, interns should be given substantive, authentic, and real activities that they will encounter in their eventual administrative assignments.

Although internships can be designed in an infinite variety of formats, whatever the format, care should be taken to provide extended field experiences that closely replicate daily administrative life, while maintaining a balance between the competing demands of the clinical requirements and the intern's full-time employment. Permitting a full-time teacher to merely compile clinical hours in small increments—during preparation periods and before school—trivializes this activity. A poorly designed internship will likely be only marginally better than no clinical experience at all, if the intern only passively "logs hours," completing trivial projects or clerical activities (Hart & Pounder, 1999) such as folding newsletters, answering phones, supervising detentions, and recording attendance.

Aspiring school leaders must observe the ebbs and flows of administration as they occur throughout the academic year, in addition to participating in significant activities that occur only during some seasons. Examples of these responsibilities might include the following: developing the school budget, hiring faculty and staff, participating in the collective negotiations process, reaching decisions on staff reductions, creating the master schedule, conducting a school bond election, developing a school improvement plan, arranging student orientation activities, and/or scheduling athletics events. Interns must have the opportunity to see their projects through to completion, experiencing either the consequences of a poorly designed and implemented event or the satisfaction of a well-conceived and structured activity. Either occurrence represents a significant learning event.

THE HIGH-QUALITY INTERNSHIP EXPERIENCE

A year-long full-time placement is considered to be optimal, especially "for those students who lack significant administrative experience" (NPBEA, 1989, p. 18). Noting that this ideal cannot always be arranged, NCATE recommends that the internship should "generally include a six-month (or equivalent), full-time mentored experience, preferably involving two or more settings and multiple levels" (NPBEA, 2001). However, NCATE even backs off from this recommendation, stating that alternatives can be developed, including such options as two three-month internships "or another combination of experiences that equates to the total culmination" (NPBEA, 2001).

Rather than attempting to attain the elusive ideal internship, the university should have as its goal ensuring that each student receives a *high-quality experience* (Hackmann & English, 2001). Although some may desire a more structured definition of the internship, the clinical component must be based within the context of each state's and university's requirements. For example, an informal survey determined that slightly fewer than half of the states mandate some type of clinical experience for administrative licensure, with the remaining states leaving this decision to the university's discretion (Hackmann & English, 2001). States with internship requirements were not uniform in their expectations: hourly requirements ranged between 75 and 740 clock hours, while some listed course credit requirements with no minimum clock hours stated.

We will not define a universal standard for the minimum number of clock hours (or days) necessary for a *high-quality clinical experience* because we believe that these decisions rightly belong in the hands of the program faculty. Administrator preparation programs must operate within the confines of state policies, university mandates, and regulations of accreditation agencies. For example, a decade ago UCEA-member institutions averaged 280 clinical hours, but the range was between 100 and over 800 (Paulter, 1990). In contrast, institutions affiliated with the Danforth Principal Preparation Program required an average of 632 internship hours (Cordeiro, Krueger, Parks, Restine, & Wilton, 1993). Clearly, clinical requirements vary widely among institutions.

Although not stating a minimum number of hours, we do believe that the more time devoted to clinical experiences, the better. Milstein and Krueger (1997) believe that sufficient time on task is mandatory for an effective internship. They state, "Internships should take place over the school year, during the school day, and with sufficient regularity and frequency to insure that interns are able to internalize the administrative role" (Milstein & Krueger, 1997, p. 108).

To provide some guidance, we will share the requirements at Iowa State University (ISU). The ISU requirements are not listed as the ideal but as one example. The ISU educational administration faculty reached their clinical decisions after carefully examining the state of Iowa rules and regulations for administrator preparation programs, as well as considering students' concerns of balancing the competing responsibilities of full-time employment, part-time coursework, and family needs.

At the initial level of licensure, the principalship, ISU students are required to participate in 50 days (the equivalent of 400 hours) of clinical experiences throughout their two-year program. Students complete the equivalent of five internship days in each of the fall and spring semesters, with an additional 15 days in each of two summer sessions. In addition to engaging in clinical activities in the buildings in which they are employed, students also are matched with one or more mentor principals in neighboring districts. Since the mentoring principals work in districts with different academic calendars, interns can accumulate clinical hours on days when their schools are not in session (such as winter breaks, spring breaks, and other school-scheduled holiday or vacation periods). Consequently, they do not need to use their personal days and are not called away from their classrooms and students.

Individuals enrolled in the superintendent licensure program at ISU are required to complete 100 clock hours of field experiences, with an additional 30 hours in the grade levels in which they do not hold their building-level licensure. (For example, an individual holding the elementary principal's license would complete 30 clinical hours at the secondary level.) Individuals in the state of Iowa must have a minimum of three years of building-level administrative experience before they may apply for their superintendent's endorsement. Because candidates have already proved their effectiveness as leaders at the building level, they are not required to put in as many clinical hours for district-level administrative licensure. This practice reflects the ISU educational administration faculty's belief that the superintendency program builds upon the knowledge and skills that students have learned through their initial licensure program and their ongoing administrative employment.

The following suggestions are intended to provide some guidance as university personnel and administrative mentors strive to develop comprehensive high-quality field experiences.

1. *Rather than being targeted only to an internship of a specified duration (such as a three- or six-month practicum), clinical activities should be integrated throughout the program.* Griffiths et al. (1988b) maintain that field experiences should start almost from the first day of enrollment in the administrator preparation program. In each course, instructors should identify activities to be completed in a clinical setting to integrate theory and practice. For example, during a school law course, students could be required to observe their building principal handle a student disciplinary situation. During an instructional supervision course, students could conduct teacher observations and facilitate pre- and post-observation conferences. Certainly, a culminating internship also would be beneficial, so students could practice their craft after completing all required coursework, but this should not be the only clinical opportunity provided.

2. *Clinical activities must be of significant duration and intensity.* If students simply drop in and out of the clinical setting for brief activities, they do not receive the full benefit of the experience, since they do not have sufficient background information on each situation to be fully effective. These brief encounters also place an undue burden on mentors, who feel they must stop whatever they are doing either to assign a task or explain the activity in which they are currently engaged. Candidates need exposure to administrative life on an extended basis, so they have a full understanding of the demands of the position (Hackmann & English, 2001).

3. *Clinical experiences should occur in multiple settings.* As a matter of convenience, most students complete their internships in the same schools where they teach (Daresh & Playko, 1992). Proximity alone is not a reason to select a mentor, since one's supervisor may not necessarily be an ideal tutor. Mentors and interns should be matched carefully, with close attention paid to the identification of exemplary and supportive school leaders who will serve as role models. Interns will probably be more willing to share weaknesses, concerns, and their personal feelings with a mentor who is not their immediate supervisor, since they may fear possible retribution (Jacobson, 1996).

So they may have broad-based experiences, interns should observe several administrators working in varied settings, gaining exposure to a variety of leadership styles and a range of grade levels (Milstein, 1993). Furthermore, an exposure to diverse settings helps the intern determine the leadership style that is most closely aligned with her or his personality and educational philosophy (Hackmann et al., 1999), as well as identifying the grade level (elementary, middle, or secondary) that is most appealing.

4. *Clinical activities must be authentic and engaging, increasing in complexity as the intern gains confidence and skills.* This practicum must not simply consist of busy work and relatively low-order activities. Quality experiences must be provided, so that the candidate is well prepared to assume an administrative position af-

ter completing the internship. Activities should be scaffolded (Cordeiro & Smith-Sloan, 1995), moving from simple to increasingly complex assignments as the intern demonstrates mastery of skills and gains confidence in his or her abilities (Peper, 1988). The intern may initially shadow the mentor and other school leaders, observing how they address routine matters and learning the organizational culture. Observations can be enhanced when the mentor debriefs with the intern, explaining how decisions were reached, the underlying rationale, and why the decisions were appropriate in each unique situation.

Few attempts should be made to shield the aspiring leaders from the harsh realities of school leadership. When appropriate, interns also should be placed in confrontational situations, so they can practice their conflict resolution skills and receive immediate feedback from their mentors on their effectiveness in handling these situations.

One or more long-term, multilayered projects should be assigned, either as a joint administrator-intern project or as the exclusive responsibility of the intern, so the student can follow a project from inception to implementation (Hart & Pounder, 1999). Through these activities, administrator candidates should have opportunities to work with a variety of constituents, including teachers, students, parents, other administrators, and representatives from various businesses and social service agencies. When time is provided for significant projects, these activities actually can promote changes in policies and practices within the organization (Pounder, 1995).

ROLES AND RESPONSIBILITIES OF ALL PARTICIPANTS IN THE INTERNSHIP

The internship is too critical a part of administrator preparation to simply be left to chance. Therefore, to ensure that the clinical experience is of the highest quality, all parties should be made fully aware of their roles. Each party—the university supervisor, mentor, and intern—has significant responsibilities in this activity.

University Supervisor Responsibilities

The higher education institution, through the university supervisor, should take great care in facilitating a positive and educationally rewarding internship activity for the aspiring school leader. Among the supervisor's responsibilities are the following:

1. Careful selection of the mentor and site is essential. The internship requires "a relationship between the trainees and their mentors that is intense, intellectually stimulating, and trusting" (NPBEA, 1989, p. 22). Due to the close and sometimes stressful interactions that will occur during these clinical hours, mentors should be selected not only for their expertise, but also for their ability to nurture the intern's progress. If there is a strong likelihood that the individuals' personalities or philosophical beliefs may clash, the supervisor should continue the search for a more compatible match.

The selection of a compatible school or district setting also is vital because the site must provide opportunities for growth (Cordeiro & Smith-Sloan, 1995). Supervisors should avoid placing the student only in her or his home school or district because there will be no opportunities to experience diverse settings or to learn alternative policies and procedures.

2. Inform all parties of their individual and shared responsibilities in ensuring the success of the field experience. Expectations for each partner in this activity should be outlined clearly, preferably both in writing and orally through an initial meeting. At this initial conference, the intern should share his or her identified growth areas with the mentor and supervisor (which are based upon a self-analysis of the ISLLC standards), and the three can collaboratively develop a set of internship goals and activities. Sufficient structure should be provided so that both mentor and intern understand what activities would be appropriate and those that would not (such as busy work, low-order clerical tasks, or activities that merely reinforce skills that the intern has already internalized and mastered.

As appropriate, the field supervisor should conduct on-site orientation activities with mentor administrators, especially for those working with interns for the first time. Mentors also should be aware that flexibility should be inherent in the field activities so that interns can benefit from unanticipated learning activities as they may arise.

3. *Approve the student's planned internship goals and activities.* The university supervisor is accountable for ensuring that the student's activities satisfy the program's clinical expectations. Hence, the supervisor must make certain that the intern's goals focus on areas in which strength is desired, in addition to providing experiences in all six of the ISLLC strands. Once the goals have been approved, the supervisor occasionally should check the intern's clinical activities to verify that the goals are being addressed. In addition, the supervisor should assist the intern in identifying artifacts to include in the portfolio, documenting successful goal attainment.

4. *Keep communication channels with the mentor open.* After the initial conference, the supervisor should maintain regular contact with the mentor but without excessive intrusion into the school setting. Educational leaders are busy individuals; hence, fewer than one in five state that they desire close university supervision of the internship process (Reynolds, 1997). Feedback from the mentor can be obtained through e-mail messages and telephone calls, with occasional field visits so that the supervisor can receive feedback on the intern's performance through face-to-face visits with the mentor.

Occasionally it may become apparent that the intern is making insufficient progress or has been placed in a setting that does not appear to be leading to success. The university supervisor should intervene as appropriate, meeting with the intern and mentor to reinforce the clinical goals, identify new activities, and attempt to resolve any issues or conflicts that may have arisen. Although it should be reserved as a last resort, it may become necessary to terminate the placement or identify a new site for the intern, if it is decided that this action is in the best interests of the student or school district.

5. *Maintain regular communication channels with the intern.* Telephone calls, direct observations, and e-mail messages certainly should be utilized to sustain regular contact. In addition, the intern should maintain a daily log detailing all activities with occasional entries in which she or he reflects on significant learning opportunities. Through perusing the daily log, the supervisor can be assured that the student is fulfilling the identified clinical goals and is continuing to enhance skills. Some educational administration programs require interns to participate in seminars, so that several students can collectively debrief and engage in collaborative problem solving related to their intern activities. The university supervisor should act as a consultant to the intern, sometimes serving as a sympathetic ear and at other times being an additional resource through suggesting professional readings or additional activities to enrich the experience.

6. *Provide constructive feedback to the mentor and the intern.* The reflective journal can be a highly efficient and effective means to assess the intern's development and pose reflective questions to the intern (Hackmann et al., 1999). If the supervisor learns that the mentor is not assigning high-quality tasks or is not taking time to talk with the mentor, he or she should tactfully suggest ways for the mentor to improve the quality of interactions and activities. Likewise, the supervisor should provide constructive feedback when the intern is not satisfactorily completing assignments. As the university's representative, it becomes the supervisor's responsibility to ensure that all parties fulfill the university's expectations for the clinical experience.

7. Complete an evaluation of the intern's performance. Working in consultation with the mentor(s), the supervisor will need to evaluate the intern's performance and determine a final grade. It is recommended that a concluding meeting be held with the intern, mentor, and supervisor in attendance. At this meeting the intern's clinical goals can be reviewed and progress noted. The supervisor can provide additional suggestions for the aspiring school leader to continue to improve her or his skills after the internship has been completed.

Administrative Mentor Responsibilities

School leaders who consent to host an intern should not take this responsibility lightly; this activity can directly affect the student's decision regarding whether or not to seek an administrative position. Among the mentor's responsibilities are the following:

1. Approach the mentoring role with sincerity and commitment. The clinical experience is valuable only if it avoids "the temptation to show newcomers 'how we do it around here,' without giving an opportunity to construct better ways of 'doing it'" (Daresh & Playko, 1992, p. 51). An outstanding learning environment must be created (Hackmann et al., 1999) so that the potential school leader can take advantage of every possible learning opportunity that comes along. When the intern completes this requirement, the mentor should be convinced that this person has been prepared— as fully as possible—to face the myriad challenges of administrative life.

The mentor should be a positive role model, so that the intern can learn through observing the mentor's actions and daily interactions with others. The intern should be introduced to the best administrative practices by being permitted to observe not only the mentor but also other outstanding administrators in the district and region. The mentor should continually assume the role of teacher, openly explaining actions and discussing the reasons for

those actions. In addition, mentors should discuss the many rewards and personal sacrifices inherent in educational administration. Because leadership is not an exact science, interns must learn
that incorrect decisions occasionally will be made and have an opportunity to observe how successful leaders correct these errors.

2. *Become familiar with the ISLLC standards.* Many veteran
practitioners are not aware of the ISLLC standards for school leaders because they completed their professional training prior to the
development of these indicators. So that they are as knowledgeable as their interns, mentors will need to familiarize themselves
with these standards. The remaining chapters of this book will be
helpful in introducing and explaining each of the six standards.

3. *Transition the intern into and out of the internship setting.* As
an outsider, the intern will need to be formally introduced into the
school setting (Hackmann et al., 1999) through all appropriate communication channels, including school newsletters, student an-
nouncements or assemblies, faculty meetings, parent meetings, and
administrative councils. Introductions should include information
regarding the intern's professional preparation and work experience,
so that faculty, staff, students, and parents will have confidence in
the person's ability to handle administrative assignments.

The intern should be welcomed as part of the leadership team,
not held at arm's length and dismissed when it is time to discuss
delicate matters. She or he should immediately be provided with
faculty handbooks, student handbooks, and a board policy manual,
so that policies and procedures can be quickly learned. Staff and
students also should be made aware of the intern's responsibilities
(and the boundaries of these duties), so that additional explana-
tions will be unnecessary when the intern is assigned to work on
projects that affect them. Finally, all school constituents should be
notified when the clinical requirements are completed, and the intern departs.

4. *Delegate challenging tasks to the intern.* A high-quality clinical activity does not consist simply of another set of eyes to super-

vise a football game or pair of hands to attach mailing labels to envelopes. Mentors must delegate significant responsibilities that assist in preparing administrator candidates to be change agents and instructional leaders (Milstein et al., 1991), not activities that simply give the intern something to do while fulfilling their required hours. Particular attention should be paid to providing opportunities for the intern to strengthen any perceived areas of weakness, as well as ensuring that he or she is exposed to varied administrative tasks.

Initially, as the intern becomes acclimated to the role and responsibilities inherent in the position, it is recommended that the mentor closely supervise his or her work. Immediate feedback and assistance should be provided so that the intern can learn the proper procedures, correct any errors, and gain self-confidence. As proficiency and skills increase, direct supervision should diminish accordingly, with the expectation that the intern will become a self-sufficient and contributing member of the leadership team (Hackmann et al., 1999).

Some assigned projects may be relatively solitary in nature (such as revising a student handbook or reviewing school policies), but most assignments should require the intern to interact with others in the school environment, since the essence of leadership is working with and through others to achieve desired results. Such activities as chairing a building- or district-level committee, working with department chairs or principals to finalize budget requests, interviewing teacher applicants, facilitating a meeting to resolve a parent's concern, and presenting a proposal to the school board all provide the intern with authentic opportunities to showcase talents and to hone communication and interpersonal skills.

5. *Embrace opportunities to learn from the intern.* The mentor-mentee pairing should be a two-way learning partnership. Because the intern is enrolled in an administrator training program, the individual is being exposed to recent educational innovations and provided with information related to best practices in this era of

school reform. Veteran leaders who are not conversant on the current educational literature can learn about recent trends from their interns. Furthermore, practicing administrators will benefit simply by taking time to engage in reflective practice, talking through their performance with the interns.

6. Provide honest, constructive feedback when assessing the intern's performance. Because the intern is working alongside the mentor, the mentor will possess the greatest amount of observational data and knowledge regarding the intern's completion of the clinical responsibilities and potential success as a future educational leader. The mentor should provide candid feedback to the intern on a continuous basis, so the intern is fully aware of the quality of her or his work and has numerous opportunities to improve any areas in which growth is warranted.

An honest appraisal should be provided to the university supervisor, so that the intern's final evaluation will be an accurate reflection of the clinical performance. Potential employers may desire feedback on the applicant's field experiences, and an inflated grade will reflect negatively on both the mentor and the educational administration program.

Intern Responsibilities

It should go without saying that the clinical experience is primarily intended to benefit the would-be school leader. The intern has numerous responsibilities, including those listed below.

1. Learn as much as possible. The intern must be open to any potential learning activities that may be presented, even if they may be stress-filled or exceedingly challenging. Clinical experiences should be viewed as one's final opportunity to practice with a safety net in place, since the mentor will be continually available to provide advice and support when the intern questions the wisdom and viability of a potential decision. The intern should think of himself/herself as a sponge (Hackmann et al., 1999), soaking up every possible learning episode through observing and participating in the clinical setting.

When completing the self-assessment of strengths and potential areas of growth in preparation for the initial meeting with the supervisor and mentor, the intern should be fully candid regarding preparation, knowledge, and skills. The internship must be viewed as an opportunity to remediate any deficiencies or to master skills in areas to which the intern has not been previously exposed. By openly acknowledging potential growth areas, the intern can be assured that clinical activities will be tailored to his or her individual needs, thereby strengthening or eliminating areas of weakness.

2. *Operate within the policies and practices of the internship site.* Just as with any employment placement, the intern must adhere to the organization's rules and regulations and should consider the mentor as the immediate supervisor. Occasionally, the intern may have ideological disagreements with the mentor or may not agree with the policies of the host district. The internship, however, is not an appropriate venue for challenging organizational policies and practices. Learning to operate within the confines of policies is yet another skill that can be learned during the clinical activity, one that definitely will be needed when the student assumes the initial administrative appointment.

During this activity, the aspiring leader will be made privy to a great deal of confidential data at the host site, including student records, personnel records, and a variety of information shared in personal conferences with the mentor, staff, and students. Just as is true with the intern's place of employment, professional ethics dictate that confidentiality must be maintained at all times.

3. *Be professional, dependable, and consistent.* Even if the internship is unpaid, the administrator candidate should approach the assignment with the same level of dedication as if it were a fully compensated position. All commitments should be honored and addressed as if the individual were employed in the host district. For example, in the case of illness or an unanticipated conflict, the

intern should notify the mentor in advance, making arrangements to have any administrative responsibilities covered or to report on an alternate date. Professional dress is required at all times, and the intern should consult with the mentor to determine any expectations for dress.

At times the intern will be acting in place of the mentor and will be called upon to make administrative decisions. These decisions should be consistently aligned with the mentor's practices and should not substitute the intern's judgment in place of the mentor's.

4. Be self-confident, proactive, and assertive. Especially when the administrator is embarking on an initial mentoring arrangement, the mentor may not be fully aware of the responsibilities that can be assigned to the intern, may be reluctant to give up control of a project, or may not be efficient in utilizing the intern's time to the best advantage. However, the intern should not simply sit and wait for an assignment. The intern must be assertive in asking for assignments, notifying the mentor when he or she has completed a task and is ready for another, and offering to assist when it is apparent that additional hands are immediately needed to resolve the latest crisis. There should be little, if any, downtime during this clinical experience.

As the intern builds skills and gains confidence in the position, she or he should be capable of completing increasingly difficult projects or should be assigned new areas of responsibility. If tasks do not increase in complexity after a sufficient period of time, the intern should initiate a discussion with the mentor. Additional time demands are incurred when one assumes the mentoring responsibility, and the mentor simply may not have taken the time to assess the intern's readiness for new assignments or has not had an opportunity to identify more interesting and engaging projects. Of course, the mentor may believe the intern has not demonstrated proficiency and is not yet prepared to give more challenging assignments. In any case, the intern has the most to gain—or to lose—through this clinical experience. Consequently, continual dialogue and feedback are critical to ensure that the intern attains the maximum benefit from this experience.

5. *Consult with the university supervisor.* The mentor occasionally may wish to consult others external to the internship setting for their perspective, expertise, or advice. One of the university supervisor's responsibilities is to be a resource for the intern. Because this supervisor is working with mentors and interns in multiple locations (and most likely is teaching educational administration courses), the supervisor will be able to provide guidance, suggest additional readings, or connect the intern to others who have experienced a similar situation.

If the student believes that the clinical experiences are not living up to his or her expectations or may be ready for another placement, the supervisor should be informed. The supervisor then can speak with the mentor to restructure the experience or may initiate a change in placement (at a different grade level or in a school with different demographics) so that the intern can continue to experience new schools or school districts.

6. *Fulfill all university obligations in a timely fashion.* As the intern is immersed in the clinical setting, he or she may feel more like an administrator than a student. Nevertheless, the field experience is a course requirement, and all university expectations must be met. Some university supervisors may require that all clinical hours be logged in daily journals and submitted monthly, along with reflective papers documenting how classroom theory has been translated into practice. Other programs may require the intern to develop a portfolio noting their successful completion of internship goals, showcasing completed projects, and documenting skills learned as a result of the field experience. The challenges of leadership responsibilities may make completing these requirements difficult, but they must be accomplished on time.

At the conclusion of the internship, it is recommended that the student complete a final ISLLC self-assessment, comparing this document with the assessment carried out in preparation for the internship. Because professional development is a career-long pursuit, the student should be encouraged to complete a Professional Growth Plan, noting improvement goals for their first few years as a novice educational leader.

SUMMARY

A high-quality internship experience results in long-lasting benefits for the aspiring administrator, mentor administrator, host school and district, and university preparation program. To reach this goal, however, all parties must fully embrace their mutual roles and responsibilities in designing a well-structured experience. To promote theory-to-practice connections, clinical activities should be integrated throughout the student's program of studies, should occur in diverse settings, and should provide challenging, engaging learning opportunities.

Clinical activities should not simply train interns to be school managers. Instead, high-quality clinical activities prepare aspiring educational leaders to be change agents and instructional leaders for schools of the future. The six remaining chapters of this text provide a detailed explanation of the ISLLC standards. Clinical experiences framed around these standards will help ensure that interns are better prepared for immediate success when assuming their initial administrative appointments.

SELF-ASSESSMENT, PERSONALIZED INTERNSHIP PLAN, AND CLINICAL ACTIVITIES

The activities listed below are intended to assist the intern, mentor(s), and supervisor in structuring a quality internship experience, designed to address the intern's self-identified areas in which improvement is desired.

1. Self-Assessment. Complete the ISLLC self-assessment included in Appendix B. Closely examine indicators that you believe reflect your greatest strengths, then identify indicators in which you feel you would like to improve. Next, examine your mentors' job descriptions, matching position responsibilities with your self-identified improvement areas. Tentatively identify five or six potential growth areas in which you wish to initially focus your internship activities. As you consider these areas, concentrate on activities that are comprehensive, requiring extensive practice and mastery of multiple skills, rather than simply one-shot learning events.

2. Supervisor Meeting. Meet with your university supervisor, either individually or with other classmates who are completing their internship assignments. As you discuss your tentatively identified improvement areas, continue to expand upon this listing of potential goal areas that you would like to address with your clinical activities.

3. Draft Internship Plan. After meeting with your field supervisor, narrow your list of possible growth areas to three. Develop a tentative Personalized Internship Plan (PIP) for each goal, using the format that is provided in Appendix C. During your initial meeting with your mentor and supervisor, these draft goals will be used as a starting point as you collaboratively begin to structure your internship activities.

4. Three-Way Conference. Bring copies of your draft PIPs to your planning conference with your supervisor and mentor. In addition, provide a copy of your resumé to your mentor, so that he or she will become more knowledgeable about your academic preparation and employment history. During this initial meeting, you should be open to any additional learning opportunities that may be recommended by your mentor and supervisor. However, do not hesitate to suggest activities that you believe are essential to enhancing your knowledge of the position and your leadership skills. As the meeting progresses, all parties should agree to a minimum of three goals on which the internship will focus initially. At the conclusion of the clinical experience, *the intern will be expected to demonstrate competency in all six ISSLC standards.* Therefore, target dates should be established for completion of these initial goals, and additional goals should be identified as appropriate to ensure that the student's experiences encompass all ISSLC standards.

5. *Final Personalized Internship Plans.* After the internship goals have been identified, it is the intern's responsibility to develop the finalized PIPs. Copies of these PIPs and the ISLLC self-assessment should be provided to the mentor(s) and university supervisor as soon as they have been developed.

6. *Reflective Logs.* Internship journals serve three purposes: a) they provide documentation of daily responsibilities and experiences the intern has fulfilled during the clinical component, indicating how they relate to the identified goals; b) they stimulate the intern to engage in systematic, in-depth reflection regarding significant learning opportunities; and c) they provide diagnostic feedback to the university supervisor, who can use the journal as one means to document that the intern is engaging in substantive and sustained clinical activities.

With each activity and its subsequent journal entry and reflection, you should consider how your participation in this experience better prepares you to fulfill your responsibility as a change agent and instructional leader. Reflective entries also should include unanswered questions about the experience, since these questions may assist in the identification of new activities to enhance the internship. Discuss with your supervisor the expectations for the format of the journal entries; a sample reflective log is included in Appendix C. Of course, the reflective journals should represent professional standards, including being computer-generated or typewritten and grammatically correct. Reflective logs should be submitted at regular intervals to your supervisor.

7. *Portfolio Development.* Interns should develop a portfolio that documents their mastery of PIP goals and successful attainment of

the ISLLC standards. Each PIP should denote artifacts that can be used to demonstrate attainment of each goal. At the conclusion of the clinical experience, the intern's portfolio should include the following materials at a minimum: a) the initial ISLLC self-assessment, b) Personalized Internship Plans for each goal, c) artifacts related to each PIP, d) a field experience log summary (see Appendix C), e) reflective papers related to selected clinical activities, f) a final ISLLC self-assessment completed at the conclusion of the internship, and g) a Professional Development Plan noting additional professional growth activities in which the student wishes to engage in preparation for his or her initial administrative appointment.

IDENTIFYING SIGNIFICANT LEARNING EXPERIENCES THROUGHOUT THE INTERNSHIP

At the beginning of the internship, it will be quite difficult for students to accurately identify every significant activity that they wish to complete throughout this clinical experience. This is especially true since no individual, including the mentor(s) and university supervisor, will be able to predict all learning opportunities that will present themselves throughout the duration of this experience. Consequently, although the clinical experiences should be carefully structured, they also should be sufficiently flexible to allow interns to identify and select new learning goals as they gain knowledge and skills, and to take advantage of unanticipated learning experiences as they may arise.

The remaining chapters provide a more complete explanation of each of the six ISLLC standards. At the end of each chapter is a listing of possible internship activities related to the individual standard to assist the intern in identifying and selecting experiences that will facilitate skills development. In addition, suggested readings and Web sites are included. As the intern and mentor become more knowledgeable about the ISLLC standards, they should work with the university supervisor to modify the Personalized Internship Plan, either adding or eliminating goals, so that these clinical activities provide the best possible learning experiences for the aspiring leader.

SUGGESTED READINGS

Hayes, W. (2001). *So you want to be a superintendent?* Lanham, MD: Scarecrow.

Hoyle, J. R., English, F. W., & Steffy, B. E. (1998). *Skills for successful 21st century school leaders: Standards for peak performers.* Arlington, VA: American Association of School Administrators.

Milstein, M. M., and associates. (1993). *Changing the way we prepare educational leaders.* Newbury Park, CA: Corwin Press.

Murphy, J. (1992). *The landscape of leadership preparation: Reframing the education of school administrators.* Newbury Park, CA: Corwin Press.

National Policy Board for Educational Administration. (1993). *Principals for our changing schools: The knowledge and skill base.* Lancaster, PA: Technomic.

REFERENCES

Clark, D. C., & Clark, S. N. (1996). Better preparation of educational leaders. *Educational Researcher, 25*(8), 1820.

Cordeiro, P. A., Krueger, J. A., Parks, D., Restine, N., & Wilton, P. T. (1993). Taking stock: Learnings gleaned from universities participating in the Danforth program. In M. M. Milstein & associates (Eds.), *Changing the way we prepare educational leaders* (p. 1738). Newbury Park, CA: Corwin Press.

Cordeiro, P., & Smith-Sloan, E. (1995, April). *Apprenticeships for administrative interns: Learning to talk like a principal.* Paper presented at the annual meeting of the American Educational Research Association, San Francisco. (ERIC Document Reproduction Service No. ED 385 014).

Cuban, L. (1996). Reforming the practice of educational administration through managing dilemmas. In S. L. Jacobson, E. S. Hickcox, & R. B. Stevenson (Eds.), *School administration: Persistent dilemmas in preparation and practice* (pp. 3–17). Westport, CT: Praeger.

Daresh, J. C., & Playko, M. A. (1992). *The professional development of school administrators: Preservice, induction, and inservice applications.* Needham Heights, MA: Allyn and Bacon.

Doud, J. L, & Keller, E. P. (1998). *A ten-year study: The K–8 principal in 1998.* Alexandria, VA: National Association of Elementary School Principals.

Elmore, R. (2000). *Building a new structure for school leadership.* Washington, DC: Albert Shanker Institute.

Griffiths, D. E., Stout, R. T., & Forsyth, P. B. (Eds.). (1988a). *Leaders for America's schools: The report and papers of the National Commission on Excellence in Educational Administration.* Berkeley, CA: McCutchan.

Griffiths, D. E., Stout, R. T., & Forsyth, P. B. (1988b). The preparation of educational administrators. In D. E. Griffiths, R. T. Stout, P. B. Forsyth (Eds.), *Leaders for America's schools: The report and papers of the National Commission on Excellence in Educational Administration* (pp. 284–304). Berkeley, CA: McCutchan.

Hackmann, D. G., & English, F. W. (2001, Spring). About straw horses and administrator shortages: Confronting the pragmatics of the administrative internship. *UCEA Review, 50*(2), 12–15.

Hackmann, D. G., Russell, F. S., & Elliott, R. J. (1999). Making administrative internships meaningful. *Planning and Changing, 30,* 2–14.

Hart, A. W., & Pounder, D. G. (1999). Reinventing preparation programs: A decade of activity. In J. Murphy and P. B. Forsyth (Eds.), *Educational administration: A decade of reform* (pp. 115–151). Thousand Oaks, CA: Corwin Press.

Interstate School Leaders Licensure Consortium. (1996). *Standards for school leaders.* Washington, DC: Council of Chief State School Officers.

Jacobson, S. L. (1996). School leadership in an age of reform: New directions in principal preparation. *International Journal of Educational Reform, 5*(3), 271–277.

Krueger, J. A., & Milstein, M. M. (1995). Promoting excellence in educational leadership: What really matters? *Planning and Changing, 26,* 148–167.

Leithwood, K., Jantzi, D., Coffin, G., & Wilson, P. (1996). Preparing school leaders: What works? *Journal of School Leadership, 6,* 316–342.

Milstein, M. (1990). Rethinking the clinical aspects in administrative preparation: From theory to practice. In S. L. Jacobson & J. Conway (Eds.), *Educational leadership in an age of reform* (pp. 119–130). New York: Longman.

Milstein, M. M., and associates. (1993). *Changing the way we prepare educational leaders.* Newbury Park, CA: Corwin Press.

Milstein, M. M., Bobroff, B. M., & Restine, L. N. (1991). *Internship programs in educational administration: A guide to preparing educational leaders.* New York: Teachers College Press.

Milstein, M. M., & Krueger, J. A. (1997). Improving educational administration preparation programs: What we have learned over the past decade. *Peabody Journal of Education, 72*(2), 100–116.

Murphy, J. (1992). *The landscape of leadership preparation: Reframing the education of school administrators.* Newbury Park, CA: Corwin Press.

National Commission on Excellence in Education. (1983). *A nation at risk: The imperative for educational reform.* Washington, DC: U.S. Department of Education.

National Policy Board for Educational Administration. (1989). *Improving the preparation of school administrators: An agenda for reform.* Charlottesville, VA: University of Virginia Press.

National Policy Board for Educational Administration. (1993). *Principals for our changing schools: The knowledge and skill base.* Lancaster, PA: Technomic.

National Policy Board for Educational Administration. (2001). *New NCATE standards for educational administration.* [On-line]. Available Internet: http://www.npbea.org/projects/NCATE_materials.html.

National Staff Development Council. (2000). *Learning to lead, leading to learn.* Oxford, OH: Author. [On-line]. Available Internet: www.nsdc.org.

Paulter, A. (1990). *A review of UCEA member institutions' clinical experiences/internships/field experiences for educational leaders.* Paper presented at the annual meeting of the University Council for Educational Administration, Pittsburgh, PA.

Peper, J. B. (1988). Clinical education for school superintendents and principals: The missing link. In D. E. Griffiths, R. T. Stout, & P. B.

Forsyth (Eds.), *Leaders for America's schools: The report and papers of the National Commission on Excellence in Educational Administration* (pp. 360–366). Berkeley, CA: McCutchan.

Pounder, D. G. (1995). *Theory to practice: A description and multidimensional evaluation of the University of Utah's educational administration Ed.D. program.* (ERIC Document Reproduction Service No. ED 384 113)

Reynolds, J. C. (1997). Designing the internship for small and large schools. *Rural Educator, 18*(3), 12–15.

University Council for Educational Administration. (2001). *Policy governing membership in UCEA.* [On-line.] Available Internet: http://www.ucea.org.

2

A VISION FOR SUCCESS

Standard 1: A school administrator is an educational leader who promotes the success of all students by facilitating the development, articulation, implementation, and stewardship of a vision of learning that is shared and supported by the school community.

INTRODUCTION

A close look at successful organizations and individuals reveals that a plan developed around specific, measurable goals is central to their success. These goals drive organizational activities, create the image of the organization in the future, and establish the benchmarks against which progress is measured. The degree of critical attention focused upon educational issues in contemporary political and corporate arenas, particularly in this age of competition and choice, emphasizes the need for a clear, compelling image of purpose imperative for schools today, perhaps more so than ever before (Bracey, 2000).

What are the essentials that students must learn at each grade level and how should they be assessed? What is the appropriate response for schools when students fail to meet established benchmarks? How well prepared for adult life roles and the workplace are the graduates of our schools? Questions such as these appear regularly, not only in educational publications, but also in the popular media. Underlying these questions is another, implicit question: What are the goals of elementary and secondary education, and how will they be realized? Educational leaders cannot begin to answer these questions for the public until they have answered the most basic one for themselves as educators: "What is the vision that is driving our schools?"

Nanus (1992) notes, "There is no more powerful engine driving an organization toward excellence and long-range success than an attractive, worthwhile, and achievable vision of the future, widely shared" (p. 3). In simple terms, a vision is a picture of what the organization would look like if operating at its maximum potential in achieving its common goal. Essential to developing, embracing, and nurturing the critical vision is skilled leadership, which builds coalitions and collaboration among the individuals and elements within the organization to create the dynamics of success. Williams (1993) states, "Environments that promote vision web human beings together in teams so that human minds can be in dialogue with other human minds. One person's visions of possibility are linked with other people's visions of possibility" (p. 2).

To develop a way of understanding of ISLLC Standard 1, this chapter will focus upon the theories, concepts, and strategies of systems thinking, strategic planning, and consensus building. It will do so as these elements relate to the development of an organizational vision. It will also consider the process by which the vision is articulated; identify the challenges of implementing the change necessary to realize the vision; and suggest strategies for nurturing and sustaining the vision within the organization.

SYSTEMS THINKING

One of the critical elements of skilled leadership is a recognition of the systemic nature of the school organization. A school is a social system that is embedded within a larger system of the community and is shaped by those forces that result from the interaction of various community entities. To construct and promote a vision that truly responds to the needs of the schools, the skilled educational leader operates with a clear understanding of the interdependence that is characteristic of complex social systems. Effective leaders recognize schools "as open and dynamic systems and subsystems, as interrelated across functional boundaries, as interactive combinations and as integrative processes" (Razik & Swanson, 2001, p. 41).

Conceptual skills are key to leadership in this area. Patterson (1993) offers the following guidelines to assist organizations in recognizing and operating within the implications of systems thinking:

- Focus on the system, not the people.
- Learn how the current system evolved and how it connects to related systems.
- Expect the system to resist interventions meant to disrupt the stability of the current system.
- Evaluate the system against the organization's core values.
- Look beyond symptomatic solutions to fundamental systems issues.
- Think whole-system, long-term solutions and allow time for the solutions to take effect.
- Anticipate new systems problems arising from current systems solutions. (pp. 67–68)

Systems thinking and the constructs it presents are essential in developing a comprehensive vision for an organization. According to Senge (1990), visions without systems thinking end up painting lovely pictures of the future with no deep understanding of the forces that must be mastered to reach that future. Once cognizant and comfortable with the implications of systems thinking and the inherent need to bring people together in a common purpose, the effective educational leader must seize the opportunity to begin building toward a shared, organizational vision centered on student success.

Closely connected to systems thinking is Total Quality Management (TQM). W. Edwards Deming, commonly called the "Father of TQM," noted that 85% of an organization's problems can be attributed to the organization itself, with workers only responsible for 15% (Deming, 1986). TQM focuses on improving the organization through such practices as teamwork and collaboration among management and workers. Quality improvement becomes the goal of every individual, and "the focus of everyone's work in the TQM model is excellent, quick, high-quality, and flawless service" (Cunningham & Cordeiro, 2000, p. 181).

When applied to education, TQM addresses the continuous improvement of schools and school systems. Bonstingl (2001) notes that the Japanese refer to this dedication to mutual improvement as *kaizen*. To ensure quality in the school setting, leaders must work closely with their staffs to transform the culture to one that promotes a willingness to continually analyze every aspect of the organization, with an eye toward quality.

Many schools have implemented School-Based Management (SBM), also called Site-Based Management, to build upon the TQM leadership principles. Through empowering faculty, staff, and parents in the school governance process, all partners become committed to improving schools and promoting student achievement (National Association of Secondary School Principals [NASSP], 1996). School leaders should encourage faculty members to be innovative and take risks, as they strive to identify approaches that successfully meet students' learning needs (NASSP, 1996).

STRATEGIC PLANNING

Strategic planning provides organizations with the opportunity to involve stakeholders in the process of creating and promoting policies, procedures, and programs that position and enable the organization to respond to the needs of an increasingly complex global economy and information society. Strategic planning is a proven method of positioning an organization to realize its goals in an inclusive, participatory manner, using different models of the process that have evolved over the past decade.

Strategic planning is defined in several ways. Seyfarth (1999) states that it is "a technique by which planners scan the environment of an organization to identify trends that seem likely to affect its ability to accomplish its mission" (p. 53). Goodstein, Nolan, and Pfeiffer (1992) emphasize the element of futuring when they state that strategic planning is "the process by which the guiding members of an organization envision the future and develop the necessary procedures and operations to achieve that future" (p. 3). Cook (1990) simply and directly defines strategic planning as "the means by which an organization constantly recreates itself to achieve extraordinary purpose" (p. 84).

Each of these definitions contributes something of value when applied to the educational setting. Strategic planning is a dynamic process that is both linear and cyclical. It is formulated by the combined expertise of members within the organization and stakeholders outside of the organization, focusing on their common interests. The process is future-oriented, identifies goals that are measurable, thus making the organization accountable, and seeks to create the promotion of rational decision-making toward the deployment of resources that are focused on fixed goals and priorities (Cook, 1990).

Strategic planning is different from long-range planning in that it emphasizes change rather than stability (Valentine, 1997). According to Valentine (1997), strategic planning must do two things: (1) It clarifies what the organization is attempting to accomplish, and (2) it identifies and uses means to determine how the organization is doing and whether or not it is achieving organizational goals. Alexander and Serfass (1999) provide a practical model for strategic planning for educators as shown in Figure 2.1. A

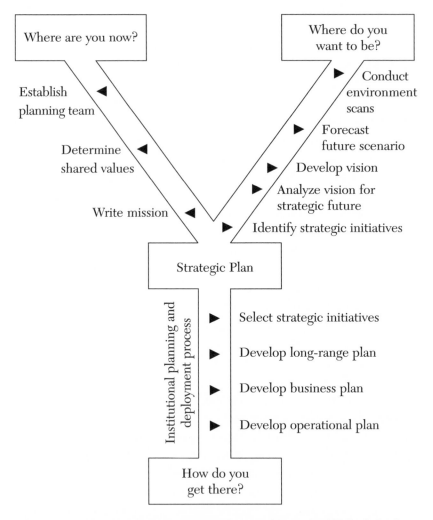

Figure 2.1   Strategic Planning Model. *Source:* **Alexander, W. F., & Serfass, R. W. (1999).** *Futuring tools for strategic planning in education.* **Milwaukee, WI: ASQ Quality Press, p. 18. Reprinted with permission.**

Y-shaped model is used to emphasize the three major considerations required for planning: (1) Where are we now? (2) Where do we want to be? (3) How do we get there?

DEVELOPING A VISION

The process of developing a vision for schools and school systems begins with identifying the characteristics of successful schools. This approach provides the school community with a definition of its "ideal" self as a starting point. Contemporary literature on effective schools can be extremely useful in this essential, but potentially tedious, task, since "[a] professional learning community will *always* begin its exploration of an issue by gathering relevant background information and compiling the best thinking on that issue" (DuFour & Eaker, 1998, p. 69).

A review of the research conducted by Edmonds (1979), Newmann and Wehlage (1995), and Lezotte (1997) yields specific indicators of what constitutes an organization that incorporates good teaching and learning and productive instructional environments. These indicators include developing a clear school mission, providing a safe and orderly learning environment, holding high expectations for students, creating maximum opportunity to learn, frequently assessing students' progress, working toward collaborative home-school-community relations, and having strong principal leadership. The mission statement is the formal explanation of the organization's purpose, which serves as the foundation for its activities (Valentine, 1997).

In their summary of research on effective school cultures, Saphier and King (as cited in Sagor, 1992) focus on the human relations skills necessary for success in this arena. They report the following 12 norms that distinguish schools where growth and development are most likely to occur: (1) collegiality; (2) experimentation; (3) high expectations; (4) trust and confidence; (5) tangible support; (6) reaching out to the knowledge bases; (7) appreciation and recognition; (8) caring, celebration, and humor; (9)

involvement in decision making; (10) protection of what's important; (11) traditions; and (12) honest, open communication (p. 6).

An outgrowth of the effective schools research has been the development of what is commonly known as the school improvement process (SIP). This process puts into action the components identified as important to improve the quality of schools. Effective leaders of the school improvement process focus on addressing the needs of, and expectations for, *all* students through planning and monitoring continuous improvement. By holding high standards for personal and organizational performance, such leaders promote student self-reflection, as well as the use of assessment data to ensure that every student is challenged to perform at the highest possible level. School improvement is orchestrated through collaborative efforts of a school improvement team that includes teachers, other school staff, and community members, and is empowered by the school leader.

Recognizing that schools exist to meet the educational needs of the entire community that they serve, it is important to bring together representatives of as many interested and invested groups (stakeholders) as possible for the purpose of building a shared vision. Stakeholders can be divided into two distinct entities: the internal public and the external public.

The internal public of a school organization includes the board of education members, school administration, professional teaching staff, students, support staff consisting of secretarial, custodial, paraprofessionals, food service and transportation employees, and parents of students. The external public is made up of business and industrial leaders, community service groups, community members without children in public schools, including senior citizens, government and political leaders and power brokers, key communicators, and school liaison groups such as alumni organizations and booster groups.

Effective educational leaders guide these stakeholders through a process of examining relevant data about the current status of the school's programs, its successes as well as its areas of need, demographic data specific to the community it serves, and sources of potential resources. "Strategically, the organization (i.e., the school) must know of the existence of resources, employ managerial talent to import and organize their use, and then call upon organizational intelligence to make sure that the entire system, including its environments, is well served" (Razik & Swanson, 2001, p. 37).

CONSENSUS BUILDING

The consensus process is an effective model for engaging stakeholders in planning. In seeking mutual agreement, this process fosters individual differences; personal self-reliance and self-esteem; creativity and innovation; cooperative attitudes; and improved interpersonal communications and relationships, responsibility, and accountability (Saint & Lawson, 1994). Saint and Lawson (1994) suggest the following strategies to promote and support the consensus process: (a) create unity, (b) value diversity, (c) involve everyone, (d) promote imagination, (e) look for the third way, (f) use internal rewards, (g) promote value of learning, (h) encourage self-reliance, and (i) encourage empathetic listening (p. 67–70).

In his book *More Than 50 Ways to Build Team Consensus,* Williams (1993) cites additional ways to facilitate the consensus process. He describes simple strategies to form committed teams, including the following: visualizing the common direction, activities that create visible documentation toward the goal, and suggested processes for illuminating the total framework for action.

The goal throughout the stage of creating a vision is to capture the best thinking of everyone involved. The strength of the consensus process lies in the quality of the group's decision as it is rooted in input and ownership, to provide the inspiration for those in the group to embrace and follow. As Williams (1993) reports, "The process of experiencing consensus is deeply energizing" (p. 3).

It is expected that throughout the vision development process, the stakeholders involved in the critical review are engaged in on-going communication with the groups they represent. Following this two-way communication, everyone involved in the development process is expected to utilize existing communication vehicles and, where necessary, create new avenues to share the results of their efforts. Building deeper understanding and consensus within the representative stakeholder bodies achieves the grassroots ownership that supports and sustains the vision over time. Weller and Weller (2000) further suggest, "Vision unites the leader and the followers to achieve common, agreed-upon ends and provides the strong sense of commitment, purpose, and direction necessary to achieve quality outcomes" (p. 49).

ARTICULATING THE VISION

The next stage of implementation is to effectively communicate the vision within the larger organization and throughout the greater community. Use of the visual image, the presence of the written and spoken word, and the actions of members of the school community best articulate the vision of the organization. The vision statement needs to be visible in daily/weekly staff bulletins, in newsletters and handbooks, on monthly calendars and bulletin board notices, and prominent on Web and home pages and in the school and newspapers. Banners, school marquees, and displays are other avenues for visibility.

School leaders must effectively use the opportunities presented to them daily to articulate and model the vision of the schools. To do so, they must carefully consider the message that they wish to communicate and the way in which it will be communicated. They need to observe the reactions, both verbal and nonverbal, of those to whom they are speaking. Understanding the background of the audience, the interest they have in the message, and the amount of

time available to share with the audience are all abundantly important to one's effectiveness in the articulation process. Good communicators speak with clarity and conviction, show passion and enthu-
siasm for their message, take the time to be appropriately prepared,
and are honest and consistent with their public. In practice, a good
leader becomes both the defender of, and the cheerleader for, the
school's vision. Wallace (as cited in Hoyle, 1995) notes that leaders
"must envision strengthened schools and be able to energize professionals and the community to bring about the conditions that will ensure a high-quality educational product" (p. 60).

An even more powerful statement of the school's vision is embedded in the underlying philosophy and beliefs that are the
sources of support for leadership behaviors. As Kouzes and Posner
(1993) note, "We learn whether or not we can count on our leaders by watching them operate in a wide variety of settings. Consistency reveals to us both a depth of conviction and an internal integration of words and actions" (p. 195).

IMPLEMENTATION OF THE VISION

Implementing the vision through the strategic planning process
can be accomplished only if there is "emphatic and relentless support of the plan from those at the top of the organization" (Cook,
1995, p. 147) and also acceptance and ownership of the vision on
the part of everyone within the organization. The responsibility for
helping those within the individual school building understand and
commit to their part in making the school vision "real" rests with
the building-level leadership.

The steps needed to move from identification to ownership are
many. First, as each individual school community attempts to construct its future, it begins with the district's vision statement as a
basis upon which to develop its own school mission and goal statements. Often this is designated as "staff development," a process

through which leadership becomes a shared commitment, and a sense of responsibility focused on student success becomes central for everyone involved. Kouzes and Posner (1993) assert, "If we are to clarify values, build understanding and commitment to shared values, and create communities where people perceive cooperative goals and mutual respect, then we must concurrently establish the capacity of people and work teams to take on their new leadership responsibilities" (p. 155).

The mission statement generated through this process is a detailed message to constituents describing "what" the vision of the organization is and "how" it will be realized. Educational programs, plans, and actions are the products of the mission statement. Goal statements should follow naturally from the mission and should always include standards or benchmarks by which the school can measure progress and success.

In each case participants absolutely must utilize existing resources to implement the vision, mission, and goals, and build toward the development of new resources or the redistribution of existing resources to support future growth. In this way, the organization has "built capacity" for achieving its goals by enlarging the understanding and abilities of the people within the organization and identified areas where it needs and acquires new resources.

LEADING CHANGE

As educational organizations grow and respond to the demands of an ever-changing complex external environment, leaders must understand the challenges salient in collective reactions to change. Bolman and Deal (1991) identify these issues as the following:

- Change causes people to feel incompetent, needy, and powerless.
- Change creates confusion and unpredictability throughout the organization.

- Change generates conflict.
- Change creates loss. (p. 397)

Understanding these dimensions of change, particularly as they apply to and affect their own organization, is perhaps the most difficult and daunting task for a leader. The challenge is to create an internal environment that is supportive and proactive and also has in place cultural norms, policies, and procedures that anticipate these reactions to change, thus minimizing and mitigating the heightened anxiety inherent in substantive organizational change. Combs, Miser, and Whitaker (1999) indicate that:

> In a school where concern for learning and change dominates the vision and the daily reality of school life, people see learning as a journey that is taken together in a climate that supports risk taking. This kind of school does not see learning as an arrival point predetermined by others, for others. Instead, the school arranges itself so that learning needs are met; people feel free from threat; passion for the learning of all people is encouraged; honest communication through supportive dialogue links people in common, aligned goals; and all people feel included through the expectation of cooperative and collaborative work. (p. 94)

Schwahn and Spady (1998) summarize the steps involved in vision development, articulation, and implementation. They address the following conditions that are essential for change to occur in organizations:

Purpose—*"It has meaning for me."* Purpose is the deep reason that the organization exists, which employees must share to find value and meaning in their work, and constituents must endorse to identify with organizational aims.

Vision—*"It's clear and exciting."* Vision is the Total Leader's blueprint and road map for change.

Ownership—*"I want to be part of it."* Ownership is the strong identification with, investment in, and commitment to the organization's purpose and vision statement.

Capacity—"I can do it." Capacity is the knowledge, skills, resources, and tools needed to successfully make the changes implied in the organization's stated purpose and vision statement.

Support—"Our leader is helping us do it." Support comprises the policies, decisions, attention, resources, and procedures that enable employees and constituents to make and sustain the changes implied in the purpose and vision. (pp. 22–23)

STEWARDSHIP OF THE VISION

District-level leadership plays a key role in the successful implementation of the vision. Beyond this, district leaders serve as stewards guarding and protecting the school's purpose and vision and empowering building-level leaders to create and maintain the mission and goals of the school. "Being the steward of a vision shifts a leader's relationship toward her or his personal vision. It ceases to be a possession, as in 'this is *my* vision,' and becomes a calling" (Senge, 1990, p. 352).

A critical element of stewardship is the regular monitoring, evaluation, and revision process related to the vision, mission, and goals. One method of achieving this is through the support of action research on the part of educational professionals.

DEVELOPING SCHOOL IMPROVEMENT PLANS

In the current era of school reform, school leaders must go beyond simply establishing mission statements, developing a vision, and creating strategic plans. An increasing number of states are holding school administrators and teachers accountable for students' success and demonstrating improved student achievement at the building level. Many schools now are required to develop Comprehensive School Improvement Plans, which describe their strengths and weaknesses, specify their annual learning goals, and establish benchmarks for ensuring success (Jackson & Davis, 2000). State statutes typically require schools to annually communicate their progress toward their learning goals to their constituents and the state departments of education. Some educators may be uncomfortable with reporting this information through school district newsletters and local newspapers, but it is a natural outcome of the accountability movement.

It would be difficult to argue with the statement that, when teachers and administrators target their efforts toward student learning, improved student achievement likely will result. School leaders must be committed to educational equity for all students. To assist leaders in this aim, teachers and administrators must be proficient in disaggregating achievement data by ethnicity, race, gender, socioeconomic levels, and special education status to determine whether different groups of students are achieving at substantially similar levels (Jackson & Davis, 2000).

School leaders cannot assume their schools will automatically improve when they develop a data-driven School Improvement Plan because barriers frequently impede school initiatives. In a survey of 287 faculty members participating in a school improvement program, the most frequently identified obstacles for teachers were lack of time, staff conflict, and lack of funding (Hackmann, Tack, & Pokay, 1999). Leaders must make certain that adequate resources are provided to assist faculties with their school improvement goals. Additionally, they will need to continue to identify ways to promote faculty collaboration and consensus.

Jackson and Davis (2000) recommend that school faculties develop a detailed, concise action plan that clearly describes the school's goals. The plan should do the following:

- Describe specific activities, strategies, or actions to be taken
- Identify who is responsible for implementation
- Set a timeline with target dates
- Identify financial, professional development, and other resources
- List the expected results in concrete and specific terms

- Determine how progress will be measured
- Describe how information will be shared.

By creating a detailed School Improvement Plan, all parties will be informed of their individual and collective responsibilities for students' success.

ACTION RESEARCH

In educational terms, action research is the engagement of a network of professional educators in the improvement of their own craft of teaching. It represents the behaviors of educators that most visibly demonstrates that schools are learning organizations. Schmoker (1999) states, "It is time for teams of practitioners to tap into the power of best practice while continuously engaging in results-oriented 'action research' " (p. x). By encouraging and supporting these professionals in this discovery process, leaders empower their professional staff to initiate the changes necessary to ensure success for their students and themselves.

Keefe and Jenkins (1997) list several key assumptions that serve as the basis for conducting action research at the school level:

- Theory about practice is generated by data collected in the practical arena where educators are trusted professionals, empowered to make local decisions.
- Schools are the laboratories where research in school practice is the direct result of educators' questions about instruction.
- Action research is both a process and a product.
- Recommendations for school improvement grounded in the school setting engender greater commitment on the part of educators.

Schools that operate on these assumptions see themselves as engaged in "intellectual professional pursuit," (Sagor, 1992, p. 4) with staff members intimately involved "in generating the knowledge that informs their practice" (p. 5).

Collaborative action research incorporates five sequential steps (Sagor, 1992). The first step is problem formulation, in which the practitioner(s) identify the issues that are of greatest concern, reflect on what they know about them, and identify the gaps in their knowledge base.

Step two is the data collection process. In this process the researchers plan the use of instruments and methods that will accurately measure the phenomena that they are studying and engage in the data collection process through the use of these instruments and methods.

Analyzing the data collected is the third step. This phase involves a systematic approach of developing themes and patterns that are revealed by the data. Sharing the discovery with colleagues is the fourth step, which creates a heightened awareness of the research and its usefulness to the school. Lastly, because the purpose of this endeavor is professional improvement, action plans must be put into place to incorporate the new knowledge in professional practice.

Engagement in the action research process provides a platform for teachers to move from the professional role of mechanic/technician to the professional role of creative investigator and problem solver. "This new vision rejects the mindless application of standardized practices across all settings and contexts, and instead advocates the use of contextually relevant procedures formulated by inquiring and resourceful practitioners" (Stringer, 1996, p. 3).

SUMMARY

Educational leaders who can successfully meet ISLLC Standard 1 can expect substantive and meaningful change in their organization, resulting in increased student learning and success. A key factor that frequently is overlooked in sustaining such change is the need to recognize and celebrate success throughout the entire process. Participants in all dimensions of the vision development, articulation, implementation, and stewardship phases of the improvement process need to be congratulated and their efforts validated at every opportunity. This, too, is the responsibility of a leader. Only when people feel that their efforts are recognized, appreciated, and valuable can there exist any expectation of continued progress and expanded effort. School improvement is a job that is never finished. Indeed, it is a continuous, cyclical process requiring the renewal of commitment in each new cycle of endeavor. Without the recognition and celebration of *past* success, *future* achievement is jeopardized. The future, after all, is what vision is all about.

SUGGESTED INTERNSHIP ACTIVITIES RELATED TO STANDARD I

Review the present skill levels you noted on your ISLLC Standards Self-Assessment under Standard 1. Note areas in which you wish to improve your skills, and working with your mentor and supervisor, identify activities that you can complete during your internship. The following listing of activities related to Standard 1 is provided to help you identify projects that may be appropriate for your clinical experience:

1. Participate in the district-level strategic planning process that includes community members, school staff, and students.
2. Lead your individual school in the process of implementing the district vision at the building level.
3. Engage in a resource assessment process in the community for the purpose of identifying existing and potential resources—human, economic, and cultural—that might be directed toward the attainment of the school's vision.

4. Oversee a campaign to garner additional financial resources needed to achieve the school district's vision and mission.

5. Review the school's or district's mission statement, and conduct a faculty discussion related to the organization's success in achieving the mission.

6. Create an action research team around a student learning/ school building challenge, collect and analyze data related to the challenge, and present a plan to apply your new knowledge.

7. Review the district's organizational chart. Research the evolution of the organization and the role that each entity plays in supporting student learning.

8. Identify the district's core values. Meet with key leaders within the organization and ascertain how the system functions to mirror these core values.

9. Serve as a chairperson of the School Improvement Team in your building for at least one academic year or volunteer to chair or serve on the School Improvement Team for the elementary school where you reside.

10. Compile necessary data and complete school reports (i.e., district, state, or national reports; accreditation reports).

11. Evaluate the extent to which school improvement goals are being accomplished.

12. Identify the constituencies that compose your internal and external publics. Select an individual from each of these representative groups and start a "key communicators/ informants" process.

13. Lead a consensus-building exercise to address a specific challenge(s) facing your school.

14. Critique a variety of communication vehicles used in your district or school regarding messages that are being conveyed about the vision and mission of your school.

15. Identify the cultural norms of the community and prepare an analysis of how these are reflected in the educational program of the school.

16. Conduct research to determine how the building school improvement plan relates to the districtwide vision of success for all students. Examine disaggregated data to see how different groups are performing within the school. Prepare a summary for the school improvement team with recommendations for implementation.

17. Based on your ISLLC Standards Self-Assessment under Standard 1, select one or two books from the suggested readings that will help expand your knowledge of topics related to this standard. In addition, select one of the Web site resources listed, review the information available, and identify how this resource can assist you in your professional development.

SUGGESTED READINGS

Barth, R. (1990). *Improving schools from within.* San Francisco: Jossey-Bass.

Bolman, L., & Deal, T. (1995). *Leading with soul: An uncommon journey of spirit.* San Francisco: Jossey-Bass.

Bonstingl, J. J. (2001). *Schools of quality: An introduction to Total Quality Management in education* (3rd ed.). Alexandria, VA: Association for Supervision and Curriculum Development.

Bridges, W. (1991). *Managing transitions: Making the most of change.* Reading, MA: Addison-Wesley.

Deming, W. E. (1986). *Out of crisis.* Cambridge: MA: MIT Center for Advanced Engineering Studies.

Elliot, J. (1991). *Action research for educational change.* Bristol, PA: Open University Press.

Fullan, M. (1993). *Change forces: Probing the depths of educational reform.* Bristol, PA: The Falmer Press.

Fullan, M. (1999). *Change forces: The sequel.* New York: Falmer Press.

Gardner, J. W. (1990). *On leadership.* New York: The Free Press.

Glasser, W. (1992). *The quality school.* New York: HarperCollins.

Glickman, C. (1996). *Renewing America's schools: A guide for school-based action.* San Francisco: Jossey-Bass.

Goodstein, L., Nolan, T., & Pfeiffer, J. W. (1992). *Applied strategic planning: How to develop a plan that really works.* New York: McGraw-Hill.

Haller, E. J., & Kleine, P. F. (2001). *Using educational research: A school administrator's guide.* Needham Heights, MA: Allyn and Bacon.

Hargraves, A. (Ed). (1997). *Rethinking educational change with heart and mind.* Alexandria, VA: Association of Supervision and Curriculum Development.

Lashway, L. (1997). *Leading with vision.* Eugene, OR: ERIC Clearinghouse on Educational Management.

McDonald, J. P. (1996). *Redesigning school: Lessons for the 21st century.* San Francisco: Jossey-Bass.

Nanus, B. (1992). *Visionary leadership: Creating a compelling sense of direction for your organization.* San Francisco: Jossey-Bass.

O'Toole, J. (1995). *Leading change: The ideology of comfort and the tyranny of custom.* San Francisco: Jossey-Bass.

Ramsey, R. D. (1999). *Lead, follow, or get out of the way: How to be a more effective leader in today's schools.* Thousand Oaks, CA: Corwin Press.

Senge, P. (1990). *The fifth discipline: The art and practice of the learning organization.* New York: Doubleday.

Senge, P., Cambron-McCabe, N., Lucas, T., Smith, B., Dutton, J., & Kleiner, A. (2000). *Schools that learn.* New York: Doubleday.

Sergiovanni, T. J. (1992). *Moral leadership: Getting to the heart of school improvement.* San Francisco: Jossey-Bass.

Slavin, R. E. (1996). *Every child, every school: Success for all.* Thousand Oaks, CA: Corwin Press.

Schwahn, C., & Spady, W. (1998). *Total leaders: Applying the best future-focused change strategies to education.* Arlington, VA: American Association of School Administrators.

Speck, M. (1999). *The principalship: Building learning community.* Upper Saddle River, NJ: Prentice-Hall.

Valentine, E. P. (1997). *Strategic management in education* (2nd ed.). Baltimore: The Pasteur Center for Strategic Management.

Williams, R. B. (1993). *More than 50 ways to build team consensus.* Palatine, IL: IRI/Skylight Publishing.

WEB SITE RESOURCES

Phi Delta Kappa (PDK)
www.pdkintl.org/home.shtml

American Association of School Administrators (AASA)
www.aasa.org

The Coalition of Essential Schools
www.essentialschools.org

National School Boards Association (NSBA)
www.nsba.org

University Council for Educational Administration (UCEA)
www.ucea.org

REFERENCES

Alexander, W. F., & Serfass R. W. (1999). *Futuring tools for strategic quality planning in education.* Milwaukee, WI: ASQ Quality Press.
Bolman, L., & Deal, T. (1991). *Reframing organizations: Artistry, choice, and leadership.* San Francisco: Jossey-Bass.
Bonstingl, J. J. (2001). *Schools of quality: An introduction to Total Quality Management in education* (3rd ed.). Alexandria, VA: Association for Supervision and Curriculum Development.
Bracey, G. W. (2000). Tenth annual Bracey report on the condition of public education. *Phi Delta Kappan, 82,* 133–144.
Combs, A., Miser, A., & Whitaker, K. (1999). *On becoming a school leader: A person-centered challenge.* Alexandria, VA: Association for Supervision and Curriculum Development.
Cook, W. J. (1995). *Strategic planning for America's schools* (Rev. ed.). Arlington, VA: American Association of School Administrators.

Cunningham, W. G., & Cordeiro, P. A. (2000). *Educational administration: A problem-based approach.* Needham Heights, MA: Allyn and Bacon.

Dufour, R., & Eaker, R. (1998). *Professional learning communities at work: Best practices for enhancing student achievement.* Bloomington, IN: National Educational Service.

Edmonds, R. (1979). Effective schools for the urban poor. *Educational Leadership, 37*(1), 15–18, 20–24.

Goodstein, L., Nolan, T., & Pfeiffer, J. W. (1992). *Applied strategic planning: How to develop a plan that really works.* New York: McGraw-Hill.

Hackmann, D. G., Tack, M. W., & Pokay, P. H. (1999). Results oriented school improvement: Lessons from practice. *International Journal of Educational Reform, 8*(1), 8–14.

Hoyle, J. R. (1995). *Leadership and futuring: Making visions happen.* Thousand Oaks, CA: Corwin Press.

Jackson, A. W., & Davis, G. A. (2000). *Turning points 2000: Educating adolescents in the 21st century.* New York: Teachers College Press.

Keefe, J., & Jenkins, J. (1997). *Instruction and the learning environment.* Larchmont, NY: Eye on Education.

Kouzes, J., & Posner, B. (1993). *Credibility: How leaders gain it and lose it, why people demand it.* San Francisco: Jossey-Bass.

Lezotte, L. (1997). *Learning for all.* Okemos, MI: Effective School Products.

Nanus, B. (1992). *Visionary leadership.* San Francisco: Jossey-Bass.

National Association of Secondary School Principals. (1996). *Breaking ranks: Changing an American institution.* Reston, VA: Author.

Newmann, F., & Wehlage, G. (1995). *Successful school restructuring: A report to the public and educators by the Center for Restructuring Schools.* Madison, WI: University of Wisconsin Press.

Patterson, J. L. (1993). *Leadership for tomorrow's schools.* Alexandria, VA: Association for Supervision and Curriculum Development.

Razik, T. A., & Swanson, A. D. (2001). *Fundamental concepts of educational leadership* (2nd ed.). Upper Saddle River, NJ: Prentice-Hall.

Sagor, R. (1992). *How to conduct collaborative action research.* Alexandria, VA: Association for Supervision and Curriculum Development.

Saint, S., & Lawson, J. R. (1994). *Rules for reaching consensus: A modern approach to the age-old process of making decisions.* San Diego, CA: Pfeiffer & Company.

Schmoker, M. (1999). *Results: The key to continuous school improvement* (2nd ed.). Alexandria, VA: Association for Supervision and Curriculum Development.

Schwahn, C., & Spady, W. (1998). *Total leaders: Applying the best future-focused change strategies to education.* Arlington, VA: American Association of School Administrators.

Senge, P. M. (1990). *The fifth discipline: The art and practice of the learning organization.* New York: Doubleday.

Seyfarth, J. T. (1999). *The principal: New leadership for new challenges.* Upper Saddle River, NJ: Prentice-Hall.

Stringer, E. T. (1996). *Action research: A handbook for practitioners.* Thousand Oaks, CA: Sage Publications.

Valentine, E. P. (1997). *Strategic management in education* (2nd ed.). Baltimore: The Pasteur Center for Strategic Management.

Weller, L. D., & Weller, S. (2000). *Quality human resources leadership: A principal's handbook.* Lanham, MD: Scarecrow Press.

Williams, R. B. (1993). *More than 50 ways to build team consensus.* Palatine, IL: IRI/Skylight Publishing.

③

A CULTURE FOR
LEARNING AND GROWTH

Standard 2: A school administrator is an educational leader who promotes the success of all students by advocating, nurturing, and sustaining a school culture and instructional program conducive to student learning and staff professional growth.

INTRODUCTION

Creating and sustaining a culture for learning and growth is the process through which leaders operationalize the mission and vision of the educational organization. Instructional leadership is at the heart of this process and embedded in this leadership is the requirement to engage the organization in the process of change at every level. At the individual level, this approach requires staff development focused on lifelong learning and on improving student achievement. At the school-building level, a culture must be established that supports collaboration and recognizes diversity in learners and curriculum. At the district level, leaders must make a commitment to providing the resources that support professional staff development and improvement efforts across the organization.

This chapter will discuss the four major elements involved in creating and sustaining a culture for learning and growth in schools: school culture, the instructional program and curriculum development, student learning, and professional staff development. These are the elements that compose ISLLC Standard 2.

SCHOOL CULTURE

Schools, like other organizations, are defined by patterns of behavior and structure that are commonly referred to as "culture." Schein (1984) defines culture as:

> [A] pattern of basic assumptions—invented, discovered, or developed by a given group as it learns to cope with its problems of external adaptation and internal integration—that has worked well enough to be considered valid and, therefore, to be taught to new members as the correct way to perceive, think, and feel in relation to those problems. (p. 9)

Such patterns provide school staff members with a framework. This framework gives "meaning, passion, and purpose" (Deal & Peterson, 1999, p. 1) to the day-to-day activities of the organization and, as a result, it is valued by those within the organization. Deal and Peterson (1999) note, "Cultural patterns are highly enduring, have [a] powerful impact on performance and shape the ways people think, act, and feel" (p. 4). To put it simply, culture is the way things are done in an organization that make it different, unique, and compelling.

Strategic planning and vision development, discussed in Chapter 2, are, along with culture building, three related tasks required for effective school leadership. A strong culture is formed through opportunities to share what is important about one's work, through structured interaction that highlights both common elements and diversity, and through supportive risk-taking that builds trust as well as personal and professional growth. "Culture pervades people's minds and forms their model for perceiving, relating, and interpreting their management, their work, and their selves. The professional lives within a school culture derive importance, meaning, identity, and belongingness from this culture" (Cunningham & Gresso, 1993, p. 32).

Pervasive throughout effective school cultures are high expectations of performance for leaders, students, and staff. Everyone in the organization is treated with dignity and respect; their contributions are valued and important; and their accomplishments are recognized and celebrated. Educational leaders are charged with the responsibility of ensuring that programs and processes are aligned for success and that the climate and culture of the organization are regularly assessed. The organization and its people are focused both on the commitment that "all children can learn" and the responsibility for preparing students to be outstanding contributors to society. Unfortunately, some educators interpret the word "all" to mean "most"; as a result, some children with disabilities are excluded from this statement. Understanding that "all," indeed, refers to *every* child, effective educators are committed to all children's success, regardless of their disabilities (Jackson & Davis, 2000).

Deal and Peterson (1999) report that school principals and superintendents who have successfully developed strong, supportive cultures concentrate their efforts on the following elements:

- A mission focused on student and teacher learning
- A rich sense of history and purpose
- Core values of collegiality, performance, and improvement that engender quality, achievement, and learning for everyone
- Positive beliefs and assumptions about the potential of students and staff to learn and grow

- A strong professional community that uses knowledge, experience, and research to improve practice
- An informal network that fosters positive communication flow
- Shared leadership that balances continuity and improvement
- Rituals and ceremonies that reinforce core cultural values
- Stories that celebrate successes and recognize heroines and heroes
- A physical environment that symbolizes joy and pride
- A widely shared sense of respect and caring for everyone. (p. 116)

Such leaders provide multiple occasions for staff to work together on projects that have both significance for and an impact on the organization. Each occasion is characterized by collaboration and teamwork to ensure ownership and is recognized by a specific tie-in to the instructional goals of the group.

Ultimately, school leaders who develop strong, positive cultures become aware of the direct link between these cultures and improved teaching and learning. "Numerous studies of school change have identified the organizational culture as critical to the successful improvement of teaching and learning" (Deal & Peterson, 1999, p. 5). Instructional improvement thrives in an environment of mutual support and growth for both staff and students. Lambert (1998) notes that:

> [L]eadership is about learning together, and constructing meaning and knowledge collectively and collaboratively. It involves opportunities to surface and mediate perceptions, values, beliefs, information, and assumptions through continuing conversations; to inquire about and generate ideas together; to seek to reflect upon and make sense of work in the light of shared beliefs and new information; and to create actions that grow out of these new understandings. (pp. 5–6)

INSTRUCTIONAL PROGRAM

The importance of and basis for the leadership of schools correspond to the purpose of the schools themselves—the delivery of effective instructional programs resulting in student gains. Thus, those who aspire to such leadership must have a thorough, solid grounding in both the theory and practice of effective instruction. Conceptual skills in this area require understanding of the content of the program as well as the nature of the learner.

Successful instructional leadership recognizes that society and the times have changed, and that practices that were effective in the past, even the recent past, need to be reexamined in light of today's societal realities. Most prominent among the challenges confronting today's principals is the mandate "to provide a positive learning environment for a highly diverse student population" (Ferrandino, 2001, p. 441). Not only is the mix of students in our schools more culturally, ethnically, and economically heterogeneous than ever before, but it also is characterized by numerous societal stressors.

A study conducted in 1995 by the American Association of School Administrators (AASA) about how students have changed since the 1960s revealed the following trends:

- The number of "dysfunctional" families has grown.
- Advanced technology has influenced school, work, and home life.
- Children are threatened by crime, violence, ignorance, and poverty.
- Communities are changing and becoming more diverse.
- Mass media grip our children, giving them more knowledge at an earlier age.
- Children shun authority, traditional values, and responsibilities.
- A hurry-up society often lacks a sense of community.
- Changing workplace demands create a need for higher levels of literacy.
- Knowledge about learning styles demands new kinds of education.
- Peers exert a powerful influence on values. (Uchida, Cetron, & McKenzie, 1996, pp. 4–5)

As administrators work with teachers who instruct diverse students coming to schools shaped by these factors, they must be thoroughly conversant with multiple ways of analyzing the various facets of the work of the teacher, from the initial planning stages of lessons, through the creating of a culture for learning in the classroom, to actual teaching-learning activities and the assessment of student learning.

Promoting Sound Instructional Planning

Good planning of any kind begins with a mental image of what is necessary for success in the venture. Recent research on what constitutes effective teaching has helped to define the elements of teacher behaviors that are most likely to promote positive results. Successful teaching begins with the analysis of lesson structure, information about learning styles, brain research, multiple intelligences, authentic assessment, and constructivist classrooms to shape instructional decision-making about the content and the process of learning (Caine & Caine, 1991; Danielson, 1996; Gardner, 1991; Hunter, 1982; Jacobs, 1997; Jensen, 1998; Newmann, Secada, & Wehlage, 1995).

Planning for this kind of teaching uses clear principles of child and adolescent psychology to structure classroom time so as to engage the learner in curriculum-based, relevant, and developmentally appropriate activities. These activities create meaning for the learner, unite instructional elements, and build a bridge from the known to the unknown. Tomlinson (1999) notes, "Thus, in a healthy classroom, what is taught and learned is relevant to students; it seems personal, familiar, connected to the world they know" (p. 30).

The skill necessary to engage in this kind of planning is not gained solely from information found in books but is honed through classroom experience and teachers' reflections on their work. As the instructional leader, the principal must help teachers develop an array of teaching tools from which to select those methods most likely to succeed, based on knowledge of both students and curriculum. This type of planning for instruction is improved when the principal and teachers form a learning community and together "focus on the elements of design that are most likely to engage students, using our knowledge of the student-user and the subject as the basis" (Wiggins & McTighe, 1998, pp. 118–119).

Plans also need to include a variety of strategies for the ongoing assessment of students' learning. Here, again, it is the role of the administrator to help teachers grow in their knowledge of when and how to use these strategies (Danielson & McGreal, 2000). Administrators should identify and use both traditional and more recent authentic assessment models to inform and manage the instructional process in both formative and summative modes. The sources of student assessment also need to be broad-based. Fenwick and Parsons (2000) note,

> Too often, teachers and learners equate evaluation with something done at the end of a program of study, as useful to get a grade. However, to be effective, evaluation must be ongoing, continuous, and completely integrated into the learning process. It can come from a peer, an instructor, the consequences of the task itself, or oneself— through comparing one's performance with a model or set of standards or through sudden insight. (p. 113)

The analysis of the total picture evident through examination of these many sources is the key to effective and sustained learning resulting from informed instruction.

Supporting a Positive Classroom Environment

One of the major elements of teachers' professional practice is skill in creating a classroom environment that is based on mutual respect and strong organizational standards (Danielson,

1996). These standards are characterized by a focus on learning and reflect the culture of the school. The role of the educational leader in defining and supporting this learning culture is paramount.

A positive classroom environment emphasizes success rather than failure, as well as the value of learning from taking risks. This environment must be a place where it is all right, even expected, for students to use trial and error methods to learn. This is so because "[i]n a healthy classroom climate the teacher avoids using learning as a threat or a punishment" (Oliva & Pawlas, 2001, p. 189). Students need teachers who "inspire them with *confidence* that they can learn, accomplish, and interact successfully, design experiences that will impart the *competencies* needed for academic and social successes . . . create *chances* to use their skills" (Elias et al., 1997, p. 31).

To approach their students within this frame of reference, teachers need to feel a similar relationship with their instructional leader, the principal. The role of the principal in this situation "is to regularly reinforce and recognize improvement efforts, both privately and publicly" (Schmoker, 1999, p. 111), of their staff members, to build "the social capital that allows people to trust, depend on, and learn from one another" (Fink & Resnick, 2001, p. 606). Thus, teachers will experience, firsthand, the inner strength and growth that they are attempting to develop in their students.

Assessing Instruction and Learning

Instructional leadership most often is visible in how the principal interacts with teachers regarding actual classroom activities. Many have referred to this interaction as "classroom observation" and have thought of it as constituting the whole of teacher evaluation. It is actually only a part, albeit an important one, of the entire process of promoting the professional growth of the teacher, as discussed throughout this chapter.

Over the past few decades, the focus on teacher evaluation has shifted away from the act of teaching to the process of learning. The principal who works effectively with teachers interacts with them regularly about what they are teaching, how they are teaching it, and what the results are, as they relate to students' achievement. Thus, before visiting a classroom and watching the teacher with students in that setting, the instructional leader has talked with the teacher about the specifics of what he or she has been doing, what the teacher expects to take place during the classroom visit, and how these activities support the formal school curriculum. This dialogue will give the principal evidence of the teacher's instructional planning and classroom management techniques. Additionally, it also will create a higher level of consciousness and understanding on the part of the teacher regarding his or her use of various instructional strategies, some of which may be intuitive and never previously addressed deliberately and consciously.

Instructional leaders and teachers can also collaborate using the contemporary emphasis on student assessment and testing, to use various data to analyze what is really happening with achievement, and to use the new insights to inform the instructional practices of the teacher. In this way, both the principal and the teacher share the responsibility for gains in student achievement.

With the great diversity among students in most classrooms today, and the immense volume of curricular content to be explored and mastered, one of the hallmarks of effective instruction is the ability of the teacher to use a variety of teaching-learning methods. Instructional leaders are charged with helping teachers to grow in their ability to use these tools in the classroom. Teaching approaches may be methodological, such as using direct questioning with some content or students, and more activity-based learning with other curricula or individuals. These tools could also be content-based, such as employing the synergistic impact of interdisciplinary lessons that use more than one content area to enhance understandings across the curriculum. "As teaching objectives shift from instilling facts to improving students' thinking skills, educators find their roles in the classroom also change. Increasingly, teachers must prepare for instruction that guides rather than directs, that poses questions rather than provides answers" (Davis, Hawley, McMullan, & Spilka, 1997, p. 42).

One of the most significant changes in today's classrooms is the use of technology, specifically the computer, in the instructional process. Because the role of the school is to help students gain the skills they will need to succeed in life, educational leaders must know about and be skilled in using technology, in its many forms, to enhance human potential. These instructional leaders must also help teachers reach this level of skill.

The impact of the computer and microchip on learning and the use of information across every facet of life have tremendous implications for the definition of effective teaching. The use of the computer in the classroom to assist textbook and teacher-defined learning that was prevalent in the 1980s has evolved to today's use of the computer as a primary source of information and a tool for defining what students must learn (Means, 2000). Rather than being considered an add-on to the curriculum, technology should be integrated into classroom instruction, as Brogan (2000) notes,

> Those who argue that classroom computers take up time that could be spent more valuably on developing academic and social skills miss the point. Guided use of the Internet for research develops a child's critical-thinking skills. Children learn to collaborate, consider multiple points of view, and evaluate various forms of information. (p. 58)

These are extremely valuable academic and social skills. Thus, the use of technology to support, enlarge, and shape the world of the classroom has become an essential skill for the successful teacher, regardless of the content area.

CURRICULUM DEVELOPMENT

Oliva and Pawlas (2001) believe, "Without a curriculum there can be no instruction: without instruction a curriculum is lifeless" (p. 273). The heart of the instructional program in any school is the curriculum that defines those "learnings" that the school accepts as its *raison d'être*. For schools to be successful, the curriculum must be both structurally sound and continuously reviewed and refined.

Review and revision of the curriculum, commonly referred to as curriculum development, is a major element in the effective leadership of the school. It is a process that includes multiple phases and emphases—curriculum audit, curriculum articulation, curriculum alignment, curriculum coordination—but one that essentially brings teachers and community together to determine what is to be taught and how it should be presented to maximize its impact. It insures that the curriculum is coherent and truly addresses the needs of the community that the school serves. As Beane (1995) notes: "A 'coherent' curriculum is one that holds together, that makes sense as a whole; and its parts, whatever they are, are unified and connected by that sense of the whole" (p. 3).

To promote improved student achievement in the school system, instructional leaders must require full alignment between the written, taught, and tested curriculum. English and Larson (1996) caution that when curriculum alignment is not part of this process, "the creation of a curriculum may provoke lowered achievement by directing teachers to select content that is not part of the test content. Children are then tested on what they have not been taught" (pp. 107–108). Furthermore, standardized tests that are not aligned to the curriculum tend to measure socioeconomic status: As a group, poor students do worse on these tests than their more affluent classmates. However, when tests are fully aligned to the written and taught curriculum, the influence of the socioeconomic factor is greatly diminished (English & Larson, 1996).

The curriculum development process requires the school leader to address three essential areas to be effective. First, she or he must be sensitive to the culture of the community. Because the curriculum is intended to prepare students to be productive members of their communities, what is taught in schools must be shaped and viewed through the lens of that community, reflecting its uniqueness as well as its integration within the larger society. "Schools used to be considered the hubs of their communities, and they need to take up that critical role again. Today's schools can no longer function apart from the larger society" (Ferrandino, 2001, p. 442).

To achieve this relevance, principals and superintendents must be in regular contact with various constituent groups in the community through participation in groups such as the Rotary, the Chamber of Commerce, and especially through inclusive parent groups. Such a group would insure a dialogue with parents of students from all geographical areas as well as grade levels of the school. "The heart of school leadership lies in developing positive personal and community relationships" (Azzara, 2000–01, p. 63) through this type of regular, ongoing communication.

Second, instructional leaders must know about the standards that make up the content of contemporary discussion about effective schools and how these standards and their accompanying benchmarks relate to their students. Although some spurn the standards and testing movements as attempts to make students pass in lockstep through the educational process, others have noted that standards help educators clearly identify goals with high levels of student achievement for themselves and their schools (Carr & Harris, 2001; Darling-Hammond, 1997; Glickman, 2000–01; Larabee, 2000).

School administrators need to work with teachers to address these standards in light of the assumptions upon which they are based and what they advocate for educational practice. They must also evaluate these standards on the basis of societal and community needs as evidenced in their own school settings and use their collaborative professional skills to define a curriculum that develops the individual capabilities of the student while simultaneously achieving a clearly articulated set of educational outcomes that support democratic ideals. Leadership to accomplish this work recognizes the need to make time and resources available to critically review what is taught, what is learned, and what can be done to improve the process, based upon the collaboratively defined vision of the school. Using this process, "leadership is more than just shared, it is fostered, nurtured, controlled, and held by all facets of the education community" (Neuman & Simmons, 2000, pp. 10–11).

Finally, effective school leaders are informed about the best practices to be used in delivery of instructional content. To keep their knowledge current in this area, instructional leaders must be avid consumers of professional literature and also be active in professional circles where such practices are debated and demonstrated. Educators have been justifiably criticized for not applying the results of research in their schools. Especially relevant here is action research that comes directly from the experience of classroom teachers and interaction with students. Having such first-hand knowledge of the best how-to's in instruction will provide the leader with a solid basis for continuous dialogue with teachers about the curriculum and its deployment in the classroom. The ultimate result of the entire curriculum development process, then, is to cause improvement throughout the learning organization. As English (2000) notes, "Curriculum development that does not challenge what schools do and how they do it is naïve" (p. 28).

STUDENT LEARNING

As noted above, effective school leaders, especially building-level leaders, must be thoroughly knowledgeable about how students learn, as defined in theories of human growth and development, about how to ignite the passion for learning through the students' motivation, and about how to address the great diversity in students' learning styles as well as in their backgrounds. Only with such knowledge as the foundation for action can principals provide the structure, facilitate the processes, and develop the programs that truly meet the needs of the students and the staff who serve them.

One of the most educationally significant areas of research affecting concepts of human growth and development that has developed in the last decade is that of brain research and brain-based learning. Caine and Caine (1997) state, "Although brain research is often so narrowly focused that it appears to have little to offer educators, when findings of neuroscientists are matched with findings in other domains, the implications are breathtaking" (p. 6). Educators are beginning to realize that the interconnectedness and relational aspects of acquiring new knowledge constitute the foundation of true learning as examined in light of brain research. Learning is a much more complex process than the mere collection of facts. It is a dynamic process requiring students to be critical thinkers and sophisticated consumers of information.

The advances in understanding how the brain functions have led to the emergence of a new learning theory called constructivism. Direct-instruction methods, which reinforce the lecture method, increasingly are being de-emphasized in favor of approaches that promote the active engagement of students in the learning process. Derived from the field of cognitive psychology and building on the work of Jean Piaget and Lev Vygotsky, constructivist theory is based on the belief that individuals actively create new knowledge and learning from their existing beliefs and personal experiences (Brooks & Brooks, 1993).

Constructivism rests on the following core assumptions: (a) the learner must be actively engaged in learning; (b) knowledge is constructed through social interaction; (c) knowledge is context-based, requiring students to be involved in real-world problem solving; (d) effective learning involves conceptual change; and learning involves metacognition, in which the individual reflects on his or her own learning experiences (Glatthorn, 1994). Such recent catchphrases as "student as worker," "teacher as coach," and "depth over breadth" reflect the movement to develop constructivist learning environments.

Another research-based concept that has recently entered into classroom practice is that of "emotional intelligence," as defined by Goleman (1995) and others. Helping students to understand their own emotions as well as those of others, and using students' emotional connections to various ideas and concepts to enhance their understanding of those ideas and concepts are major additions to instructional goals and objectives in schools today. "Emotion . . . is our biological thermostat and central to cognition and educational practice" (Sylwester, 2000, p. 20). Service learning, another new concept being used in the schools, is an extension of this idea of connecting emotion with learning activities. The result of both is greater personal meaning and cognition on the part of the student. One of the key roles of the principal is to help teachers identify major emotional factors and concepts and to incorporate them into their lessons and activities.

Two other important and related concepts that have greatly influenced teaching and learning in the past decade are those of learning styles and multiple intelligences. Gardner (1999) describes eight different kinds of intelligence: verbal-linguistic, logical-mathematical, musical, interpersonal, intrapersonal, spatial, bodily-kinesthetic, and naturalistic. Each of these "intelligences" and their combination within each individual results in preferred ways of learning that are unique to the individual. When this research is correlated with Carl Jung's psychological types (Jung, 1923), the result is a powerful theoretical base for recognizing and using various classroom approaches, giving students multiple opportunities to work within their unique learning patterns.

Here, again, it is important to note the role of the principal as instructional leader in helping teachers to learn about and apply these research tools in the classroom.

Instructional leaders and teachers frequently grapple with problems and situations related to the lack of student motivation. The key to unlocking the power of motivation lies in creating an environment in which students' self-interest and the learning objectives of the school come together. If instructional activities and school structure are grounded in the basic premises of the brain-based and learning-style research, teaching and learning would be characterized in understanding of the individual student and the meanings that he or she connects to the process and curricular content.

Many teachers must shift their methodology to incorporate the idea of teaching to establish meaning for students about what is being learned. These teachers have been trained in the stand-and-deliver "imparting of knowledge" concept of teaching. Jensen (1998) warns, "Never assume that because something is relevant to you, it's relevant to your students. Help them discover relevance, but don't impose your connections" (pp. 92–93). Teaching is also best done in a social context, as Jensen further suggests:

> Teachers who continue to emphasize one-sided lecture methods are violating an important principle of our brain: Essentially we are social beings and our brains grow in a social environment. Because we often forge meaning through socializing, the whole role of student-to-student discussion is vastly underused. . . . Talking, sharing, and discussing are critical; we are biologically wired for language and communicating with one another. (p. 93)

Principals and superintendents will find it necessary to help teachers understand and become comfortable with this approach to their role—some more than others. The reward, however, of the time and effort expended to create this understanding is a reduction of student problems caused by lack of motivation.

PROFESSIONAL STAFF DEVELOPMENT

School district personnel devote significant time and attention to the conceptualization and understanding of how students learn and grow. Similar time and effort is needed to identify how the adults in schools learn and grow and how they develop the skill and ability to assert their new knowledge in the practice of teaching. This is the role of professional staff development. As defined by Guskey (2000), professional staff development is composed of:

> . . . those processes and activities designed to enhance the professional knowledge, skills, and attitudes of educators so that they might, in turn, improve the learning of students. In some cases, it also involves learning how to redesign educational structures and cultures. It is an extremely important endeavor and central to education's advancement as a profession. (p. 16)

Indeed, most contemporary definitions of professional staff development have as their central themes and cornerstone the focus on the improvement of student learning and development of human potential. (Bradley, Kallick, & Regan, 1991; Guskey, 2000; Orlich, 1989; Weller & Weller, 2000; Zepeda, 1999).

Effective professional staff development addresses adults as life-long learners and begins with the focus on the individual staff member. Levine (1989) reports:

> We know that growth starts from within, the most effective forms of staff development begin with the self. The more you know about yourself, the better able you are to model effective learning, support the growth of others, and create a climate conducive to individual and group growth. (p. xv)

Speck and Knipe (2000) begin this process with the use of the "personal cycle of inquiry," with the school leader helping individual teachers to identify unique learning goals based on their career development and their students' instructional needs. The process continues by implementing a focused plan that applies teacher learning in classroom instruction and follows through with reflective evaluation. Fink and Resnick (2001) note that "the job of culture building and of guiding individual teachers regarding which . . . professional development opportunities to use belongs to the principal" (p. 602).

Research in the area of adult developmental theory has shown that adult learners are rich in experience, concerned about their personal development, problem-focused, self-directed, and desirous of having immediate application of their new knowledge. Because adults are at different stages in their development, leaders must customize staff development programs to address the differing dispositions of these adult learners. Bradley, Kallick, and Regan (1991) concur that "[t]he content and process of [staff development] programs that are most likely to promote developmental learning in adults have certain ingredients: real experiences, careful and continuous guided reflection, ongoing duration, and challenge and support" (p. 67). These elements are woven into several different effective models for helping teachers grow professionally.

STAFF DEVELOPMENT MODELS

Zepeda (1999) and Brouillette (1999) promote the use of a variety of staff development models using different embedded methods to achieve successful results. These models are best described in five general categories: the individually guided model of staff development; the observation/assessment model; the development/improvement process; the training model; and the inquiry model of staff development.

The individually guided model of staff development is characterized by self-directed learning, which is either a stand-alone

process or a part of a district's overall program. This process is focused on the individual taking responsibility for the identification
of his or her learning needs or interests, development of a plan to
address the needs/interests, engagement in the planned process,
and assessment of whether the process achieved the desired
goals.

The observation/assessment model of staff development,
which most educators associate with the teacher/classroom evaluation process, can be a very powerful opportunity for growth
and development when coupled with reflection and analysis.
Contemporary methods frequently used within this model are
peer coaching, mentoring, and clinical supervision. Critical to
these models' success is that district and building leaders are mutually committed to these processes as viable professional development for everyone involved. Danielson and McGreal (2000)
promote a three-track teacher evaluation model that focuses on
the formative aspects of evaluation, with professional learning
opportunities targeted at each individual teacher's identified areas of professional growth.

When teachers engage in problem-based learning activities associated and addressed in such forums as school improvement
committees, site-based decision-making bodies, and accreditation
efforts, they have the opportunity to focus on real-life issues that
are used to create active, learner-oriented environments for
growth. These are examples of the development/improvement
process model for professional development. The intense level of
participation in this model enhances the opportunity and potential
for true change and growth. One of the most popular models of
staff development is the training model, which is predominately
associated with in-service, workshop, or professional conference
participation. To succeed, training programs must have clear objectives and desired learner outcomes. To increase the opportunity
for skill development, such training programs need to include "exploration of theory, demonstration or modeling of a skill, practice

of the skill under simulated conditions, feedback about performance, and coaching" (Brouillette, 1999, p. 164). Such training
must also be part of a long-term, well-planned effort to provide ongoing training and practice in the skills to be developed.

Action research and study group/cluster are examples of the inquiry model of staff development. Action research is a systematic approach to the following: problem identification; research instrument
development; collection, organization and analysis of data; and action plans resulting from the findings. The study group/cluster
model uses a group of participants who have come together to explore and focus on topics chosen by the group. This model addresses
issues of immediate relevance and offers the opportunity for peer interaction as it relates to common professional interests.

Orlich (1989) synthesized research findings of several studies
conducted in the 1980s to identify the following 15 empirically
based traits for successful staff development programs: (1) needs
derived, (2) clearly stated objectives, (3) diverse groups with different needs, (4) collaborative planning, (5) flexibility in scheduling,
(6) relevant protocols, (7) options for individual and groups, (8) intensity of training, (9) problem-solving orientation, (10) involvement of principal, (11) concrete activities, (12) participant skills
practice, (13) assistance for classroom transfer, (14) long-range development, and (15) rewards and incentives structure
(p. 13). The level to which these traits are embedded in the specific
staff development model will vary with the processes used. Effective school leaders know that the strength and legitimacy of any
profession, especially education, depend on the continued growth
and development of its members. It is a leadership responsibility to
organize the time, resources, and effective avenues for self-assessment, reflection, consultation, and training toward that end.

DuFour and Eaker (1998) use the National Staff Development
Standards as the basis for their recommendations on the content,
the process, and the context of effective staff development programs. The content should:

- Be based on research
- Focus on both generic and discipline specific teaching skills
- Expand the repertoire of teachers to meet the needs of students who learn in diverse ways

The process of effective staff development should:

- Attend to the tenets of good teaching
- Provide the ongoing coaching that is critical to the mastery of new skills
- Result in reflection and dialogue on the part of participants
- Be sustained over a considerable period of time
- Be evaluated at several different levels, including evidence of improved student performance.

The context of effective staff development should:

- Be focused on individual schools and have strong support from the central office
- Be so deeply embedded in daily work that it is difficult to determine where the work ends and the staff development begins
- Foster renewal (pp. 276–277)

SUMMARY

District- and building-level leaders have as their central responsibilities creating and sustaining a culture for growth and development focused upon students and adults in schools. These responsibilities are the essence of ISLLC Standard 2. Commitment to these goals must be embedded in the vision and mission of the schools and operationalized in all daily activity. As Levine (1989) states, "Without supportive structures and a fertile school culture, growth will be isolated and idiosyncratic, its impact minimal and unstained" (p. xv).

SUGGESTED INTERNSHIP
ACTIVITIES RELATED TO STANDARD 2

Review the present skill levels you noted on your ISLLC Standards Self-Assessment under Standard 2. Note areas in which you wish to improve your skills and, working with your mentor(s) and supervisor, identify activities that you can complete during your internship experience. The following listing of activities related to Standard 2 is provided to assist you in identifying projects that may be appropriate for your clinical experience:

1. Chair a school professional development committee and utilize a needs assessment process to determine individual/group needs. Identify new strategies for engaging faculty/staff in development activities.
2. Research several climate instruments that would assist the principal or superintendent in assessing the school's or district's overall climate. Select one and administer it, to assess your organization's climate and culture.
3. Identify an instructional improvement plan, the sources of student data that support the plan and the strategies for implementing the plan.
4. Gather and analyze relevant student profile data to educate staff in changing demographic trends among school district students.
5. Work with building-level leaders to disaggregate student assessment data. Prepare a gap analysis for staff that identifies strategies to incorporate this information in future school improvement activities.
6. Review the district's teacher/classroom observation process and suggest strategies for an enhanced professional development focus in the process.

7. Review the district's supervision/evaluation process for support staff, noting any areas in which the models can be improved.
8. Identify the elements of toxic school culture and work with building-level leaders to create strategies to address them.
9. Volunteer to chair a building/districtwide subject area curriculum committee that is working through a curriculum alignment process.
10. Participate in an Individual Education Plan (IEP) committee for a special needs student.
11. Present a workshop for staff on three authentic assessment models of instruction.
12. Develop a process to evaluate the implementation of a new instructional program.
13. Organize, promote, and administer a "student of the week" program.
14. Shadow your mentor in the formal teacher evaluation process for at least two faculty members. Participate in all phases of the process, i.e., preobservation meeting, observation, and postconference activity.
15. Organize a "technology sharing" forum for faculty and staff. Have participants present current strategies related to technology usage in their classrooms. Summarize these strategies for presentation to the school board.
16. Become a school representative to a local community group such as Rotary, Exchange Club, Kiwanis, or Chamber of Commerce.
17. Form a study group or action research team around a relevant issue or challenge facing your school staff.
18. Work with a teacher to assist in the development of an individually guided staff development plan.
19. Observe several classrooms and scan for teaching that demonstrates the application of brain-based research and multiple intelligences research. Present evidence of the use of these exemplary practices at a staff meeting.

20. Review submitted teacher applications, recommend candidates for interviews, participate in the interviews, and (to the extent possible) make hiring recommendations to your mentor.
21. Implement a peer coaching model with teachers who are interested in piloting it.
22. Based on your ISLLC Standards Self-Assessment under Standard 2, select one or two books from the suggested readings that will help expand your knowledge on topics related to this standard. In addition, select one of the Web site resources listed, review the information available, and identify how this resource can assist you in your professional development.

SUGGESTED READINGS

Danielson, C., & McGreal, T. L. (2000). *Teacher evaluation to enhance professional practice.* Alexandria, VA: Association for Supervision and Curriculum Development.

Deal, T. E., & Peterson, K. D. (1999). *Shaping school culture: The heart of leadership.* San Francisco: Jossey-Bass.

English, F. W. (2000). *Deciding what to teach and test: Developing, aligning, and auditing the curriculum* (Millennium ed.). Newbury Park, CA: Corwin Press.

Erickson, H. L. (1998). *Concept-based curriculum and instruction: Teaching beyond the facts.* Thousand Oaks, CA: Corwin Press.

Glatthorn, A. A. (2000). *The principal as curriculum leader: Shaping what is taught and tested* (2nd ed). Thousand Oaks, CA: Corwin Press.

Glatthorn, A. A. (1994). *Developing a quality curriculum.* Alexandria, VA: Association for Supervision and Curriculum Development.

Glatthorn, A., & Fox, L. (1996). *Quality teaching through professional development.* Thousand Oaks, CA: Corwin Press.

Guskey, T., & Huberman, M. (Eds.). (1995). *Professional development in education.* New York: Teachers College Press.

Jensen, E. (1998). *Teaching with the brain in mind.* Alexandria, VA: Association for Supervision and Curriculum Development.

Newmann, F., Secada, W., & Wehlage, G. (1995). *A guide to authentic instruction and assessment: Vision, standards and scoring.* Madison, WI: Wisconsin Center for Education Research.

Osterman, K., & Kottkamp, R. (1993). *Reflective practice for educators: Improving schooling through professional development.* Newbury Park, CA: Corwin Press.

Pellicer, L. O. (1999). *Caring enough to lead: Schools and the sacred trust.* Thousand Oaks, CA: Corwin Press.

Sapp, S. E. (2000). *Guide to best practices for new school administrators.* Lanham, MD: The Scarecrow Press.

Sarason, S. (1996). *Revisiting the culture of the school and the problem of change.* New York: Teachers College Press.

Schmoker, M. (1999). *Results: The key to continuous school improvement* (2nd ed.). Alexandria, VA: Association for Supervision and Curriculum Development.

Silver, H. F., Strong, R. W., & Perini, M. J. (2000). *So each may learn: Integrating learning styles and multiple intelligences.* Alexandria, VA: Association for Supervision and Curriculum Development.

Sparks, D., & Hirsh, S. (1997). *A new vision for staff development.* Alexandria, VA: Association for Supervision and Curriculum Development.

Tanner, D., & Tanner, L. (1995). *Curriculum development: Theory and practice* (3rd ed.). Englewood Cliffs, NJ: Merrill-Prentice Hall.

Wiggins, G., & McTighe, J. (1998). *Understanding by design.* Alexandria, VA: Association for Supervision and Curriculum Development.

WEB SITE RESOURCES

ERIC Clearinghouse on Educational Management
www.eric.uoregon.edu

Association for Supervision and Curriculum Development (ASCD)
www.ascd.org

North Central Regional Education Library
www.ncrel.org

National Staff Development Council
www.nsdc.org

Assessment and Evaluation on the Internet—sponsored by ERIC
http://ericae.net/ninbod.htm

National Center for Conflict Resolution Education
www.nccre.org

Office of Educational Research and Improvement
www.ed.gov/offices/OERI

Achieve—Searchable database of state and international standards
www.achieve.org

National Center for Research on Evaluation, Standards, and Student
Testing (CRESST)
www.cse.ucla.edu

REFERENCES

Azzara, J. R. (2000–01). The heart of school leadership. *Educational Leadership, 58*(4), 62–64.

Beane, J. A. (1995). Introduction: What is a coherent curriculum? In J. A. Beane (Ed.), *Toward a coherent curriculum* (pp. 1–14). Alexandria, VA: Association for Supervision and Curriculum Development.

Bradley, M. K., Kallick, B. O., & Regan, H. B. (1991). *The staff development manager: A guide to professional growth.* Needham Heights, MA: Allyn and Bacon.

Brogan, P. (2000). Educating the digital generation. *Educational Leadership, 58*(2), 57–59.

Brooks, J. G., & Brooks, M. G. (1993). *In search for understanding: The case for constructivist classrooms.* Alexandria, VA: Association for Supervision and Curriculum Development.

Brouillette, L. (1999). In L. W. Hughes (ed). The principal as leader (p. 164). Upper Saddle River, NJ: Prentice Hall., Inc.

Caine, R. N., & Caine, G. (1991). *Making connections: Teaching and the human brain.* Alexandria, VA: Association for Supervision and Curriculum Development.

Caine, R. N., & Caine, G. (1997). *Unleashing the power of perceptual change.* Alexandria, VA: Association for Supervision and Curriculum Development.

Carr, J. F., & Harris, D. E. (2001). *Succeeding with standards: Linking curriculum, assessment, and action planning.* Alexandria, VA: Association of Supervision and Curriculum Development.

Costa, A. L., & Kallick, B. (Eds.). (2000). *Discovering and exploring habits of mind.* Alexandria, VA: Association for Supervision and Curriculum Development.

Cunningham, W. C., & Gresso, D. W. (1993). *Cultural leadership: The culture of excellence in education.* Needham Heights, MA: Allyn and Bacon.

Danielson, C. (1996). *Enhancing professional practice: A framework for teaching.* Alexandria, VA: Association for Supervision and Curriculum Development.

Danielson, C., & McGreal, T. (2000). *Teacher evaluation to enhance professional practice.* Alexandria, VA: Association for Supervision and Curriculum Development.

Darling-Hammond, L. (1997). *The right to learn: A blueprint for creating schools that work.* San Francisco: Jossey-Bass.

Davis, M., Hawley, P., McMullan, B., & Spilka, G. (1997). *Design as a catalyst for learning.* Alexandria, VA: Association for Supervision and Curriculum Development.

Deal, T. E., & Peterson, K. D. (1999). *Shaping school culture: The heart of leadership.* San Francisco: Jossey-Bass.

DuFour, R., & Eaker, R. (1998). *Professional learning communities at work: Best practices for enhancing student achievement.* Bloomington, IN: National Educational Service.

Elias, M., Zins, J., Weissberg, R., Frey, K., Greenberg, M., Haynes, N., Kessler, R., Schwab-Stone, M., & Shriver, T. (1997). *Promoting social and emotional learning: Guidelines for educators.* Alexandria, VA: Association for Supervision and Curriculum Development.

English, F. W. (2000). *Deciding what to teach and test: Developing, aligning, and auditing the curriculum* (Millenium ed.). Newbury Park, CA: Corwin Press.

English, F. W., & Larson, R. L. (1996). *Curriculum management for educational and social service organizations* (2nd ed.). Springfield, IL: Charles C. Thomas.

Fenwick, T., & Parsons, J. (2000). *The art of evaluation.* Toronto: Tompson Educational Publishing.

Ferrandino, V. L. (2001). Challenges for 21st-century elementary school principals. *Phi Delta Kappan, 82,* 440–442.

Fink, E., & Resnick, L. (2001). Developing principals as instructional leaders. *Phi Delta Kappan, 82,* 598–606.

Gardner, H. (1991). *The unschooled mind: How children think and how schools should teach.* New York: Basic Books.

Gardner, H. (1999). *Intelligence reframed: Multiple intelligences for the 21st century.* New York: Basic Books.

Glatthorn, A. A. (1994). Constructivism: Implications for curriculum. *International Journal of Educational Reform, 3,* 449–455.

Glickman, C. D. (2000–01). Holding sacred ground: The impact of standardization. *Educational Leadership, 58*(4), 46–51.

Goleman, D. (1995). *Emotional intelligence.* New York: Bantam.

Guskey, T. R. (2000). *Evaluating professional development.* Thousand Oaks, CA: Corwin Press.

Hickman, C. R., & Silva, M. A. (1984). *Creating excellence: Managing corporate culture, strategy, and change in a new age.* New York: New America Library.

Hughes, L. (1999). *The principal as leader* (2nd ed.). Upper Saddle River, NJ: Prentice-Hall.

Hunter, M. C. (1982). *Mastery teaching.* Thousand Oaks, CA: Corwin Press.

Jackson, A. W., & Davis, G. A. (2000). *Turning points 2000: Educating adolescents in the 21st century.* New York: Teachers College Press.

Jacobs, H. H. (1997). *Mapping the big picture: Integrating curriculum and assessment K–12.* Alexandria, VA: Association for Supervision and Curriculum Development.

Jensen, E. (1998). *Teaching with the brain in mind.* Alexandria, VA: Association for Supervision and Curriculum Development.

Jung, C. (1923). *Psychological types* (H. G. Baynes, Trans.). New York: Harcourt Brace.

Lambert, L. (1998). *Building leadership capacity in schools.* Alexandria, VA: Association for Supervision and Curriculum Development.

Larabee, D. F. (2000). Resisting educational standards. *Phi Delta Kappan, 82,* 28–33.

Levine, S. L. (1989). *Promoting adult growth in schools.* Needham Heights, MA: Allyn and Bacon.

Means, B. (2000). Technology in America's schools: Before and after Y2K. In R. S. Brandt (Ed.), *Education in a new era* (pp. 185–210). Alexandria, VA: Association for Supervision and Curriculum Development.

Neuman, M., & Simmons, W. (2000). Leadership for student learning. *Phi Delta Kappan, 82,* 8–12.

Newmann, F., Secada, W., & Wehlage, G. (1995). *A guide to authentic instruction and assessment: Vision, standards and scoring.* Madison, WI: Wisconsin Center for Education Research.

Oliva, P., & Pawlas, G. (2001). *Supervision for today's schools* (6th ed.). New York: John Wiley & Sons.

Orlich, D. C. (1989). *Staff development: Enhancing human potential.* Needham Heights, MA: Allyn and Bacon.

Schein, E. H. (1984). *Organizational culture and leadership.* San Francisco: Jossey-Bass.

Schmoker, M. (1999). *Results: The key to continuous school improvement* (2nd ed.). Alexandria, VA: Association for Supervision and Curriculum Development.

Speck, M., & Knipe, C. (2000). *Why can't We get it right? Professional development in our schools.* Thousand Oaks, CA: Carwin Press.

Sylwester, R. (2000). Unconscious emotions, conscious feelings. *Educational Leadership, 58*(3), 20–24.

Tomlinson, C. A. (1999). *The differentiated classroom: Responding to the needs of all learners.* Alexandria, VA: Association for Supervision and Curriculum Development.

Uchida, D., Cetron, M., & McKenzie, F. (1996). *Preparing students for the 21st century.* Arlington, VA: American Association of School Administrators.

Weller, L. D. & Weller, S. (2000). *Quality human resources leadership: A principal's handbook.* Lanham, MD: Scarecrow.

Zepeda, S. J. (1999). *Staff development: Practices that promote leadership in learning communities.* Larchmont, NY: Eye on Education.

4

MANAGING CHANGE

Standard 3: A school administrator is an educational leader who promotes the success of all students by ensuring management of the organization, operations, and resources for a safe, efficient, and effective learning environment.

INTRODUCTION

If school administrators are to effectively lead and manage schools, they must strive to balance the responsibilities inherent in each of these roles. Leadership roles typically are identified with those activities that enhance the development, articulation, and stewardship of the school district's vision and mission. These roles tend to be people-oriented and focused on the essential relationships and interactions with stakeholders that are critical to leading change. Management roles, in contrast, are most often concerned with the supervision of day-to-day operations where special knowledge, training, and expertise in specific areas are critical to success. Although difficult to separate, "leadership is something earned over time, something you build on, with power bestowed by *followers*. A manager, on the other hand, exercises power bestowed by *superiors* and is usually limited to responsibilities and accountabilities for resources" (Dunklee, 2000, p. 109).

This chapter will focus primarily on distinct management functions and tasks that constitute essential subsystems of the organization as reflected in ISLLC Standard 3. The discussion begins with an introduction to basic organizational theory and development as they relate to operating policy and governance, problem-analysis, decision-making based on data, and the focus on continuous improvement. The remaining subsystems to be discussed include human resource management; infrastructure concerns such as school facility planning and use, school safety and security; fiscal operations and resource allocation and alignment; risk and liability; and technology planning, development, and maintenance.

ORGANIZATION DEVELOPMENT

Common to all healthy organizations is a positive and growth-producing process for responding to opportunities for change. The opportunities for change in the educational arena today are myriad and multifaceted. Public schools face unprecedented challenges to both the "what" and the "how" of their operations. To respond to these challenges, educational leaders must cultivate various strategies for developing and enhancing the overall strength of the organization.

One of the leadership processes that helps ensure a positive response to challenges is that termed "organization development." First developed in business and governmental organizations in the 1950s, the process of organization development (OD) was conceptualized as a way for the change and improvement process to take place within the context of the work group. Organization development encourages the members of a specific work group to examine their interactions and on-the-job performance in light of the defined function of the group within the larger organization and that of the individual within the group. In this way, the entire organization benefits and improves.

Organizational change as defined by OD is based on major underlying assumptions about the importance of the individual within the organization, but as a member of a work group, thus reflecting an interaction of the contingency and systems theorists regarding how organizations are best structured (Morgan, 1997). The systems theory elements of OD include analysis of the unit's relationship to the other parts of the organization (larger system) while simultaneously examining current levels of success as defined for the entire organization as well as for the individuals within the unit (contingency factors).

A good example of applying this concept of OD to the educational setting is one in which students in an individual school within the school district are not performing well in standardized tests. Using the school as the unit of analysis, the instructional leader/principal creates opportunities for the staff to examine their teaching processes in light of what they are doing individually, and as grade level subgroups, that is not bringing about the anticipated success (higher student achievement). In this process "[t]eachers are looking for the right combination of leadership and autonomy. A good mix provides an atmosphere where they can focus on instruction and student achievement, while participating in important decisions that affect their practice and professional growth" (Wyman, 2001, p. 3).

Another example, more related to management, would be the situation wherein an individual school decided to implement a new curriculum or program as part of its overall school improvement process, but the faculty were stymied in their efforts to do so by the lack of financial support from the business office of the school district. In this case, the OD process would encourage each unit, the school and the business office, to examine how their actions affect one another, and what the resulting impact is on the organization's overall vision and mission. The resolution of this situation might well require a review of operating policies within the organization, and the examination of the specific governance powers assigned each unit or subsystem of the district. "The obvious challenge related to the operating policy/governance sub-system is to establish and maintain effective communications channels capable of involving all stakeholders in the school system's policy and governance processes" (Dembowski, 1999, p. 10).

Problem Analysis

In many respects OD can be considered as one of several possible responses that might be appropriate in a problem situation. When results do not match expectations, leaders look for ways to make the changes necessary to improve. Advocates of the problem analysis process suggest several strategies for investigating both probable causes and possible solutions. According to Achilles, Reynolds, and Achilles (1997), the process of problem-analysis "includes both problem finding and problem solving" (p. 6), and "will lead to decisions, sharing of the problem and solution, initiation of some course of action, and eventual assessment of the outcomes of implementing a solution" (p. 6). These strategies encompass both good management behaviors (problem solving) and good leadership actions (problem finding), with the clear identification of the problem paramount before determination of appropriate solutions. Patterson (1997) notes,

> When people want to jump quickly into a discussion of solutions or outcomes, leaders must return the focus to core values. After acknowledging that a discussion of outcomes is important, leaders must first make sure the group has a clear understanding of and commitment to the reasons why they are doing what they are doing. (p. 36)

Included within the major steps of problem finding and problem solving are all the subprocesses traditionally discussed in problem-related structures. These include the analysis of information and data related to the problem; the preliminary determination of causes; the identification of possible solutions; an analysis of implications if solutions are implemented; the selection and deployment of the best remedy; and, finally, the evaluation of results. The entire process is complexly interwoven and heuristic in nature. One subprocess sometimes leads back to another, or other times jumps forward, as the results of one step generate new paths to pursue in quest of what is ultimately the best course of action. What cannot be overstated is the importance of the role of the leader in conceptually guiding this process and using key interpersonal skills to bring all relevant elements of the organization together in productive problem-analysis.

Data-Based Decision-Making

Data-based decision-making is yet another leadership response to directing change and growth within the organization. This process, although similar in many respects to problem-analysis, focuses primarily on accessing and using multiple sources of information as catalysts for insight into ways to improve the organization. Applying this process to schools, Bernhardt (1998) notes that:

> We want to see data gathered throughout the school on a regular basis—not just when an external force requires it, and we want members of the school community to understand how to use data to accurately inform individuals, within and external to the school, of how the school is doing. (p. 8)

The process is ongoing, rather than driven by crisis. In this sense, it is more of a proactive way of doing business, not an analysis focused on a reaction to a particular situation.

A key skill needed by an effective school administrator in data-based decision making is understanding the systemic nature of the organization—that is, the interrelationships among its various components. Using this conceptual skill the principal or superintendent then realizes that making improvement in one facet of the school, or in one phase of a plan, has an immediate and fundamental impact upon all the other facets of the organization and phases of the plan. Changes are not undertaken lightly, and the intended, as well as the unintended, results of modifications are regularly reviewed and incorporated into the planning process. "The savvy principal will be as careful to follow a process or model in implementing the decision as she or he was thorough in using a problem-analysis model to guide the problem-analysis process" (Achilles et al., 1997, p. 134). Understanding of the continuous and cyclical process of using a constant stream of analytical information to generate ongoing improvement is the essence of leadership for building and sustaining positive growth and change. This, in turn, leads to review of the managerial functions that support the continuous school improvement process.

THE MANAGERIAL CYCLE

Contemporary perspectives describe the field of management (Kaufmann, Majone, & Ostrom, 1986) not as an isolated event, but rather as a series of linked activities. These activities commonly are described as the management cycle and consist of three components: planning, controlling, and evaluating. These parts are sequential and cyclic in nature, as shown and defined in Figure 4.1.

During the planning phase of the managerial cycle, specific direction is set and organizational goals and objectives are established, as shaped and filtered by the organization's vision. In the process of carrying out these established goals, "attention is given to establishing control systems to record and report activity, compare results against intentions, and detect deviations" (Dembowski, 1999, p. 8), the functions included in the control phase of the cycle. Finally, the evaluation phase of the cycle consists of the

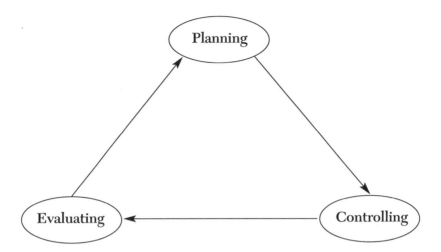

Planning: Information collection, analysis, forecasting, and proposing courses of action leading to decision making.

Controlling: The process of implementing a program and the associated methods of increasing the alignment of actions with intentions.

Evaluating: The process of determining the results of program action in order to use this information to inform future action, continuing action, revised action, or abandoning an activity.

Figure 4.1   The Managerial Cycle. *Source*: Dembowski, F. (with Ekstrom, C. D.). (1999). *Effective school district management: A self-review instrument and guide.* Arlington, VA: American Association of School Administrators, p. 7.

comparison of results with intended goals (effectiveness), and the organizational cost of these results (efficiency).

As school administrators perform the various management duties involved in planning, controlling, and evaluating, they must be mindful of the relationship of these responsibilities to their overarching leadership role. "Management is not by itself bad or less important than leadership. Paradoxically, leadership is not likely to occur easily unless management provides consistency and a nurturing status quo in which there are few surprises" (Achilles, Keedy, & High, 1999, p. 28). Effective principals' management behaviors must always be informed by solid conceptual skills and infused with the human relations' dimensions necessary to be effective in managing the organization.

HUMAN RESOURCE MANAGEMENT

The most valuable resource an organization has is its people. In schools, this resource includes teachers, support staff, administration, students, parents and patrons, and the board of education. With the recent shift in authority to site-based managed schools, the responsibility for leading and managing these valuable human resources has become a major responsibility of the principal. In order for "the principal to develop and devise mechanisms to produce more effective student results and provide higher quality programs and levels of teacher performance," new skills and additional knowledge in the area of human resource management must be developed (Weller & Weller, 2000, p xi).

Transforming the Culture

Creating and sustaining a culture for learning and growth in schools is critical to student success. Central to cultivating this environment are effective communications and human relations, team building and teamwork, staff development for continuous improvement, and proper, timely rewards and recognition. Weller and Weller (2000) report:

Effective principals lead through persuasion and influence, and must have an ability to communicate accurately and concisely for achieving quality outcomes. Good human relations skills are central to motivating people, attaining their cooperation and sustaining their unity and commitment. Principals have to build strong communication networks among their staff to minimize misunderstanding and conflict and to maximize trust and credibility. (p. 63)

However, the process of building this kind of trust relationship cannot be rushed or compressed. It is the result of an investment of both considerable effort and significant time on the part of the principal, and the quality of the resulting relationship will be directly proportional to these two factors.

Effective communication and human relations skills also provide the added opportunity to develop avenues for team building and teamwork. Creating structures that support the involvement of teachers, staff, parents and students in the decision-making processes of the school further empowers this workforce and the students. This provides input, influence, and power in identifying needs and solving problems of the school environment. Thompson (2001) notes, "When principals engage parents and teachers in the decision-making process, they are employing a strategy for both arriving at better decisions and building ownership for those decisions" (p. 1). Additionally, using these collaborative processes allows participants to be involved in creating professional staff development that is focused on identified needs to bring about continuous improvement. Principals must be willing to engage in the dialogue in such a way that they expose their own values and beliefs, as well as an honest desire to embrace new ideas and challenges (Greer & Short, 1999).

Key to high employee and student morale is "a reward and recognition system that fosters quality job performance outcomes" (Weller & Weller, 2000, p. 143). Displaying respect and appreciation for the contributions and achievements of employees demonstrates how leaders value staff efforts and participation. Palestini (1999) agrees:

A transformative leader motivates subordinates to achieve beyond their original expectations by increasing their awareness about the importance of designated outcomes and ways of attaining them, by getting workers to go beyond their self-interest to that of the team, the school, the school system and the larger society, by changing or expanding the individual's needs. (pp. 54–55)

Consistent acknowledgment of individual and organizational goal attainment gives the encouragement necessary to foster continuous growth and development throughout the organization.

Skills for Developing Human Resource Potential

With the emphasis in the education organizational culture on transformation and growth, several administrative skill areas have been identified as important for effective human resource management to support and enhance this emphasis: human resource planning, recruitment and selection, induction and retention, conflict management, and appraisal and development of personnel. Each of these areas builds on the trust and collaborative relationships considered essential in a growth-focused culture.

Human resource planning. Human resource planning and districtwide strategic planning are effective when they interface with one another at the very onset of the strategic planning process. While districtwide strategic development is focused on broad organizational goals and objectives, the human resource planning process is involved with determining the personnel available both internally and externally to implement the districtwide plan. The typical role of the building administrator in this process is in compiling human resource inventories, developing enrollment projections, forecasting personnel needs, and taking action to meet human resource needs in accordance with district policies and procedures.

Recruitment and selection. Identifying and employing new staff members with updated knowledge and skills, and whose interests match the needs of the district, is one method school districts use to achieve their vision for success. Recruitment and selection of these individuals is often shared by both district-level and building-level leadership.

The purpose of recruitment is to provide a continuous supply of well-qualified professionals and support staff for current and prospective job opportunities in the school district. To accomplish this goal, foundation activities need to be in place, roles and responsibilities of the process defined, candidate sources identified, and appropriate materials developed.

Foundation activities related to the recruitment process include those identified earlier relative to human resource inventories, enrollment projections, and forecasting the human resource needs. In addition, school district policies need to be established that outline the recruitment process and address issues such as the following: responsibility for implementing the policy, centralized/decentralized/regional recruitment programs, affirmative action/no discrimination provisions, nepotism, residency requirements, posting and advertising positions, preparation and professional qualifications, information requested from candidates, penalties for information that is not truthful, and handling job inquiries (Castallo, Fletcher, Rossetti, & Sekowski, 1992, pp. 52–55).

Although the majority of this information is formulated at the district level, administrators at all levels need to be knowledgeable of their specific roles and responsibilities in recruitment foundation activity. Building administrators need to know at which points in the recruiting process to offer their input and when the district office will take the lead. Most school districts have board policies that delineate specifics in the hiring process.

The selection process begins with one clear goal in mind: ". . . select the *best* candidate for the job, the one who holds the highest promise of succeeding in the face of the demands and requirements inherent in the job" (Weller & Weller, 2000, p. 192). To facilitate this, Jensen (1987) suggests the following recommendations for personnel selection: (a) develop written policies for selection, (b) treat candidates with fairness and respect, (c) train those who select teachers, (d) involve more people in the decisions, (e) consider a variety of information about candidates, and (f) learn from successes and failures: validate your process (pp. 26–27).

Additional foundation activity includes the identification of candidate resource pools and the development of appropriate promotional materials. In many cases these activities are orchestrated at the district level. However, the professional knowledge of leaders throughout the organization in this area is essential to successfully compete for the most talented human resources in the job market.

Induction and retention. A well-planned process for employee induction serves both the employee and the organization. The employee has the opportunity to develop personal confidence in his or her ability to perform the duties necessary for the job, and the organization benefits by having high-performing, quality-producing employees in place as quickly as possible. Research in this area (McDonald, 1980; Ryan, 1980) has shown that an orientation process that recognizes the difficulty of being "the new kid on the block" and makes an effort to provide a smooth transition into the new workplace has dramatic and positive effects on the long-term retention of employees. According to Allen (2000) effective induction programs have the following features: (a) use experienced, well-trained teachers as mentors, (b) are based upon well-defined program standards, (c) are funded adequately, (d) include a good evaluation process for new teachers, (e) go beyond the first year of a teacher's career, and (f) are a part of a larger effort that includes reduced teaching loads, appropriate class placements, ample opportunity for observation of other teachers, and targeted professional development (p. 5).

Retaining qualified staff is a major responsibility of principals, since it is the school building that is the venue for service provided by the staff members. School-based leaders need to know about the causes of job dissatisfaction and provide professional development structures, growth opportunities, and various incentives to prevent, if possible, dissatisfying situations from occurring. Haggart (as cited in Weller & Weller, 2000) notes that:

> [j]ob satisfaction concerns among teachers have been identified as concerns about workload, frequent and varied new assignments, lack of adequate resources, inadequate administrator support, lack of adequate supervision for instruction, principal leadership style, stress, and lack of career opportunities. (pp. 205)

Here, again, good channels of communication between the principal and staff members are absolutely essential. Effective leaders must be attentive to these issues and provide a variety of mechanisms to address them, both within the school building and throughout the organization. Special efforts must be made to continuously monitor staff thinking and concerns as part of the continuous growth and development process for all employees.

Conflict management. Collaboration is the keystone of the successful educational organization, and a primary factor in developing the positive school culture that is so important to effectiveness in both the classroom and the boardroom. This emphasis on teamwork and cooperation is juxtaposed, however, on societal standards that often laud competition and individualism. The result is that conflicts may occur between individuals within the work group, or between work groups within the organization. School leaders need to be prepared to proactively address these situations by using a variety of conflict-management skills.

One of the first conflict-management skills that leaders need to develop is the ability to anticipate people's reactions to specific situations. The better one knows his or her staff and community, the greater the likelihood that this person will be capable of anticipating these reactions and thus have the opportunity to determine an appropriate strategy to approach the situation. When conflict does manifest itself, however, it is critical to acknowledge it, so that it may be described, defined, discussed, and managed.

Blake and Mouton (as cited in Barge, 1994) describe five basic conflict-management styles; withdrawal, smoothing, compromise, forcing, and problem-solving: "[M]ost conflict management theorists agree that the problem-solving style is the most effective because it manages conflict constructively by encouraging the two parties to share their ideas about the conflict" (p. 164). As people work together to resolve their conflicts, they can reach common ground through mutual resolution of the problem.

For the problem-solving style of conflict management to be most effective for the organization to achieve the desired collaborative environment, an overarching commitment to the philosophy of mutual gain is essential. A mutual gain approach seeks to identify shared interests, examine differences, and define the parties' preferences before trying to reach a decision. Generating options before selecting among them almost always leads to the possibility of joint gain, satisfying the interests of all sides with creative solutions (Fisher, Ury, & Patton, 1991).

It is important to acknowledge that conflict and stress are natural outcomes of everyday working relationships and inherent in all human interactions. Although no one single style of conflict management works in all circumstances, the effective school leader needs to develop the knowledge, skill, and understanding to manage conflict and ensure successful resolution. If this area is left unmanaged, the organization will suffer from lack of productivity, poor employee morale, and individual and professional animosity. In contrast, when managed appropriately, conflict can emerge as the stimulus for creative problem-solving, maximizing the opportunity for growth, development, and change for the better.

Appraisal and development of human resources. School district leaders have a legal responsibility to evaluate the individual job performance of all staff members. Effective processes for personnel appraisal allow administrators to facilitate decisions about staff deployment, staff development, and employment status. More importantly, the appraisal process provides feedback, guidance, and assistance to help school staff members better meet the expectations of their job-related duties. Weller and Weller (2000) assert, "The primary goal of performance appraisal is to improve the teaching-learning phenomena to maximize student achievement" (p. 219).

Establishing a clear outline of evaluation criteria and a joint understanding about how and when evaluation will be conducted allows the evaluator and employee the opportunity to develop mutual understanding and respect for the appraisal process. Weller and Weller (2000) believe that

> [d]esigned properly, appraisal systems can promote positive attitudes toward performance evaluation and integrate the interest of the individual with those of the organization. Additional advantages of the appraisal process are mutual goal setting, professional development, and the freedom to be creative and innovative within a system that promotes continuous improvement. (pp. 219–220)

Such a process also provides the administrator with the opportunity to share beliefs and goals and to build the collaborative aspects of the school culture.

Many appraisal system tools and professional development opportunities are available. Knowledge of these tools and opportunities will assist administrators as they lead their staff through the process of change and strive to reach their human resource potential.

INFRASTRUCTURE

Development of an environmental infrastructure offers another opportunity for leaders at the building and district levels to support their commitment to teaching and learning and the focus on student achievement. This section introduces three dimensions to be considered in developing a nurturing environmental infrastructure:

the managing of time, school facility planning and use, and school safety and security.

Managing Time

Time is another valuable resource that building-level leaders have the opportunity to manage. Effective schools research and research on alternative uses of time have revealed that the school schedule is one aspect of the learning environment that shapes the opportunity for the staff to achieve the school's mission. Seyfarth (1999) states, "The primary purpose of time management in schools is to maximize the time devoted to academic learning activities and to minimize the amount of time spent on activities that produce no achievement gains" (p. 327).

Several processes are involved with the scheduling of time in a school building. These include the preplanning stage or pre-scheduling, registration, building the master schedule, and scheduling students or student placement. These processes are not conducted in isolation, but occur simultaneously as data are collected regarding the opportunities for and interests of the students. The preplanning stage leading up to and including the actual development of the master schedule should consider several areas.

- Involvement—Provide maximum opportunity for staff and students to be involved and have input into the development of the schedule.
- Opportunity—Provide optimum course choices to accommodate students' unique interests and learning needs.
- Curriculum and Instruction—Consider curriculum and instruction design, and staff and grouping patterns to achieve optimum learning opportunity.
- Flexibility—Create as little interdependence within the schedule as possible so that changes can be made to accommodate a variety of curricular and instructional requests for change within the regular structure.

- Alternative Design—Consider alternative design patterns such as block scheduling, parallel scheduling, and extended day, to enhance learning opportunities.
- Efficiency—Minimize the availability of unsupervised learning activities like study halls, limit the amount of passing time from classroom to classroom, and examine the lunch schedules and before and after school time.
- Dependence—Limit as much as possible the degree to which your school schedule is dependent on outside influences, such as busing schedules.
- Space—Use all available space to its fullest potential. (Ubben, Hughes, & Norris, 2001)

The registration process in middle and high schools will provide students and their families with the opportunity to plan for the future and to make selections on the basis of students' needs, interests, and curricular requirements. Once this information is gathered, a master schedule can be developed and student scheduling can take place, or in the case of the elementary school, student placement can proceed. Effectively managing the time resources of a school building requires the principal to use good conceptual and technical skills. Identification of the impact that schedule changes have on both students and teachers must be done early and often in the time management and scheduling process.

School Facility Planning and Use

School facilities are the single greatest investment that districts make at one time and, therefore, are a resource that all members of the school community must preserve. Although facility programming and planning is complex, the overall goals should address issues raised by the following questions:

- Is the facility structurally sound?
- Is it healthful and safe?

- Is it efficient to operate?
- Does it support the program?
- Is it attractive and comfortable?
- Is its location convenient for the users?
- Is its space optimally used?
- Is it the right size?
- Can it be modified? (Thompson & Wood, 1998, p. 244)

Discussions addressing these issues take place with broader district-level representation, and building-level leaders also will participate in the dialogue to ensure that their voices are heard on the issues of the physical plant and implications for its use. The planning process needs to reflect conversation about the school-age population being served, program offerings of the district and the individual school, overall economic and demographic profile of the district, and the long-range needs. Drake and Roe (1999) suggest:

> The school building is often an expression of the community regarding itself and the value it places on education. Over time it can also be an expression of the principal's values in the way it is maintained, used and valued by students and staff. A key thought is that the term *facility* implies just that—the building should facilitate positive learning. The principal's challenge is, in the face of rapid changes, to seize quickly expanded opportunities to keep the building as a facilitating tool. (p. 459)

School facilities not only are used for the traditional school-day program but they also are used to deliver a multitude of services through interagency collaboration agreements. Seyfarth (1999) notes, "Among the advantages of interagency collaboration is that children receive more benefits and schools gain partners in their efforts to help children" (p. 42). Skills in working collaboratively with outside agencies are necessary and need to be developed by school leaders for the successful delivery of extended services for children and families.

School leaders also are responsible for extending new knowledge and understanding of how students learn and grow in order to influence planners on how space should be designed and for what purpose. Day (2001) suggests, "The learning environment must lend itself to multiple learning styles, the incorporation of technology, and flexible arrangements that will support project work and both large- and small-group instruction" (p. 6). The use of a planning committee that includes teachers, parents, and students will assist principals and superintendents in keeping the instructional focus of the school building in the forefront of everyone's thinking.

Attention to building maintenance offers another opportunity to extend support for teaching and learning through the physical plant. Boyd (1992) reports, ". . . on the basis of the available current research, building maintenance is one variable that school districts have control over—and one that has a measurable impact on pupil achievement" (p. 89). Holloway (2000) also points out that "[s]chool buildings, whether old or new, must be maintained and renovated for aesthetic reasons and to protect the health and safety of the staff members and students who work and learn in them" (p. 88.) Building leaders, more than anyone else, have a major responsibility to monitor the condition of their buildings relative to the teaching-learning process. Poor school environments often cause staff to become demoralized and disconnect from the ongoing and sustained efforts they must make to be effective with students.

Participation in school facility planning is critical if building-level leaders want to facilitate the learning process within the physical environment of the school. The opportunity exists to extend school facility usage to agencies that provide needed support for children and their families. Advocating for space that accommodates the latest understanding of effective teaching and learning and the tools to deliver them is also an important contribution to the planning process. Finally, promoting support for a clean, comfortable, and attractive learning environment has a positive effect on student learning and must also be acknowledged.

School Safety and Security

When the majority of schools in this country were built, relatively little concern was directed toward the issues of safety that are plaguing American schools today. Only a few decades ago, gang-related violence and school shootings seemed unimaginable to the public at large. Today, however, the development of operational procedures, rules, and policies to maintain school safety and security are a major responsibility for all school leaders. Schneider, Walker, and Sprague (2000) report that research shows safer schools tend to be places that are lead well, have positive climates and atmosphere, are inclusive of all students, and are academically effective.

School leaders must first enlist the support of teachers, parents, and the community in addressing the challenges of securing a safe environment for growth and learning. Cooperation is the foundation of order in schools and must be combined with effective control measures (Seyfarth, 1999). Determining the balance between control and cooperation is a responsibility for each individual school community and must be embraced and supported by all constituencies involved to be effective.

The schoolwide plan for discipline is an outgrowth of this commitment and helps achieve consistency in the management of student behavior. Steps in developing the discipline plan include the following: identifying the basic beliefs and values that form the foundation for managing student behavior, specifying expected behaviors, developing procedures for teaching and communicating schoolwide behavioral expectations, developing procedures for correcting problem behavior, and developing procedures for record keeping and evaluation (Seyfarth, 1999).

The philosophy driving the school discipline plan also should extend into the development of individual classroom management skills. Strategies that individual teachers utilize to encourage positive growth and development of all students must be supported schoolwide and consistent with the expectations sought throughout the school building.

A well-developed crisis communication/management plan also enhances the safety and security of the school environment. An effective crisis plan is developed by those who will be using the plan, delegates responsibility for safety and action to all adults in the building, incorporates the use of district-level and human service agency personnel for support, is easily accessible and practiced by staff and students, and is evaluated following its use.

Schiffbauer (2000) proposes the following important questions to consider in evaluating school safety measures:

- How close is the office area to the main access door?
- Are hallways safe?
- What communications systems are in place?
- What traffic patterns are feasible?
- What lighting is in place?
- Is the crisis management plan in place?
- Do in-service programs enhance staff members' coping skills?
- Do school policies emphasize safety?
- Does the school curriculum address school-safety issues?
- Does the school meet necessary legal requirements?
- Is the community a part of the school safety plan? (pp. 72–74)

Each of these questions needs to be considered by the building-level leaders as they plan a safe, secure environment for students and staff. At the conclusion of "A Checklist for Safe Schools," Schiffbauer (2000) makes the following statement:

Probably the most important factor in any school safety plan is the visibility of staff members, especially administrators. As difficult as it is to get away from the phone and reports, administrators must take frequent walks around the school building and its perimeter. Their presence tells students, staff and parents—better than any newsletter article or report could—that they value school safety. (p. 74)

MANAGING FINANCIAL RESOURCES

Administrators are responsible not only for the management of human resources in their buildings, but they also are accountable for the management of financial resources. District-level administrators must ensure that the district's financial holdings are wisely managed and that funds are collected, encumbered, and expended in accordance with statutory requirements. Building-level leaders must appropriately allocate, effectively manage, closely monitor, and accurately evaluate the use of all financial resources that reach the building level. These aims are achieved most effectively if the school staff and school community are actively involved in the process. School improvement teams or site-based decision-making teams are the entities most commonly used in this process. Seyfarth (1999) states: "Involving school personnel and parents in the schools in setting priorities and making spending decisions is intended to increase accountability and help the school reach its mission" (p. 335).

With or without site-based/school improvement teams, leaders of the financial planning process must have an overall understanding of school finance as it relates to the origin of resources available through local and state government tax structures, the federal government, private foundations, philanthropic organizations, and local business and community organizations. Knowledge and understanding of these financial resources allows the superintendent and principals to remain on top of the schools' budget and accounting processes and to speak and communicate intelligently about issues around school finance. Drake and Roe (1999) state:

An elementary knowledge of accounting and budgeting procedures, plus some simple study of the state's school finance procedures, the school's classifications system for accounting, and the school district's budget over the past five years will provide the principal the fiscal basics to be a leader in any school system. (p. 429)

Generally, funds for maintenance and operations, capital expenditures, special use funds, and student activity funds are managed at the school site. Knowledge of, and the development of, appropriate policies and procedures for handling this responsibility and process are imperative. Careful analysis of both the limitations and possibilities of each source of financial assistance is essential as well.

Before funds can be appropriately allocated, school leaders must establish a process for needs analysis to determine the overall conditions of the learning environment and student programs. Several sources of data can be used to make this assessment: student academic performance; student behavior patterns; current and projected student demographic characteristics; curricular and program needs; knowledge, skills, and attitude surveys of staff; and inventories of instructional furniture and equipment. Following the data collection process, goals should be established and strategies developed to address the current and projected needs in the building. This approach begins the budget process and provides the opportunity for the development of a systematic approach to the allocation of resources and the monitoring of their use. It is also an opportunity for evaluating the effectiveness of resource acquisition and allocation.

Financial planning at the building and district levels is an ongoing process and should always be preceded by an educational planning analysis that is focused on student learning. Sound policies, processes, and procedures enable building leaders to demonstrate competence in financial management and thus provide the foundation for the acquisition of new resources to address ongoing program needs and learning environment enhancement. "Handling the business affairs of a school well provides a credibility to internal and external publics so that other less visible or measurable results can be achieved" (Drake & Roe, 1999, p. 443).

LEGAL RESPONSIBILITY

Schools are not exempt from the litigiously turbulent environment that exists in the United States today. School leaders need a thorough understanding of the legal responsibilities inherent in managing a school site and the ability to exercise their professional educational judgment so as not to violate the law or impinge on the rights of students, parents, teachers, and others.

The school principal is directly accountable for what occurs at the building site and must take a proactive, preventative approach toward managing the legal and regulatory environment of the school. The obligation to obtain a minimal working understanding of the educational law knowledge base is fundamental and critical to leading and managing the operation and its people. Sperry (1999) suggests the following to accomplish this task: (a) complete an introductory university-level course on education law, (b) become acquainted with the state educational law code and state-level educational law rules and regulations of the state in which one is practicing, and (c) become completely familiar with the rules and regulations of the board of education and the local school district within which one is working (pp. 28–29).

Completing university-level coursework in the area of education law will give school principals a general understanding and sensitivity to potential legal problems and issues faced by education professionals. It will also extend foundation knowledge that may help prevent or minimize potential problems. The state code and state administrative rules and regulations manual generally are available in all school districts. These materials, in addition to the local board of education policy and procedure manual, are excellent information tools for practicing administrators.

To further understand the general scope of responsibility and awareness, Sperry (1999) has divided education law into the following nine topical areas: (1) church and state; (2) discrimination (sometimes referred to or expanded into separate topics of race and/or desegregation); (3) educational program (sometimes referred to as curriculum or instruction and may or may not include church-state); (4) exceptional students (sometimes referred to as students with special needs and special education law); (5) health and safety; (6) liability or tort liability; (7) organization and governance (sometimes expanded into separate topics of school boards, finance, property, and legal framework of education); (8) personnel management (sometimes expanded into separate topics of contracts, professional negotiations, teacher rights, and teacher employment); and (9) student management (sometimes referred to or expanded into separate topics of student discipline, classification of students, and student rights) (pp. 73–74). These areas represent the wide range of complex and sensitive legal issues with which administrators are faced as they work toward effectively and efficiently leading and managing their buildings and school districts. School leaders must utilize the services and support of other district professionals and the district's legal counsel when necessary to assist them in minimizing legal liability and fostering a preventative administrative approach to their leadership.

Finally, following the development of the basic knowledge and understanding of education law, it is imperative that school leaders maintain a close watch on school litigation trends. The legal terrain is continually shifting and changing at all levels: local, state, and national. Sperry (1999) recommends that leaders remain current in their knowledge of changes in policies and procedures of the local board of education and school district; they must also stay up to date on state-level actions of the legislature and state education agency, and sensitive to national developments as they pertain to new landmark cases and changing federal statutory and regulatory actions involving schools.

Ignorance of the law can carry a very high price. Therefore, continuing legal professional development is a major responsibility for districts and their leaders.

TECHNOLOGY PLANNING, DEVELOPMENT, AND MAINTENANCE

One of the most important areas in which school leaders need to have excellent "managing change" skills is that of planning and implementing the use of technology in all its applications, including instructional and administrative purposes, within the learning organization. In the last 20 years, technology, and especially the computer, has become increasingly integral to all aspects of modern society. Lumley and Bailey (1997) note that schools cannot afford to ignore technological innovation because

- Every two to three years, the knowledge base doubles. It has been said that by 2010 it will double every 72 hours!
- Every day, 7,000 scientific and technical articles are published.
- By the time they graduate from high school, today's students have already been exposed to more information than their grandparents were in a lifetime.
- There will be as much change in the next three decades as there was in the last three centuries. (p. 5)

Because schools are in the information business—generating new knowledge as well as organizing and retrieving of already developed knowledge—the use of computer technology to assist both teachers and students in their work is vital. Similarly apparent is the impact of technology on the internal operations of the school.

These functions include budgeting, facility and operations management, scheduling, and record-keeping.

Strong conceptual skills are required for effective management of this major change process. School leaders must lead the organization in strategic technology planning. As with overall strategic planning, laying the foundation for technology infusion within the organization starts with clear identification of the role technology serves in meeting the major goals of the organization. This is followed by the subsequent delineation of the steps for deployment, including policies and procedures. As Rockman (1998) notes, "Among the central elements of a good plan will be a concern for student achievement, educational equity, and workforce preparedness" (p. 1).

This planning process is best done by a group that represents all facets of the organization—teachers, technology experts, administrative staff, parents and students—as well as significant external stakeholders from the community. The group should include both avid supporters as well as critics, so that all points of view are heard and addressed right from the start. "Broad participation not only makes the workload more manageable, it also draws in diverse talents, empowers participants, and promotes ownership and buy-in, of the outcomes" (Bagby, Bailey, Bodensteiner, & Lumley, 2000, p. 10).

This district-level technology planning committee should be given clear direction and guidelines predetermined by the local school leaders (the board of education and school administrators) about the scope, type, and timeline of the plan. Attention also should be given to ensuring that the group knows how to work together and that the group has a good understanding of what is included in the "technology" for which the planning is to be done. Equally important are strong and obvious leadership and support of the administration for technology use (including both administrative and classroom uses).

The major tasks of the planning committee include assessment of the current status of technology throughout the organization, both in the instructional setting and in administrative functions; clarification of the organization's philosophy relative to technology in all areas; development of a plan for infusion of technology, including budget, schedule, facilities/infrastructure, and training requirements. They must also study areas of responsibility; and implementation of the plan, including institutionalization through policies and procedures and interface with other organizational planning documents, and a comprehensive evaluation process (Bagby et al., 2000; Lumley & Bailey, 1997). Throughout these steps, committee members must have an ongoing dialogue with the various constituencies that they represent. Such a dialogue will ensure that all voices are heard. It also will provide accurate and timely information about the process across all areas of the school and community.

Locating funding for technology is one of the major tasks that the school leader must address. In this area, the input and assistance gleaned from the technology strategic planning group is especially valuable. A major oversight that must be avoided is not planning for all the hidden and ongoing costs embedded in implementing technology. Levinson and Grohe (2001) believe,

> Technology is like building maintenance—you pay now, or you pay lots more later. Technology funding has to be ongoing, dependable and stable. Technology funding must be a planned for, and a planned on, expenditure consistently over a five-year cycle. (p. 54)

Furthermore, this budget cannot rely on one-time grants or other "soft" money. Building principals and district leaders must see to it that revenue for technology in all aspects—capital outlay, maintenance, instructional materials, and staff development—is incorporated into the schools' regular, general funding-stream budgets.

School leaders must also pay special attention to staff development as an element included in technology implementation. Many faculties incorrectly feel that it is sufficient to simply provide money for new and replacement equipment, and for maintaining it. But new equipment and software, as with any change in teaching materials or job-related tools, require time and effort to master. Appropriate and significant investment in people through training programs pays dividends in the successful realization of the school's goals. As Tenbusch (1998) notes:

> [I]f school districts don't do a better job of allocating resources for professional development—instead of putting all the budget into technology acquisition—schools will be left with the tools but not the talent to prepare youngsters for a technological world. (p. A16)

Implementation of good technology planning, then, requires that school leaders have the conceptual skills that inform the vision and the people skills that demonstrate the importance and value of the staff in realizing that vision.

SUMMARY

Many of the skills and strategies advocated in this chapter and reflected in ISLLC Standard 3 are aligned more with traditional management areas than what has come to be termed "leadership." However, if leadership is all about the change process, then the functions for ensuring that this process takes place effectively and with as much continuity as possible are also leadership functions, even though they are often called management tasks.

Attention to fostering and enhancing the major facets of program operations at both the building and district levels is crucial to being an effective administrator. First, care must be given to the development of the personnel resources that deliver programming, from concern about work groups to providing feedback for, and nurturing the talents of, each staff member. Secondly, leaders need to be closely involved in the physical operations of the buildings to ensure the support from the school environment that complements efforts to improve programs. Third, financial resources need to be allocated and carefully managed so that solid support can be given to the learning environment. Fourth, a basic understanding of education law will reduce potential liability and risk exposure to the school district. Finally, with the advent of technology and its infusion into every facet of life, it is extremely important for school leaders to make certain that technology is truly incorporated into the instructional programs and general operations of the school.

These leadership-management activities, numerous and sometimes trivial as they may seem, are essential to successful leadership. The conceptual, technical, and human skills required to do all this, though many, are ones that can and must be practiced and developed.

SUGGESTED INTERNSHIP ACTIVITIES RELATED TO STANDARD 3

Review the current skill levels you noted on your ISLLC Standards Self-Assessment under Standard 3. Note areas in which you wish to improve your skills, and working with your mentor and supervisor, identify activities that you can complete during your internship experience. The following listing of activities related to Standard 3 is provided to help you identify projects that may be appropriate for your clinical experience:

1. Structure your internship so as to have the opportunity to participate with your mentor in the opening and closing activities of a school building for a given academic year.
2. Review routine management and communication processes used in the school building or throughout the district. Submit recommendations regarding how the use of technology

would increase the efficiency and effectiveness of these processes.

3. Serve on a hiring committee for a district-level position, teaching position, and a noncertified staff position.

4. Work with central office personnel to develop an aggressive plan to recruit employees who reflect the race and ethnicity of the student population in your district. Design a recruitment brochure to assist with this plan.

5. Learn the process used to request bids for equipment items.

6. Develop a staff orientation process that includes the development of a personnel manual that reflects the information necessary for successful induction into the organization.

7. Meet with the district's chief financial officer and examine the district-wide budget process.

8. Work with the building-level administration in the development or revision of a building budget.

9. Study the process for ordering, receiving, and inventorying supplies and textbooks.

10. Track a filed grievance through the district's defined process or procedure.

11. Review the district or building safety plan. Identify one area to research for possible updating, for example, bomb threats.

12. Using the managerial cycle model, describe the major steps necessary for constructing a new school building.

13. Conduct a needs assessment of the building and grounds, identifying needed repairs, painting, and equipment replacement. Create a priority listing, keeping in mind issues of safety, cost, instructional need, and anticipated remaining life of equipment.

14. Prepare or update a Crisis Management Plan for the district or school, listing names and phone numbers of key personnel, along with assigned roles and responsibilities.

15. Develop and/or participate in activities designed to ease students' transition into the school and out of it, into the next school setting.

16. Review the district's negotiated contracts for teaching and support personnel. If possible, observe or participate in the negotiations process.

17. Interview the district budget director to identify how the institution supports curricular improvements in its resource allocation process.

18. Identify the steps taken in two different student discipline cases, one involving a special needs student. Compare and contrast the legal considerations in each case. Discuss these processes and procedural differences with the district's special education director and your mentor.

19. Form a study group with other district administrators to examine and discuss recent court decisions affecting school operations.

20. Serve on the district technology planning committee.

21. Work with your school leadership team to develop the master schedule for the building.

22. Serve as the principal of a summer school program.

23. Review the school handbook to ensure that it is consistent with district policies, state regulations, and school laws.

24. Work with teachers who are experiencing persistent discipline problems with individual students, brainstorming and developing shared solutions.

25. Prepare teacher supervision assignments for the year (restroom supervision, lunchrooms, bus duty, activities supervision, etc.).

26. Develop or revise a Student Activities Handbook that includes a listing of all student organizations, clubs, and sports, and appropriate activities policies.

27. Based on your ISLLC Standards Self-Assessment under Standard 3, select one or two books from the suggested

readings that will help expand your knowledge base on topics related to this standard. In addition, select one of the Web site resources listed, review the information available, and identify how this resource can assist you in your professional development.

SUGGESTED READINGS

Alexander, K., & Alexander, M. D. (2001). *American public school law* (5th ed.). Belmont, CA: Wadsworth.

Alvy, H. B., & Robbins, P. (1998). *If I only knew: Successful strategies for navigating the principalship.* Thousand Oaks, CA: Corwin Press.

Bailey, G. D., & Lumley, G. D. (1997). *Staff development in technology: A sourcebook for teachers, technology leaders, and school administrators.* Bloomington, IN: National Educational Service.

Canady, R., & Rettig, M. (1995). *Block scheduling: A catalyst for change in high schools.* Princeton, NJ: Eye on Education.

Creighton, T. (2000). *Schools and data: The educator's guide for using data to improve decision making.* Thousand Oaks, CA: Corwin.

Duke, D. L. (2002). *Creating safe schools for all children.* Needham Heights, MA: Allyn and Bacon.

Dwyer, K., Osher, D., & Warger, C. (1998). *Early warnings, timely response: A guide to safe schools.* Washington DC: U.S. Department of Education.

Educational Service District 105, Yakima, WA. (1997). *Quick response: A step-by-step guide to crisis management for principals, counselors, and teachers.* Alexandria, VA: Association of Supervision and Curriculum Development.

Harvey, T. R., & Drolet, B. (1994). *Building teams building people: Expanding the fifth resource.* Lancaster, PA: Technomic.

Holcomb, E. (1999). *Getting excited about data: How to combine people, passion, and proof.* Thousand Oaks, CA: Corwin.

Imber, M., & van Geel, T. (2000). *Education law* (2nd ed.). Thousand Oaks, CA: Erlbaum Press.

Lumley, D., & Bailey, G. D. (1997). *Planning for technology: A guidebook for teachers, technology leaders, and school administrators.* Blooming-ton, IN: National Educational Service.

Norton, S. M., & Kelly, L. K. (1997). *Resource allocation: Managing money and people.* Larchmont, NY: Eye on Education.

Schlechty, P. (1997). *Inventing better schools.* San Francisco: Jossey-Bass.

Schneider, T., Walker, H., & Sprague, J. (2000). *Building safety into schools.* Eugene, OR: ERIC Clearinghouse of Educational Management.

Yodorf, M. G., Kirp, D., & Levin, B. (1992). *Educational law and policy* (3rd ed.). St. Paul, MN: West.

Zirkel, P. A., Richardson, S. N., & Goldberg, S. S. (1994). *A digest of Supreme Court decisions affecting education* (3rd ed.). Bloomington, IN: Phi Delta Kappa Educational Foundation.

WEB SITE RESOURCES

National Association of Elementary School Principals (NAESP)
www.naesp.org

National Association of Secondary School Principals (NASSP)
www.nassp.org

National Middle School Association
www.nmsa.org

American Association of School Personnel Administrators (AASPA)
www.aaspa.org

National Resource Center for Safe Schools
www.safetyzone.org

Education Commission of the States (ECS)
www.ecs.org

The Council of Educational Facility Planners International (CEFPI)
www.cefpi.com

National Clearinghouse for Educational Facilities
www.edfacilities.org

ERIC Educational Resources Information Center
www.accesseric.org

Education Law Association
www.educationlaw.org

Association of School Business Officials International
www.asbointl.org

Safe and Drug Free Schools Program
www.ed.gov/offices/OESE/SDFS

Council for Exceptional Children
www.cec.sped.org

REFERENCES

Achilles, C. M., Keedy, J. L., & High, R. M. (1999). The workaday world of the principal: How principals get things done. In L. W. Hughes (Ed.), *The principal as leader* (2nd ed.) (pp. 25–57). Upper Saddle River, NJ: Prentice-Hall.

Achilles, C. M., Reynolds, J. S., & Achilles, S. H. (1997). *Problem analysis: Responding to school complexity.* Larchmont, NY: Eye on Education.

Allen, M. (2000). *Effective induction programs. The Progress of Education Reform 1999–2001* (Report of the Education Commission of the States), 2(3), 5.

Bagby, R., Bailey, G., Bodensteiner, D., & Lumley, D. (2000). *Plans and policies for technology in education: A compendium* (2nd ed.). Alexandria, VA: National School Boards Association.

Barge, K. J. (1994). *Leadership: Communication skills for organizations and groups.* New York: St. Martin's Press.

Bernhardt, V. L. (1998). *Data analysis for comprehensive schoolwide improvement.* Larchmont, NY: Eye on Education.

Boyd, V. (1992). *School context: Bridge or barrier to change?* Austin, TX: Southwest Educational Development Laboratory.

Castallo, R. T., Fletcher, M. R., Rossetti, A. D., & Sekowski, R. W. (Eds.). (1992). *School personnel administration: A practitioner's guide.* Needham Heights, MA: Allyn and Bacon.

Day, C. W. (2001). Rethinking school design. *Learning by Design, 10,* 4–6.

Dembowski, F. (with Ekstrom, C. D.). (1999). *Effective school district management: A self-review instrument and guide.* Arlington, VA: American Association of School Administrators.

Drake, T. L., & Roe, W. H. (1999). *The principalship* (5th ed.). Upper Saddle River, NJ: Prentice-Hall.

Dunklee, D. R. (2000). *If you want to lead, not just manage: A primer for principals.* Thousand Oaks, CA: Corwin.

Fisher, R., Ury, W., & Patton, B. (1991). *Getting to yes: Negotiating agreement without giving in.* New York: Penguin Books.

Greer, J. T., & Short, P. M. (1999). Restructured schools. In L. W. Hughes (Ed.), *The principal as leader* (2nd ed.) (pp. 89–104). Upper Saddle River, NJ: Prentice-Hall.

Holloway, J. H. (2000). Healthy buildings: Successful students. *Educational Leadership, 57*(6), p. 88–89.

Jensen, M. C. (1987). *How to recruit, select, and retain the very best teachers.* Eugene, OR: ERIC Clearinghouse on Educational Management.

Jones, J. J., & Walters, D. L. (1994). *Human resource management in education.* Lancaster, PA: Technomic.

Kaufmann, F. X., Majone, G., & Ostrom, V. (1986). *Guidance, control, and evaluation in the public sector.* Berlin: deGruyter.

Levinson, E., & Grohe, B. (2001). Funding: It's time to be sufficient. *Converge, 4*(4), 54–59.

Lumley, D., & Bailey, G. D. (1997). *Planning for technology: A guidebook for teachers, technology leaders, and school administrators.* Bloomington, IN: National Educational Service.

McDonald, R. (1980). The problems of beginning teachers: A crisis in training. Princeton, NJ: Educational Testing Service.

Morgan, G. (1997). *Images of organization* (2nd ed.). Thousand Oaks, CA: Sage.

Palestini, R. H. (1999). *Educational administration: Leading with mind and heart.* Lancaster, PA: Technomic.

Patterson, J. L. (1997). *Coming clean about organizational change: Leadership in the real world.* Arlington, VA: American Association of School Administrators.

Rockman, S. (1998). *Leader's guide to education technology.* Alexandria, VA: National School Boards Association.

Ryan, K. (1980). *Biting the apple: Account of first year teachers.* New York: Longman.

Schiffbauer, P. (2000). A checklist for safe schools. *Educational Leadership, 57*(6), 72–74.

Schneider, T., Walker, H., & Sprague, J. (2000). *Building safety into schools.* Eugene, OR: ERIC Clearinghouse on Educational Management.

Seyfarth, J. T. (1999). *The principal: New leadership for new challenges.* Upper Saddle River, NJ: Prentice-Hall.

Sperry, D. J. (1999). *Working in a legal and regulatory environment: A handbook for school leaders.* Larchmont, NY: Eye on Education.

Tenbusch, J. P. (1998, March). Teaching the teachers: Technology staff development that works. *Electronic School,* A16–A20.

Thompson, S. (2001). The school leadership challenge. *Strategies for School System Leaders on District-Level Change* (An issues series by the Panasonic Foundation in cooperation with the American Association of School Administrators), *8*(1), 1–2.

Thompson, D. C., & Wood, R. C. (1998). *Money and schools: A handbook for practitioners.* Larchmont, NY: Eye on Education.

Ubben, G. C., Hughes, L. W., & Norris, C. J. (2001). *The principal: Creative leadership for effective schools* (4th ed.). Needham Heights, MA: Allyn and Bacon.

Weller, L. D., & Weller, S. (2000). *Quality human resources leadership: A principal's handbook.* Lanham, MD: Scarecrow Press.

Wyman, W. (2001). *Teaching quality: School and teacher leadership. The Progress of Education Reform 1999–2001* (Report of the Education Commission of the States), *2*(4), 3.

5

DEVELOPING COLLABORATIVE PARTNERSHIPS

Standard 4: A school administrator is an educational leader who promotes the success of all students by collaborating with families and community members, responding to diverse community interests and needs, and mobilizing community resources.

INTRODUCTION

In the past decade, more than 35 students and teachers have been killed and over 75 injured in our nation's schools. In nearly every instance, the assailants were the victims' classmates (ABC News, 1999). The public is very concerned with issues related to youths' alienation and disconnection from the school community. In the 2000 Gallup Poll, lack of discipline/more control, fighting/violence/gangs, and student use of drugs/dope were identified as three of the top five problems facing public schools (Rose & Gallup, 2000).

Recalling the wisdom contained in an ancient African proverb, "It takes a village to raise a child," school officials are beginning to recognize the importance of strengthening the bonds between the school and its constituents. By forming closer alliances with parents and community, schools may become more effective in helping students feel a sense of belonging in the school setting. In addition, by working with other social service agencies, schools may also become more proficient at recognizing signs of at-risk behaviors.

In *Building Community in Schools,* Sergiovanni (1994) bemoans the loss of community in the nation's schools and within society in general. "If we want to rewrite the script to enable good schools to flourish," Sergiovanni believes, "we need to rebuild community" (p. xi). Envisioned in its broadest terms within the context of the school setting, creating a sense of community means developing partnerships among the school, the family, and the local community. To facilitate the understanding of ISLLC Standard 4, this chapter is divided into the following three sections: collaboration with family and community members, responding to diverse community interests and needs, and mobilizing community resources.

COLLABORATION WITH FAMILY AND COMMUNITY MEMBERS

One of the eight goals contained in the 1994 *Goals 2000: Educate America Act* states: "By the year 2000, every school will promote partnerships that will increase parental involvement and participation in promoting the social, emotional, and academic growth of children." Shortly after Goals 2000 was enacted, the United States Department of Education established the Partnership for Family Involvement in Education and considers the promotion of this agency as one of its four top priorities. This partnership fosters the collaboration of family, business, community organizations, and religious groups with school personnel. The National PTA (1997) also recently developed standards for parent/family involvement programs in the following areas: (a) communicating; (b) parenting; (c) student learning; (d) volunteering; (e) school decision-making and advocacy; and (f) collaborating with community.

Why is collaboration with parents and other members of the school community important? Epstein (1995) provides numerous reasons for developing collaborative partnerships, including the following: improving school programs and climate, providing family services and support, increasing parents' skills and leadership, connecting families with others in the school and community, and helping teachers with their work. However, Epstein (1995) believes that the main reason for these partnerships is "to help all youngsters succeed in school and in later life" (p. 701).

Frequent interaction and communication among the school, families, and community ensures that students will receive consistent messages throughout the community about the common values that schools promote for student success (Epstein, 1995). The following themes are likely to be reinforced: the importance of hard work; the drive to achieve academic success; empathy for the needs of others; a personal sense of self-worth; satisfaction in doing one's job to the best of one's ability; and a desire for lifelong learning.

Educators should not take it for granted that parents automatically understand their vital role in supporting their children's learning nor should they believe that parents already have the skills that they need to assist their children. School officials may consider offering parenting skills courses for interested parents, so they learn the importance of limiting television viewing, establishing study hours, monitoring use of study time, and providing children with quiet study places in the home. Research has established a positive correlation between family involvement and scholastic achievement (National Association of Secondary School Principals, 1996).

In a true school-family-community partnership, Epstein (1995) states, educators create *family-like* schools, in which every family is welcomed, and every child feels a sense of belonging. Creating *school-like* family structures, parents recognize that their children are students and reinforce homework and various school activities that promote academic success. Student academic achievement improves significantly when parents monitor and support their children's schoolwork (Lam, 1997). Communities develop *family-like* settings to reinforce and reward students' academic progress, in addition to providing services to assist families in supporting their children. Finally, *community-minded* students and families are actively involved in their neighborhoods, helping their neighbors, and serving others within the community.

In Figure 5.1, Epstein (1995) advances a framework demonstrating six types of involvement that can assist school personnel in developing comprehensive partnership programs. The six types of involvement include the following: Parenting, Communicating, Volunteering, Learning at Home, Decision-Making, and Collaborating with Community. Also included within the figure is a representative sampling of a few of literally hundreds of activities that may be developed for each type. Working collaboratively, the school, families, and community members can select effective involvement practices that are aligned with the school's goals, then collectively identify expected results for students, teachers, and parents.

Effective Community Relations

Establishing an effective communication process is an essential skill for school leaders. School systems that exhibit good public relations programs increase the likelihood that members of their community will display confidence in the quality of their schools and will place their trust in school personnel (Gallagher, Bagin, & Kindred, 1997).

An effective process for communicating with parents and community goes beyond simply establishing a passive public relations program consisting of newsletters and brochures. School principals and superintendents should implement processes that include both one-way and two-way forms of communication. One-way communication involves all noninteractive information emanating from the school, including letters to parents, grade reports, school Web pages, monthly school newsletters, news releases submitted to the local news media, calendars, and annual reports. Disadvantages of one-way communication devices include the following: (a) there is little or no way to know if the proper message has been received or understood, and (b) they are not as effective as face-to-face interaction (Ubben, Hughes, & Norris, 2001). Two-way communication permits individuals to interact with school officials in a variety of formats, including e-mail correspondence, school board meetings, parent-student-teacher conferences (assuming that parents and students are allowed to talk and ask questions), surveys, community forums, focus group meetings, and school tours. Two-way communication has the obvious advantage in that it permits the free flow of ideas and concerns between the school and its patrons. Through interactive dialogue, school officials have an opportunity to clarify any public misperceptions, in addition to obtaining feedback (both positive and negative) about the operation of the school.

Openness and honesty should be the guiding principles to follow when conceptualizing a school-community relations program. Standard operating procedure should not be to generate a myriad of "fluff" news releases for media publication, then become inaccessible to the media and parents when unflattering reports surface concerning the schools. When school officials are perceived as attempting to cover up weaknesses, members of the community will begin to view school-based communications with a certain degree of suspicion and will carefully screen future information produced by the school in an effort to uncover perceived omissions and half-truths.

It is important to recognize that not all cultures or families have an equal appreciation for communication channels traditionally

Type 1 *Parenting*	*Type 2* *Communicating*	*Type 3* *Volunteering*
Help all families establish home environments to support children as students	Design effective forms of school-to-home and home-to-school communications about school programs and children's progress	Recruit and organize parent help and support

Sample Practices	*Sample Practices*	*Sample Practices*
Suggestions for home conditions that support learning at each grade level	Conferences with every parent at least once a year, with follow-ups as needed	School and classroom volunteer program to help teachers, administrators, students, and other parents
Workshops, video-tapes, computerized phone messages on parenting and child rearing at each age and grade level	Language translators to assist familes as needed	Parent room or family center for volunteer work, meetings, resources for families
Parent education and other courses or training for parents (e.g., GED, college credit, family literacy)	Weekly or monthly folders of student work sent home for review and comments	Annual postcard survey to identify all available talents, times, and locations of volunteers
Family support programs to assist families with health, nutrition, and other services	Parent/student pickup of report card, with conferences on improving grades	Class parent, telephone tree, or other structures to provide all families with needed information
Home visits at transition points to preschool, elementary, middle and high school; neighborhood meetings to help families understand schools and to help schools understand families	Regular schedule of useful notices, memos, phone calls, newsletters, and other communications	Parent patrols or other activities to aid safety and operation of school programs
	Clear information on choosing schools or courses, programs, and activities within the schools	
	Clear information on all school policies, programs, reforms, and transitions	

Type 4 Learning at Home	Type 5 Decision Making	Type 6 Collaborating with Community
Provide information and ideas to families about how to help students at home with homework and other curriculum-related activities, decisions, and planning	Include parents in school decisions, developing parent leaders and representatives	Identify and integrate resources and services from the community to strengthen school programs, family practices, and student learning and development
Sample Practices Information for families on skills required for students in all subjects at each grade Information on homework policies and how to monitor and discuss schoolwork at home Information on how to assist students to improve skills on various class and school assessments Regular schedule of homework that requires students to discuss and interact with families on what they are learning in class Calendars with activies for parents and students at home Family math, science, and reading activities at school Summer learning packets or activities Family participation in setting student goals each year and in planning for college and work	*Sample Practices* Active PTA/PTO or other parent organizations advisory councils, or committees (e.g., curriculum, safety, personnel) for parent leadership and participation Independent advocacy groups to lobby and work for school reform and improvements District-level councils and committees for family and community involvement Information on school or local elections for school representatives Networks to link all families with parent representatives	*Sample Practices* Information for students and families on community health, cultural, recreational, social support, and other programs or services Information on community activities that link to learning skills and talents including summer programs for students Service integration through partnerships involving school; civic, counseling, cultural, health, recreation, and other agencies and organizations; and businesses Service to the community by students, families, and schools (e.g., recycling, art, music, drama, and other activities for seniors or others) Participation of alumni in school programs for students.

Figure 5.1   Epstein's Framework of Six Types of Involvement and Sample Practices. *Source:* Epstein, J. L. (1995). School/family/community partnerships: Caring for the children we share. *Phi Delta Kappan, 76,* 704.

used by school personnel. Some parents may feel uncomfortable or unwelcome in the school and will avoid parent conferences; others may not subscribe to the local newspaper or may not read school mailings. Some families may have no means of transportation, may not have access to childcare, or may be working during scheduled meeting times. School officials may consider developing relationships with neighborhood associations, local churches, and community centers and holding parent forums at these locations, which might be more parent-friendly or geographically accessible to individuals with limited resources.

School-Business Collaboration

The 1990s saw increased interest generated in the arena of school-business partnerships, partly as a result of the enactment of the federal *School-to-Work Opportunities Act of 1994*. The school-to-work initiative is based on the concept that all students—not only those preparing for vocational occupations—receive their best career preparation by applying classroom learning to real work situations. By working in partnership, states, local schools, and businesses are encouraged to develop programs that connect three core elements of classroom instruction based on academic and occupational skills; work-based learning, including career exploration; work experience and training; and connecting activities that integrate courses with on-the-job instruction and match students with mentors at the employment site (National STW Learning and Information Center, 1999).

When reaching out to businesspersons for support, some educators operate under the misguided belief that an effective partnership is simply a one-way flow of financial resources from the business to the local school. However, Bradshaw (1989) asserts that high-quality links must be established that meet learning objectives agreed upon by both parties, leave participants with the belief that the collaborative effort was worthwhile, and assist participants in understanding each other's world.

A true collaborative arrangement between school and business is *not* charity because the partnership should provide mutual benefits for all parties (Schwartz, 1990). For the school system, business involvement may result in improved student achievement, improved student attendance, or in-service training opportunities for the faculty that result in more effective teaching. Businesses may benefit by gaining a higher quality pool of prospective employees, in addition to generating positive publicity and corporate goodwill. To be successful and long-lasting, school-business partnerships should be directly related to the mission or goals of the school district, clearly state the responsibilities of each party, designate key individuals who are responsible for completing identified activities, and include an evaluation component to measure the program's success in meeting the partnership goals (Schwartz, 1990).

According to Grobe, Curnan, and Melchior (1993), school-business activities occur at three stages. In the first stage, support, the local business contributes resources to the school, such as funding, equipment, guest speakers for the classroom, and tutoring. Cooperation, the second stage, consists of such varied short-term projects as mentoring programs or school-to-work transition programs. It is at the third stage, collaboration, that the partnership assumes a life of its own (p. 9). At this point, all participants are identifying long-range goals that address school or community needs; all are committing major resources; and many activities are occurring simultaneously. The goal of effective school-business partnerships is to become institutionalized at this level of collaboration.

One of the primary elements of successful partnerships is the participation of top-level leadership (Grobe et al., 1993). The school or community leader must have the initial idea or vision, and then must work diligently to bring interested parties together to achieve the vision. As the partnership begins to solidify, an interagency planning team should be established to assist with the identification of goals and the development of an implementation plan.

School-University Collaboration

The most visible form of interaction between school systems and universities has historically been the placement of student teachers in the local school building. However, school and university personnel can, potentially, collaborate in activities that are significantly more beneficial to both institutions than simply placing a student teacher in a classroom, which tends to benefit only the university. Wilbur and Lambert (1995) identified approximately 2,200 school-university partnerships. This number has no doubt increased in the past few years as a result of the enactment of the *School-to-Work Opportunities Act in 1994.*

The critical element in school-university partnerships is the degree to which the arrangement is essential to the normal functioning of both institutions (Goodlad, 1990). Three conditions are necessary for successful collaboration to occur: awareness of the unique differences between the institutions; recognizing that both institutions' self-interests can be met; and committing to the self-interests of the other partner (Wiseman & Nason, 1995). Russell and Flynn (1992) note many benefits of school-university collaboration, including the following: involvement in joint research, evaluation, planning, and in-service efforts; joint grant-writing opportunities; input into university professional preparation programs; access to university resources; and assistance with the school improvement process.

As the school-university partnership begins to take shape, conflict may arise, "not because the organizations are so different, but because they are so similar—two bureaucracies, each with its work defined for it and each jealously guarding its turf" (Lieberman, 1992, p. 152). This conflict can be lessened, Lieberman (1992) believes, if both groups can "share an overarching vision of school improvement, renewal, and restructuring" (pp. 152–153). Rather than viewing the elementary-secondary curriculum and university curriculum as two separate entities, one vision for an effective school-university partnership is the development of a seamless preK–16 curriculum. Although this lofty goal may be difficult to achieve, it provides a conceptual framework in which both institutions can work together to achieve their shared goals.

A promising approach for reforming teacher preparation and school practice is the Professional Development School (PDS) model developed by the Holmes Group, a consortium of the nation's leading teacher education institutions (The Holmes Group, 1990). In professional development schools, educators work in collaboration

> to develop and demonstrate (1) fine learning programs for diverse students; (2) practical, thought provoking preparation for novice teachers; (3) new understandings and professional responsibilities for experienced educators; and (4) research projects that add to all educators' knowledge about how to make schools more productive. (p.1)

Although the PDS model is not entirely new—university laboratory schools have been in existence for years—this model focuses on public schools and collaboration between schools and universities. In the PDS model, all partners work to create a community of learners, for novice professionals, experienced educators (both school- and university-based), and for research and development of the teaching profession.

Not all school districts may be able to partner with local universities to develop professional development schools, but they may be able to use the PDS framework to facilitate collaborative activities in which educators engage in action research, apply knowledge gained for program improvement, and strengthen both the individual school and the teaching profession (Lecos, 1997).

Site-Based Management

Empowering parents and staff members with decision-making authority through the establishment of site-based management

(SBM) offers another opportunity to promote collaboration among the school's constituent groups. SBM councils and school-based committee assignments are an excellent opportunity to tap into the leadership potential of the school faculty and to empower teachers with decision-making responsibility.

Parents and members of the community who serve on SBM councils should be accepted as full participants in the process, not merely as figureheads or silent partners. Their comments should be welcomed, actively solicited, and taken seriously. Parents who are involved in meaningful ways with the operation of the school are more likely to feel a connection with the school and a sense of ownership in its management processes. At the secondary level, students may also serve as SBM council representatives.

School principals should be aware that the existing research base does not yet support the notion that establishing SBM councils and implementing an SBM process in a school will lead to improved student success (Miller, 1995; Murphy, 1995). To effect positive changes in student educational outcomes, SBM councils must go beyond micromanaging relatively lower-order issues such as tardy policies and keeping the lunchroom clean. The probability of success increases when staff adhere to the following principles: (a) focus on student learning outcomes, (b) address factors among the faculty that inhibit goal attainment, and (c) build professional development into the improvement process (Hackmann, Tack, & Pokay, 1999, pp. 12–13). Simply stated, efforts should be targeted toward enhanced student achievement.

RESPONDING TO DIVERSE COMMUNITY INTERESTS AND NEEDS

By the year 2010, our nation's nonwhite population is estimated to approach 38% (Hodgkinson, 1991). Changing demographics make it imperative that school officials be cognizant of the diversity that exists within their local communities and sensitive to the needs of different groups of people. Henry (1996) cautions that the school culture is more closely aligned with the white middle class than with the culture of minority or working groups. Consequently, school leaders must be acutely aware of school practices that may unintentionally alienate and exclude people because of their race or ethnicity, gender, socioeconomic status, or sexual orientation, so that they may create more accepting, inclusive school settings. For example, as schools attempt to promote a multicultural curriculum, the terms "dealing with diversity" or "addressing diversity" may have negative connotations for members of underrepresented groups, because they may imply that the issue of diversity is something to be carefully managed rather than accepted as a vital part of the cultural tapestry of our country. Terms such as "celebrating diversity" or "embracing diversity" may be viewed more positively in the eyes of many.

The term "diversity" is usually associated with race and ethnicity. However, the National Association of Secondary School Principals (NASSP, 1996) believes that "the embrace of diversity should also lead to a healthy respect for a broad range of ideas which, after all, constitute the lifeblood of any institution devoted to education" (NASSP, 1996, p. 70). In addition to monitoring the needs and interests of their diverse clientele and providing appropriate services (Henry, 1996), responsive schools also permit dialogue among those with different points of view. All children and youth are welcomed, treated with equal respect, and provided with equal opportunities to benefit from the school's curriculum and services.

Responsive school leaders also recognize that, if they are to be effective with all individuals, they must indeed "see color." Since different cultures are socialized in different ways, it is highly inappropriate to communicate in the same manner with all individuals as if everyone were raised as Caucasians. When engaged in face-to-face communication, Anglos tend to look directly at the speaker when they are listening. In contrast, Japanese Americans tend to focus on the speaker's neck. African American and Native Americans often avoid eye contact with the speaker because in their cultures, gazing directly into the speaker's eyes is considered rude and inappropriate (O'Hair & Spaulding, 1997). School officials should ensure that appropriate professional development opportunities are provided so that staff members will be more fully prepared to work with a diverse student population (NASSP, 1996).

Phelan, Davidson, and Yu (1993) present a concept of students' multiple worlds as a model to assist educators in thinking about students in a more holistic way. In the multiple-worlds model, students are envisioned as having three competing "worlds," which are described as "the cultural knowledge and behavior found within the boundaries of each student's particular families, peer groups, and schools" (p. 53). Students with congruent world types experience parallel values, beliefs, expectations, and norms across their three worlds. These students tend to be members of two-parent families who value family cohesiveness and academic achievement, and their friends reinforce the value of school, sports, and work. Because the boundaries between family, peers, and school are easily manageable, transitioning from one setting to another is relatively harmonious and uncomplicated. However, for students with incongruent worlds (with respect to culture, ethnicity, socioeconomic status, or religion), it may be extremely difficult to cross smoothly from one world to another. These students may experience conflicts with family, may have sporadic school success, and/or alternatively may engage or withdraw from family, friends, or school. Students with incongruent worlds who are able to successfully navigate between worlds must expend great energy and effort to do so. Unfortunately, teachers are frequently unaware of the personal cost for these students' success.

Teachers who are attuned to the multiple-worlds model place increased emphasis on features within their classrooms, examine their pedagogical styles to be more closely aligned with all students' needs, and understand their personal attitudes toward teaching and students will positively or negatively influence students' ability to connect with the school environment and to succeed academically (Phelan et al., 1993). Teachers must create classroom environments where students can work together and solve problems jointly. As Phelan et al. (1993) note, "This requires more than understanding other cultures. It means that students must acquire skills and strategies to work comfortably and successfully in divergent social settings and with people different than themselves" (p. 85).

MOBILIZING COMMUNITY RESOURCES

The 1950s notion of the traditional American family structure, with a working father, a stay-at-home mother, and two normal, well-adjusted children, is no longer the norm in today's society. Recent statistics note that 27.7% of children live in single-parent households (Lugaila, 1998) and many live in blended family structures, 78% of mothers with school-age children work outside the home, nearly two in five adolescents smoked a cigarette within the past month, and nearly one in eight adolescents used illicit drugs in the past month (U.S. Department of Health and Human Services, 1998). In 1997, 13.3% of the nation's population lived below the poverty line, with a disproportionate percentage for people of color in poverty (26.5% for African Americans and 27.1% for Hispanic Americans) (Dalaker & Naifeh, 1998). Approximately 15% of school-age children do not have health insurance (U.S. Department of Health and Human Services, 1998).

Dryfoos (1994) estimates that one in four children and youth engage in many high-risk behaviors, including the use of drugs, unprotected intercourse, school truancy, and poor school performance. In addition to educating children, today's schools are called upon to provide breakfast and lunch; expand their curricula to include information on the prevention of substance abuse, teen pregnancy, AIDS, and violence; provide psychological support services; offer health screenings and necessary medical referrals; cooperate with police and social service agencies; and provide before- and after-school care (Dryfoos, 1994). The schools' primary responsibility is to provide students with the essential skills necessary to fully participate in society. However, educators understand that before they can successfully address the learning needs of high-risk children, they must find ways to attend to their basic health and social service needs.

Although schools generally have more sustained contact with children and families than do other agencies, school systems are not structured to provide comprehensive support services for children. Children and families may also be served intermittently by a variety of agency workers, including social workers, drug counselors, police officials and juvenile officers, and health care providers, with little or no coordination among services. These fragmented services may not effectively meet the needs of students, and major gaps between services may occur. Kirst (1991) recommends grouping multiple support services in one place (such as a school, church, or childcare center) so that they are more accessible to the public, and the services can be coordinated. Kirst (1991) advocates, "Coordination of services enables each agency to be more effective while maintaining administrative and programmatic autonomy" (p. 617).

The positive correlation between good health and educational achievement has prompted the establishment of full-service schools in many communities, which bring a variety of health and support services into the school building. Dryfoos (1994) explains, "The vision of the full-service school puts the best of school reform together with all other services that children, youth, and their families need, most of which can be located in a school building" (p. 12). This model recognizes that a sustained package of interventions is much more likely to result in measurable changes in disadvantaged children's lives than would intermittent and disconnected support mechanisms. Figure 5.2 illustrates support services that can be collaboratively linked within the local school setting.

In the full-service school model, rather than assuming the primary responsibility for addressing disadvantaged students' multiple needs, school officials act as partners with other community agencies. As they partake of services located within the school building, community residents of all ages once again begin to recognize the school as the hub around which the community revolves. In addition to reestablishing positive connections with community inhabitants—many who may not have seen the inside

Quality Education Provided by Schools

Effective basic skills
Individualized instruction
Team teaching
Cooperative learning
School-based management
Healthy school climate
Alternatives to tracking
Parent involvement
Effective discipline

Provided by Schools or Community Agencies

Comprehensive health
  education
Health promotion
Social skills training
Preparation for the world of
  work (life planning)

Support Services Provided by Community Agencies

Health screening and services
Dental services
Family planning
Individual counseling
Substance abuse treatment
Mental health services
Nutrition/weight management
Referral with follow-up
Basic services: Housing, food, clothes
Recreation, sports, culture
Mentoring
Family welfare services
Parent education, literacy
Child care
Employment training/jobs
Case management
Crisis intervention
Community policing

Figure 5.2 Full-Service Schools: One Stop Collaborative Institutions. Source: Dryfoos, J. G. (1994). *Full-service schools: A revolution in health and social services for children, youth, and families.* San Francisco: Jossey-Bass, p. 13. Copyright 1994 Jossey-Bass. Reprinted by permission.

of a school building for decades—the school system benefits through the creation of a seamless institution that is accessible to those needing services.

If it is determined that a full-service school model cannot be effectively established in a school setting, school officials may choose instead to function under a philosophy similar to the full-service vision. The ultimate goal is to create mechanisms that respond to the needs of students and permit various agencies to interact collaboratively. For example, school officials could assume responsibility for developing of a joint task force composed of representatives of the community's service agencies, including the local police, family services department, counseling agencies, drug/alcohol treatment centers, and the juvenile office. Meeting on a regular basis, this representative group could explore opportunities to collaborate and share their combined resources in ways that respond to the identified social service needs of the community.

SUMMARY

As school leaders strive to implement their visions of success for all students, they must identify effective methods to reconnect alienated students to the indispensable triad of school, family, and community. The goal of collaboration among all three elements of this triad is to provide students with the structure that familial (that is, family in the village sense) support endows unto each individual. Communication is the essential ingredient in this ideal family. School leaders must move beyond static one-way forms of communication to facilitate broader communication among the school, parents, and community.

Responding to diverse community interests and needs is neither a simple nor a banal task. Multicultural issues should not be viewed as something to tolerate or manage, but rather as the natural outcome of embracing the variety and uniqueness that students bring to the school culture. The idiosyncratic differences link individuals together as human beings, which are the lifeblood of American culture and the multicultural experience.

Once these basic relationships have been established, the school leader is then responsible for ensuring that student health and social needs are met. Through promoting interagency collaboration and pooling various student services, educators can more readily identify and address student and family needs. Building this network of relationships will equip students with the structure they need to develop the skills necessary to participate as fully productive members of society.

SUGGESTED INTERNSHIP ACTIVITIES RELATED TO STANDARD 4

Review the present skill levels you noted on your ISLLC Standards Self-Assessment under Standard 4. Note areas in which you wish to improve your skills and, working with your mentor and supervisor, identify activities that you can complete during your internship experience. The following listing of activities related to Standard 4 is provided to help you identify projects that may be appropriate for your clinical experiences:

1. Plan the start-of-school orientation program for new students and parents.
2. Prepare an orientation videotape that describes the school's shared values and culture.
3. Prepare the school's monthly school newsletter, including articles related to parental understanding of emerging adolescent needs and young adolescent growth and development.
4. Working in collaboration with appropriate school personnel, develop the process and schedule for student-parent-teacher conferences.

5. Design a brochure for social services agencies and organizations within the community that provide support services for students and families. Include the organization's name, address, telephone number, contact person, service provided, and note charges for services, if any.

6. Prepare a staff development program related to cultural diversity.

7. Identify the student subcultures that exist within the school and assess how the school can more effectively meet the needs of all types of students.

8. Develop a series of parenting skills courses for interested parents.

9. Provide conflict resolution or team-building skills training to the staff.

10. Learn about the school's Employee Assistance Program. If no program is offered for staff, explore other schools' programs and make recommendations for an appropriate program.

11. Design or update a Web page for the school.

12. Identify community agencies and organizations that would be interested in partnership activities with the school. Make initial contact with the groups' leaders to determine their interest in working with the school.

13. Working with the school guidance staff, develop a mentor program pairing at-risk students with teachers or businesspersons.

14. Attend and participate in PTA/PTO and Booster Club meetings.

15. Attend and participate in meetings of the school's SBM Council or other governance body.

16. Along with the principal, attend meetings in which the principal represents the school (district administrative council, Chamber of Commerce, meetings with community agencies, area principals' meetings).

17. Survey the staff to determine potential areas for partnership activities with local businesses or universities. With the principal's approval, make appropriate contacts to begin to establish a working partnership with a local business or university.
18. Draft a news release for distribution to the local media (television and newspapers).
19. With the principal's approval, invite the local media to the school to report on a unique school program or activity.
20. Design a school informational brochure for distribution to area real estate agencies.
21. Give a presentation on a school program at a meeting of a local service organization (Chamber of Commerce, Optimists, Business and Professional Women's Club, Rotary, Lions, NAACP, Ministerial Alliance).
22. Conduct focus group discussions with students or parents to assess their perceptions of the school and identify their suggestions for improvement.
23. Develop a questionnaire for faculty, students, or parents.
24. Based on your ISLLC Standards Self-Assessment under Standard 4, select one or two books from the suggested readings that will help expand your knowledge base on topics related to this standard. Also, select one of the Web site resources listed, review the information available, and identify how this resource can assist you in your professional development.

SUGGESTED READINGS

Blank, M., & Kershaw, C. (2000). *Design book for building partnerships: School, home, & community.* Lanham, MD: Scarecrow Press.
Dryfoos, J. G. (1994). *Full-service schools: A revolution in health and social services for children, youth, and families.* San Francisco: Jossey-Bass.

Epstein, J. L., Coates, L., Salina, K. C., Sanders, M. G., & Simon, B. S. (1997). *School, family, and community partnerships: Your handbook for action.* Thousand Oaks, CA: Corwin Press.

Fisher, B., & Ellis, D. (1990). *Small group decision making.* New York: McGraw-Hill.

Fuller, M. L., & Olsen, G. (1998). *Home-school relations: Working successfully with parents and families.* Needham Heights, MA: Allyn and Bacon.

Gallagher, D. R., Bagin, D., & Kindred, L. W. (2001). *The school and community relations* (7th ed.). Needham Heights, MA: Allyn and Bacon.

Hughes, L. W., & Hooper, D. W. (2000). *Public relations for school leaders.* Needham Heights, MA: Allyn and Bacon.

Murphy, J. (1995). *School-based management.* Thousand Oaks, CA: Corwin Press.

National Association of Secondary School Principals. (1996). *Breaking ranks: Changing an American institution.* Reston, VA: Author.

National PTA. (1997). *National standards for parent/family involvement programs.* Chicago, IL: Author.

Pawlas, G. E. (1995). *The administrator's guide to school-community relations.* Larchmont, NY: Eye on Education.

Sergiovanni, T. J. (1999). *Building community in schools.* San Francisco: Jossey-Bass.

Warner. C. (2000). *Promoting your school: Going beyond PR* (2nd ed.). Thousand Oaks, CA: Corwin Press.

WEB SITE RESOURCES

National Service-Learning Clearinghouse
www.nicsl.coled.umn.educ

National Parent Teacher Association
www.pta.org/index.stm

National Community Education Association
www.ncea.com

National School Public Relations Association
www.nspra.org

Partnership for Family Involvement in Education
http://pfie.ed.gov

REFERENCES

ABC News. (1999, April 29). *Violence in U.S. schools* [Online]. Available Internet: http://abcnews.go.com/sections/us/DailyNews/schoolshootings 990420.html.

Bradshaw, L. (1989). Making links. In D. Warwick (Ed.), *Linking schools and industry* (pp. 63–78). Oxford, England: Basil Blackwell.

Dalaker, J., & Naifeh, M. (1998). *Poverty in the United States: 1997* (U.S. Bureau of the Census, Current Population Reports, series P60-201). Washington, DC: U.S. Government Printing Office.

Dryfoos, J. G. (1994). *Full-service schools: A revolution in health and social services for children, youth, and families.* San Francisco: Jossey-Bass.

Epstein, J. L. (1995). School/family/community partnerships: Caring for the children we share. *Phi Delta Kappan 76,* 701–712.

Epstein, J. L., Coates, L., Salina, K. C., Sanders, M. G., & Simon, B. S. (1997). *School, family, and community partnerships: Your handbook for action.* Thousand Oaks, CA: Corwin Press.

Gallagher, D. R., Bagin, D., & Kindred, L. W. (1997). *The school and community relations* (6th ed.). Needham Heights, MA: Allyn and Bacon.

Goodlad, J. (1990). *Teachers for our nation's schools.* San Francisco: Jossey-Bass.

Grobe, T., Curnan, S. P., & Melchior, A. (1993). Synthesis of existing knowledge and practice in the field of educational partnerships. Washington, DC. U.S. Department of Education, Office of Educational Research and Improvement.

Hackmann, D. G., Tack, M. W., & Pokay, P. A. (1999). Results-oriented school improvement: Lessons from practice. *International Journal of Educational Reform, 8*(1), 8–14.

Henry, M. E. (1996). *Parent-school collaboration: Feminist organizational structures and school leadership.* Albany, NY: State University of New York Press.

Hodgkinson, H. (1991). Reform versus reality. *Phi Delta Kappan, 73,* 8–16.

The Holmes Group. (1990). *Tomorrow's schools: Principles for the design of professional development schools.* East Lansing, MI: Author.

Kirst, M. W. (1991). Improving children's services: Overcoming barriers, creating new opportunities. *Phi Delta Kappan, 72,* 615–618.

Lam, S. F. (1997). *How the family influences children's academic achievement.* New York: Garland Publishing.

Lecos, M. A. (1997). The promise of professional development schools. *Principal, 77*(1), 14, 16, 18–19.

Lieberman, A. (1992). School/university collaboration: A view from the inside. *Phi Delta Kappan, 74,* 147–156.

Lugaila, T. A. (1998). *Marital status and living arrangements: March 1998* (update). (U.S. Department of Commerce Publication No. P20-514). Washington, DC: U.S. Census Bureau.

Miller, E. (1995, November/December). Shared decision-making by itself doesn't make for better decisions. *The Harvard Education Letter, 11*(6), 1–4.

Murphy, J. (1995). *School-based management.* Thousand Oaks, CA: Corwin Press.

National Association of Secondary School Principals. (1996). *Breaking ranks: Changing an American institution.* Reston, VA: Author.

National PTA. (1997). *National standards for parent/family involvement programs.* Chicago, IL: Author.

National STW Learning and Information Center. (1999, May). *What is school-to-work?* Available Internet: http://stw.ed.gov/general/whatis .htm.

O'Hair, M. J., & Spaulding, A. M. (1997). Institutionalizing public relations through interpersonal communication: Listening, nonverbal, and conflict-resolution skills. In T. J. Kowalski (Ed.), *Public relations in educational organizations: Practice in an age of information and reform* (pp.157–185). Englewood Cliffs, NJ: Prentice-Hall.

Phelan, P., Davidson, A. L., & Yu, H. C. (1993). Students' multiple words: Navigating the borders of family, peer, and school cultures. In P. Phe-

lan & A. L. Davidson (Eds.), *Renegotiating cultural diversity in American schools* (pp. 52–88). New York: Teachers College Press.

Rose, L. C. & Gallup, A. M. (2000). The 32nd annual Phi Delta Kappa/Gallup poll of the public's attitudes toward the public schools. *Phi Delta Kappan, 82,* 41–58.

Russell, J. F., & Flynn, R. B. (1992). *School-university collaboration.* Bloomington, IN: Phi Delta Kappa Educational Foundation.

Schwartz, J. B. (1990). Will your school-business partnership stand the test of time? *NASSP Bulletin, 74*(529), 99–102.

Sergiovanni, T. J. (1994). *Building community in schools.* San Francisco: Jossey-Bass.

Ubben, G. C., Hughes, L. W., & Norris, C. J. (2001). *The principal: Creative leadership for effective schools* (4th ed.). Needham Heights, MA: Allyn and Bacon.

Wilbur, F. P., & Lambert, L. M. (1995). *Linking America's schools and colleges: Guide to partnerships and national directory* (2nd ed.). Washington, DC: America's Association for Higher Education.

Wiseman, D. L., & Nason, P. L. (1995). The nature of interactions in a field-based teacher education experience. *Action in Teacher Education, 17*(3), 1–12.

6

DEMONSTRATING ETHICAL LEADERSHIP

Standard 5: A school administrator is an educational leader who promotes the success of all students by acting with integrity, fairness, and in an ethical manner.

INTRODUCTION

American institutions that historically have been viewed as unwavering pillars of moral and ethical decency visibly are beginning to deteriorate (Beck, 1996). Over the past several years, it has become more common to read newspaper accounts of police officers charged with brutality, perjury, assaulting suspects, and with the use of racial profiling as a reason for detaining and questioning citizens. State and national legislators have been reprimanded for ethical breaches. When serving as president of the United States, William Clinton was impeached for providing false grand jury testimony and obstruction of justice, a legal consequence of his moral and ethical lapses in judgment. Children frequently emulate professional athletes as their heroes and role models, yet some sports personalities seemingly are oblivious to their immense impact on impressionable youth. The news media regularly report instances in which athletes have assaulted their coaches; spat on officials; engaged in fighting on and off the playing field; and have been convicted of such crimes as drug possession, assault, rape, and possession of concealed weapons.

As "institutions that traditionally guided our moral reasoning" (Beck, 1996, p. 11) begin to develop cracks in their foundations, educators are coming under increased pressure to be the stewards of the public's morals—the prevailing norms and values of the community and nation—because children need to emulate role models who act with integrity. Because they serve as the heads of their organizations, superintendents and principals are the school system's most visible leaders and, therefore, must be exemplars of moral leadership.

A fundamental purpose of schools is to prepare students to become fully contributing members of society. Implicit in this purpose is the belief that schoolchildren must be acculturated in public values. Bull and McCarthy (1995) note, "Public values are not only what unite Americans into a single people but also, because they include commitments to toleration and equality before the law, what make it possible for them to be diverse" (pp. 623–624). As public employees, administrators and teachers have a responsibility that exceeds what is expected of other citizens: They must enforce and model public values as they carry out their daily responsibilities. Additionally, educators must use public values as reference points in making school decisions, even when these values conflict with their private, deeply held morals, values, and convictions (Bull & McCarthy, 1995).

To facilitate the understanding of ISLLC Standard 5, this chapter explains the concepts of morals and ethical behavior, describes how educational leaders act in a manner that is consistent with their ethical standards, shares how leaders create ethical schools, and provides the professional code of ethics for educational administrators.

MORALS AND ETHICAL BEHAVIOR

When discussing morals and values and their impact on ethical behavior in educational leadership, the terms "morals" and "ethics" mean different things to different individuals. French (1997) notes, "Perhaps ethics is what one should do and morals is what one actually does. Or perhaps ethics are theoretical and morality is practical" (p. 4). Although French uses the terms "morals" and "ethics" interchangeably, they are two separate terms, albeit closely connected. The concept of "morals" refers to an individual's personal beliefs about right and wrong, which frequently are tied to society's sanctioned codes and accepted values. In contrast, the concept of "ethics" molds an individual's moral beliefs into a theory of moral values and their application in practice. "Ethics" is a more expansive term, going beyond one's morals and involving complex issues of fairness and equity, as individuals struggle to reconcile their personal beliefs with issues they confront on a daily basis in their societal interactions.

A school leader who acts ethically must be sure that her or his behavior conforms to the accepted professional standards of conduct in the field of educational administration. Professional ethics emerge when an administrator examines his or her personal values and beliefs within the specific school context (McKerrow, 1997), then makes decisions based upon what is fundamentally "fair" and "right" for the students and employees in the school, both individually and collectively.

The practice of educational leadership cannot be an amoral endeavor, one that is divorced from the leader's personal sense of right and wrong. A leader's actions could be consistent with his or her set of morals, yet be unethical, but they also could be in conflict with his or her personal morals and be ethically solid. As a role model for students and faculty, the administrator's actions speak volumes, even (and sometimes especially) when the administrator refuses to speak publicly about his or her personal beliefs, values, and ultimate administrative decisions (Beck, 1996; Piper, 1993). Raywid (1986) notes,

> As administrators think and act, these behaviors have moral bearings whether the actors intend them or not. Indeed, as we have seen, even the decision *not* to intend them—i.e., to exclude moral considerations from one's thinking—is in itself a decision of profound moral bearing. (p. 162)

Consequently, a decision to take *no* action also can have immense ethical ramifications (Beck, 1996).

Certainly, leaders desire to act in ways that are consistent with both their personal beliefs and their professional ethics. Unfortunately, the reality of the matter is that because school systems do not exist in a social vacuum, ethical conflicts are ever-present. Sometimes moral dilemmas have numerous correct answers (Strike, Haller, & Soltis, 1998), and frequently simple answers to complex questions do not exist (Beck, 1996). Ethical dilemmas result not because of a choice between right and wrong, but a choice between two rights (Kidder, 1995). One example of an ethical dilemma would be a situation in which a school leader is called upon to eliminate an educational program in times of budget shortfalls. Two programs may be equally valued within the school community and viewed as essential to the school's mission, but a compromise measure of cutting funding in half would virtually doom both programs to failure. Eliminating either program would be an unpopular, albeit necessary, measure.

Even though one's personal moral compass may be pointing in the correct direction, factors beyond one's control can occasionally intervene and prevent one from following that path. Local board policies and state and federal statutes also can present ethical quandaries. For example, simply because a decision may be deemed legal (or not illegal) does not mean that it is ethically correct. When attempting to fashion an ethically solid decision, an administrative superior or the board of education may step in to overrule the leader. School principals especially can be caught in this quandary because they can be considered "middle managers." Principals' decisions must withstand the scrutiny of the board, central office administration, parents, faculty, and students. Even though a leader's action may have full support at the building level, it may not be supported at the higher levels of the administrative hierarchy. By virtue of their more visible position within the community, superintendents' decisions frequently are exposed to public scrutiny.

ACTING WITH INTEGRITY AND FAIRNESS

An educational leader must demonstrate personal integrity and honesty in working with students, faculty, parents, and constituents. As school issues are deliberated, Strike et al. (1998) note two fundamental moral conceptions that should be the foundation for all discussions: the principle of benefit maximization and the principle of equal respect for persons. Benefit maximization implies that all school decisions should result in the most good or the greatest benefit for the most people. Equal respect connotes that the equal worth of all must be respected and that we have a duty to accord others the same kind of treatment we expect them to extend to us.

These two principles can clash when a leader must make a decision that benefits the majority of people, yet still respects the rights of the individual. Teachers usually can make decisions based only on their ramifications within the classroom, but administrators must be aware of the impact of their decisions on the functioning of the entire school or school system. If an administrator makes an exception to the rules, believing it truly is in the best interest of an individual student, that administrator must do so knowing that deviating from a school policy causes others to question the validity of the policy. Will this policy universally be enforced in all circumstances, or is it only for administrative convenience, used when the leader needs a bureaucratic crutch to support his actions? Enomoto (1997) underscores this dilemma for leaders, noting that if they follow the book, they are consistent but not compassionate.

If they are caring and compassionate, they may be too accommodating and lenient.

One of the challenges of educational leadership is to ensure that the system values and considers the viewpoints of all members of the school community, especially parents, even when these viewpoints are not compatible with the prevailing norms of the community. Paul, Berger, and Osnes (1997) caution, "All who are not connected as valued, caring, and cared-for members of the school community are strangers, kept at a distance by long-established boundaries based on social class values, race, ethnicity, and gender" (p. 20). The practice of keeping individuals at a distance and ignoring their concerns—even those whose ideas are admittedly outside the mainstream—can cause constituents to correctly believe that they are outsiders. These administrative responses may prompt frustrated outsiders to have their views heard by whatever means necessary, and in the end, students will most likely be the ones to suffer. By establishing and maintaining open channels of communication, the school is more likely to ensure that all students will remain connected and will be successful. Most individuals simply want to be heard and have their views considered as part of the democratic process. They are willing to support the ultimate decision, whatever it may be, satisfied that they have had the opportunity to be included in this process.

In spite of a school's efforts to involve all parties in school decision-making, some parents still may feel uncomfortable participating in this process. Additionally, students' voices frequently are overlooked. School officials have a responsibility to consider the viewpoints of all sectors of the school community, which includes being a voice for those who are not represented in the process, for whatever reason. Examining a potential decision from the perspective of those who will be affected, especially those who have elected to remain silent during the deliberations, helps to expose the ramifications of the action on all parties.

Some groups may attempt to advance specific personal agendas that are not in the best interest of the schools, and negotiating these political minefields can be difficult. A leader who demonstrates integrity "must honor those who hold such views but not necessarily yield to them" (Beck, 1996, p. 9). Some school leaders espouse an "open door" policy, yet they routinely may dismiss teachers and parents whose ideas are not consistent with their philosophical beliefs. Listening and valuing opinions does not mean, however, that school officials must yield to unreasonable demands. The administrative challenges are to listen, include all parties in the discourse, be certain that all viewpoints are considered, value each person's opinion, and work to achieve a shared vision of what the school is to be and the students are to become. Adhering to the principles of benefit maximization and equal respect during the democratic process ensures that the positive norms of the community will prevail. Those who were unsuccessful in pushing through their political agendas must acknowledge that they had an opportunity to participate in the process and then yield to the wishes of the majority.

Although an educational leader may reach a decision in private, the decision becomes public almost immediately. In this decision-making process, administrators have procedural responsibilities to which they must adhere (Bull & McCarthy, 1995). Since leaders will be held accountable for their actions (Mijares, 1996), they should explain the moral reasoning underlying their decisions so that others may learn how the decision was reached and can better understand the factors that prompted the action. They also must be willing to submit their decisions to public moral debate, listen to criticisms, and make revisions when appropriate. Mijares (1996) cautions that "the discomfort that comes from such challenges is far less severe than the consequences of stumbling ethically. Ethical violations have ruined careers and lives" (p. 29).

LEADERS AS SERVANTS AND STEWARDS

Sergiovanni (1992) promotes a theory of servant leadership in which school leadership is based on moral authority. As moral agents (Strike et al., 1998), school leaders must understand that, although serving others is important, shaping the institution into a covenantal community is of utmost importance. Teachers and administrators become servants and stewards of the community's ideals (Block, 1993), while in the process building a covenant of shared values within the building and school system.

Block (1993) notes that the leader's choice is between service and self-interest, and "the antidote to self-interest is to commit and to find cause" (p. 10). Instead of focusing on a professional goal to move upward in the organization or promoting their personal agendas, individuals are motivated "to create an organization and culture we can believe in" (Block, 1993, p. 89). Educational leaders have a moral responsibility "to establish an ethical school environment in which education can take place ethically" (Starratt, 1991, p. 187).

CREATING AN ETHICAL SCHOOL

How can an educational leader establish an ethical school? Starratt (1991) suggests that the administrator begin by examining and joining three ethics: an ethic of critique, an ethic of justice, and an ethic of caring. The ethic of *critique* is an analysis of the school system in its bureaucratic context, examining such practices as the organizational hierarchy of the school, the adversarial mindset of unions, and technicist approaches to teaching. Many schools as they currently are structured are replete with unethical educational practices, such as reinforcing racial and sex biases in their procedures for tracking, sorting, and labeling students. Schools should "look at themselves through a moral lens, and consider how virtually everything that goes on there affects the values and character of students" (Lickona, 1993, p. 10). During the course of this critical self-examination, teachers and administrators should not be afraid to ask hard questions and answer them truthfully. When examining school issues, do school officials first consider what is best for students, or do they yield to adult convenience? Is student confidentiality protected whenever possible? Is every student and parent valued equally and treated with courtesy and respect, regardless of ethnicity or social standing?

Critique reminds the leader of her or his social responsibility to students, the education profession, and society, as the school addresses its moral responsibility to prepare students for their place in society. Through the process of critique, school administrators and teachers can identify and eliminate unethical practices that may be present in their schools. Goens (1996) recommends that schools systems define their corporate values and identify the key principles and beliefs that serve as the foundation for quality decisions and programs. Using these beliefs as anchors, ethical practices now become a certainty.

The ethic of *justice* "demands that the claims of the institution serve both the common good and the rights of the individuals in the school" (Starratt, 1991, p. 194). Justice is frequently viewed as being public, rational, and impartial. Enomoto (1997) believes that administrators are more likely to rely on the principle of justice because they normally maintain rather than challenge the status quo.

Schools should include ethical learning activities within their curricular and extracurricular programs to stimulate discussion related to individual and school needs and conflicts that can occur when attempting to satisfy both (Starratt, 1991). Starratt recommends that schools provide workshops for faculty and students on such topics as active listening, conflict resolution, group dynamics, and problem solving, so that all will have a better understanding of how the ethic of justice can be realized in their school. Through learning activities focused on this ethic, students begin to understand that the greater needs of society sometimes must supersede the rights of the individual.

The ethic of *caring* honors each person's dignity, acknowledges their right to be themselves, and promotes loyalty to one's relationship with another (Starratt, 1991). Gilligan (1982) has been instrumental in advocating that a commitment to care is critical to the creation of an ethical, principal-driven organization. Noddings (1988) agrees, noting that a caring framework likely would influence many changes related to the process of teaching and learning in schools. Entomoto (1997) further notes that care is private, compassionate, and sensitive to context. The school leader can promote this ethic by attending to the school's culture, assuring that school songs, symbols, and award ceremonies emphasize cooperation, teamwork, service, and caring for others. The concept of a "symbolic frame" advocated by Bolman and Deal (1991) is consistent with the ethic of caring: they note that an organization's culture is communicated most clearly through its symbols and rituals.

An institution with a strong understanding of itself and its purpose will not merely passively accept newcomers into the group. Instead, new members (students, parents, and faculty) will be initiated into the organization, and in the process gain an understanding of the culture and the expectations that the organization places on them for their full participation. Although Starratt places equal value on each of the ethics, Beck (1992) believes that caring is the most important ethic.

To fully develop these three ethics, all members of the school community must come together to articulate a shared view of the ethical foundation of their school and school system (Enomoto, 1997). This common vision helps to resolve any contradictions between the school's philosophy and function. Through the process of developing a shared vision, the members of the school community begin to create a moral community in which students and faculty respect and care about one another as valued members of the group (Lickona, 1993). In addition, members of the school community develop a sense of trust and openness to one another (Goens, 1996). As Sergiovanni (1996) notes, students "learn virtue by being around virtuous people and by being part of social networks that represent webs of meaning with moral overtones"(p. 125).

THE ADMINISTRATORS' PROFESSIONAL CODE OF ETHICS

Integrity is the cornerstone of a leader's personal platform and professional practice. An administrator who displays an unwavering sense of self—making decisions that are congruent with a personal ethical code—is viewed by parents, students, and teachers as credible and reliable. Goens (1996) notes, "Professional credibility depends on ethics because without ethical practice parents and children have little security" (p. 13).

Unfortunately, not all superintendents and principals act in an ethical manner. In his dissertation study, Fenstermaker (1996) surveyed 242 school superintendents, asking them to respond to borderline ethical dilemmas by selecting an appropriate course of action from among several choices. The results were disheartening; nearly 52% of their responses were judged to be unethical. Fenstermaker (1996) concluded that either there was severe confusion regarding ethical standards, or the superintendents chose to disregard their code of ethics when making school-based decisions. He believed that a combination of both factors contributed to the low scores. Fenstermaker (1996) warned:

> As the American people become increasingly skeptical of all persons in positions of power and authority, it will become more necessary for superintendents to know and conscientiously apply ethical principles in their work roles. The alternative will be a gradual degradation of the profession as a whole—a loss of trust eventually extending not only to superintendents, but to the entire public school system that they represent. (p. 24)

Recognizing that educational leaders must abide by a consistent set of ethical principles guiding their professional conduct, six educational administration organizations have adopted the *Statement of Ethics* that is listed in Figure 6.1. These 10 ethical principles are consistent with the knowledge, skills, and dispositions related to ISLLC Standard 5.

An educational administrator's professional behavior must conform to an ethical code. The code must be idealistic and at the same time practical, so that it can apply reasonably to all educational administrators. The administrator acknowledges that the schools belong to the public they serve for the purpose of providing educational opportunities to all. However, the administrator assumes responsibility for providing professional leadership in the school and community. This responsibility requires the administrator to maintain standards of exemplary professional conduct. It must be recognized that the administrator's actions will be viewed and appraised by the community, professional associates, and students. To these ends, the administrator subscribes to the following statements of standards. The educational administrator:

1. Makes the well-being of students the fundamental value in all decision making and actions.
2. Fulfills professional responsibilities with honesty and integrity.
3. Supports the principle of due process and protects the civil and human rights of all individuals.
4. Obeys local, state, and national laws and does not knowingly join or support organizations that advocate, directly or indirectly, the overthrow of the government.
5. Implements the governing board of education's policies and administrative rules and regulations.
6. Pursues appropriate measures to correct those laws, policies, and regulations that are not consistent with sound educational goals.
7. Avoids using positions for personal gain through political, social, religious, economic, or other influences.
8. Accepts academic degrees or professional certification only from duly accredited institutions.
9. Maintains the standards and seeks to improve the effectiveness of the profession through research and continuing professional development.
10. Honors all contracts until fulfillment, release, or dissolution mutually agreed upon by all parties to contract.

This Statement of Ethics was developed by a task force representing the National Association of Secondary School Principals, National Association of Elementary School Principals, American Association of School Administrators, Association of School Business Officials, American Association of School Personnel Administrators, and National Council of Administrative Women in Education.

Figure 6.1 Statement of Ethics.

The development of a code of ethics, in and of itself, is not a simple "quick fix" for the problem of ethical dilemmas. Unethical administrators can play semantics games, discovering creative ways to work around both the letter and the spirit of the ethics laws in order to get their way. "Codes of ethics for a profession such as educational administration," Beck (1970) says, "are no substitutes for honesty, decency, courtesy, competence, common sense, and good taste" (p. 56). However, as the recognized ethical code for the educational administration profession, school leaders should embrace these principles and use them as the ethical foundation for all decisions.

LEARNING AND PRACTICING ETHICAL BEHAVIOR

Only individuals with personal integrity will adhere to a professional code of ethics. This statement begs the question: Can ethics be taught? According to the experts, the answer is "yes" (Sergiovanni, 1996; Strike et al., 1998). The ethics issue is not a subjective matter, and Strike et al. (1998) say that objective ethical reasoning is not only possible, it is vitally important. Educational administration preparation programs have a sober and challenging task "to develop a curriculum that fosters not only ethical reflection but also the formation of moral courage" (Parks, 1993, p. 49). In addition to the use of such methods as case studies and problem-based learning modules, English and Steffy (1997) recommend using film as a teaching medium. Viewing films of great leaders, not limited to the field of educational administration, but also covering all areas of history, helps aspiring administrators understand each leader's moral code and realize the connection between the leader's beliefs and actions.

As educational leaders struggle to discover the correct answers to ethical dilemmas, they may consider utilizing the "Ethics Check" questions that are listed in Figure 6.2. Blanchard and Peale (1988) acknowledge that a large gray area lies between the two extremes of right and wrong. This "Ethics Check" can help leaders be sure that they are applying objective ethical reasoning when making decisions, and, it is hoped, eliminating the gray areas in the process.

Because decisions are exposed to public scrutiny, educational leaders should consider carefully the third question: "How will it make me feel about myself?" Even when faced with emotionally charged and gut-wrenching issues, the leader must do what he or she believes is morally and ethically correct. Leaders must be able to go to sleep at night knowing that they have remained true to their moral convictions. As Blanchard and Peale (1988) warn, "There is no right way to do a wrong thing" (p. 19). Good leaders not only do things right, they also do the right thing.

1. *Is it legal?* Will I be violating either civil law or company policy?
2. *Is it balanced?* Is it fair to all concerned in the short term as well as the long term? Does it promote win-win relationships?
3. *How will it make me feel about myself?* Will it make me proud? Would I feel good if my decision was published in the newspaper? Would I feel good if my family know about it?

Figure 6.2   The "Ethics Check" Questions. *Source:* **Blanchard, K., & Peale, N. V. (1988).** *The power of ethical management.* **New York: William Morrow, p. 27. Copyright Blanchard Family Partnership and Norman Vincent Peale. Reprinted with permission.**

Immegart and Burroughs (1970) suggest that a leader also can employ the concept of an ethical screen as an input-output model. In this model, the input refers to the event, situation, or problem that is causing ethical conflict. The administrator then chooses the appropriate ethical screen to guide his or her action, which might be societal ethics, personal ethics, professional ethics, organizational ethics, or means ethics. Finally, the leader determines the output, which is the identified course of action to resolve the ethical problem.

In addition to being an unwavering exemplar of ethical conduct, the educational leader must monitor ethical practices within the organization and be willing to take action should ethical breaches occur (Goens, 1996). Principle-centered leaders care deeply about their schools' and school systems' underlying values and commitments, and they become outraged when they observe these values being violated or ignored (Sergiovanni, 2001). Ethical leaders cannot remain silent or look the other way when these violations occur. Leadership by outrage as a symbolic act touches people at a deeper level than when leadership is merely viewed as a predictable, routine act. People understand that they must not violate the ethical norms of the organization, and they in turn become outraged if others attempt to do so.

ASSESSING ORGANIZATIONAL INTEGRITY

It is good practice to periodically assess the integrity of the school organization and those who are involved with it. Goens (1996) recommends that school officials conduct summit meetings, surveys of parents and staff members, and audits to ascertain whether the organization is remaining consistent to its values, principles, and beliefs. "The degree to which a disparity exits between practice and ethical principles," Goens (1996) notes, "is the degree to

which the schools lack integrity. Without integrity, there is no credibility. Without credibility, there is no support" (p. 14).

To be certain that a school faculty is continually examining its
practices for ethical purity, a school may decide to form an ethics
committee (Sichel, 1993). The creation of such a committee can
assure that the entire school faculty, not only the principal, is
continually aware of the importance of moral and ethical decisions within the school. Although new to the field of education,
ethics committees are routine practice in hospital settings.
These committees can develop ethical codes regulating the
school, identify potential ethical conflicts, and help raise awareness of ethical issues within the school. If there is a disparity between practice and principles, educators should examine their
individual and collective behavior, challenge the wisdom of their
prior actions, and make any necessary corrections in policies or
practices.

SUMMARY

Displaying exemplary moral and ethical behavior is a necessary,
ambiguous and difficult role for the school leader, especially
when considering the shifting and conflicting positions that
moral subjectivism can take. In spite of this difficulty, the reality
of the situation is that parents, students, and the community at
large desire educational leaders who demonstrate high standards
of ethical and moral behavior, in both their professional and personal actions. A school leader is expected to model the ethical
standards set forth by the school district, consistent with the
community's beliefs.

Forfeiting one's personal conviction to permit the automation of
the laws and policies is neither a moral nor a comforting thought.
In an ideal world, the school leader's personal convictions and beliefs would be fully aligned with school policies and practices.

However, educational leaders are confronted with ethical dilemmas in school systems daily. Negotiating through these conflicts is no small task.

SUGGESTED INTERNSHIP ACTIVITIES RELATED TO STANDARD 5

Review the current skill levels that you noted on your ISLLC Standards Self-Assessment under Standard 5. Note areas in which you wish to improve your skills and, working with your mentor and supervisor, identify activities that you can complete during your internship experience. The following listing of activities related to Standard 5 is provided to help you identify projects that may be appropriate for your clinical experiences:

1. Examine the school's procedures for selecting and assigning students into remedial and advanced courses.
2. Working with the principal, establish an ethics committee for the school, consisting of administrators, teachers, students, and parents. Assist the committee with assessing and examining the school's ethical practices.
3. Review the school's or school system's budget and budgeting process, noting any instances in which funds may not be equitably distributed.
4. Prepare a presentation to the school faculty on ethics, sharing educators' professional codes of conduct with the faculty and staff. Lead a discussion related to ethical practices within the school and any potential ethical conflicts.
5. Examine your personal ethical conduct, rating your professional performance against the *Statement of Ethics* in Figure 6.1.
6. Create your personal administrative platform, which includes your personal values and beliefs and explains how

you will ensure that the school or school system you lead will consistently function in an ethical manner.

7. Review the school handbook or board policy manual, noting any instances in which policies may not be consistent with the professional code of ethics.

8. Ask your administrative mentor to explain her or his personal moral and ethical beliefs, describe instances in which she or he was faced with ethical dilemmas, and explain how they were resolved.

9. Observe a student disciplinary procedure with an "ethical eye," noting any conflicts that may exist between the student's rights as an individual and the need to maintain consistency. Is the student treated with dignity and respect? Is the student's personal honesty and integrity challenged?

10. Examine the school's or school system's practices related to the sharing of confidential information.

11. If it is not already present in the school or school system, develop a conflict resolution training program for teachers and/or students.

12. Examine the school's symbols and traditions that demonstrate a culture of caring. In collaboration with the principal and faculty, develop new programs that help to build a unified and caring school culture.

13. Hold focus group meetings with students, asking them to describe ways in which teachers, administrators, and students demonstrate that they care for all individuals in the school. Report the results to the principal or the school's ethics committee, providing recommendations for addressing issues raised by the students.

14. Based on your ISLLC Standards Self-Assessment under Standard 5, select one or two books from the suggested readings that will help expand your knowledge of topics related to this standard. In addition, select one of the Web site resources listed, review the information available, and

identify how this resource can assist you in your professional development.

SUGGESTED READINGS

Beck, L. G., & Murphy, J. (1994). *Ethics in educational leadership programs: An expanding role.* Thousand Oaks, CA: Corwin Press.

Block, P. (1993). *Stewardship: Choosing service over self-interest.* San Francisco: Jossey-Bass.

DeRoche, E., & Williams, M. (2000). *Character education: A guide for school administrators.* Lanham, MD: Scarecrow.

Gaddy, B. B., Hall, T. W., & Marzano, R. J. (1996). *School wars: Resolving our conflicts over religion and values.* San Francisco: Jossey-Bass.

Hodgkinson, C. (1991). *Educational leadership: The moral art.* Albany: State University of New York Press.

Immegart, G. L., & Burroughs, J. M. (1970). *Ethics and the school administrator.* Danville, IL: The Interstate Printers and Publishers.

Katz, M. S., Noddings, N., & Strike, K. A. (1999). *Justice and caring: The search for common ground in education.* New York: Teachers College Press.

Kidder, R. M. (1995). *How good people make tough choices.* New York: William Morrow.

Kozol, J. (1991). *Savage inequalities: Children in America's schools.* New York: Crown Press.

Noddings, N. (1992). *The challenge to care in schools.* New York: Teachers College Press.

Oakes, J., Quartz, K. H., Ryan, S., & Lipton, M. (1999). *Becoming good American schools: The struggle for civic virtue in education reform.* San Francisco: Jossey-Bass.

Paul, J. L., Berger, N. H., Osnes, P. G., Martinez, Y. G., & Morse, W. C. (Eds.). (1997). *Ethics and decision making in local schools.* Baltimore: Paul H. Brookes Publishing.

Rebore, R. W. (2001). *The ethics of educational leadership.* Upper Saddle River, NJ: Prentice Hall.

Ryan, K., & Bohlin, K. E. (1998). *Building character in schools: Practical ways to bring moral instruction to life.* San Francisco: Jossey-Bass.

Sergiovanni, T. J. (1992). *Moral leadership: Getting to the heart of school improvement.* San Francisco: Jossey-Bass.

Sergiovanni, T. J. (1999). *The lifeworld of leadership: Creating culture, community, and personal meaning in schools.* San Francisco: Jossey-Bass.

Shapiro, J. P., & Stefkovich, J. (2000). *Ethical leadership and decision making.* Mahwah, NJ: Lawrence Erlbaum Associates.

Strike, K. A., Haller, E. J., & Soltis, J. F. (1998). *The ethics of school administration* (2nd ed.). New York: Teachers College Press.

Willower, D. J., & Licata, J. W. (1997). *Values and valuation in the practice of educational administration.* Thousand Oaks, CA: Corwin Press.

WEB SITE RESOURCES

Character Counts Coalition
www.charactercounts.org

UCEA Center for the Study of Leadership and Ethics
http://curry.edschool.virginia.edu/curry/center/ethics/home.html

Centre for the Study of Values and Leadership
www.oise.utoronto.ca/~pbegley

Living Values: An Educational Program
www.livingvalues.net

REFERENCES

Beck, L. G. (1992). Meeting the challenge of the future: The place of a caring ethic in educational administration. *American Journal of Education, 100,* 454–496.

Beck, L. G. (1996). Why ethics? Why now? Thoughts on the moral challenges facing educational leaders. *The School Administrator, 9*(54), 8–11.

Beck, L. W. (1970). Professions, ethics, and professional ethics. In G. L. Immegart & J. M. Burroughs (Eds.), *Ethics and the school administrator* (pp. 43–56). Danville, IL: The Interstate Printers and Publishers.

Blanchard, K., & Peale, N. V. (1988). *The power of ethical management.* New York: William Morrow.

Block, P. (1993). *Stewardship: Choosing service over self-interest.* San Francisco: Berrett-Koehler Publishers.

Bolman, L., & Deal, T. (1991). *Reframing organizations: Artistry, choice and leadership.* San Francisco: Jossey-Bass.

Bull, B. L., & McCarthy, M. M. (1995). Reflections on the knowledge base in law and ethics for educational leaders. *Educational Administration Quarterly, 31,* 613–631.

English, F. W., & Steffy, B. E. (1997). Using film to teach leadership in educational administration. *Educational Administration Quarterly, 33,* 107–115.

Enomoto, E. K. (1997). Negotiating the ethics of care and justice. *Educational Administration Quarterly, 33,* 351–370.

Fenstermaker, W. C. (1996). The ethical dimension of superintendent decision making: A study of AASA members finds a lack of awareness of association's code of ethics. *The School Administrator, 9*(54), 16–24.

French, P. A. (1997). Moral principles, rules, and policies. In J. L. Paul, N. H. Berger, P. G. Osnes, Y. G. Martinez, & W. C. Morse (Eds.), *Ethics and decision making in local schools* (pp. 85–97). Baltimore: Paul H. Brookes.

Gilligan, C. (1982). *In a different voice: Psychological theory and women's development.* Cambridge, MA: Harvard University Press.

Goens, G. A. (1996). Shared decisions, empowerment, and ethics: A mission impossible for district leaders? *The School Administrator, 9*(54), 12–14.

Immegart, G. L., & Burroughs, J. M. (1970). *Ethics and the school administrator.* Danville, IL: The Interstate Printers and Publishers.

Kidder, R. M. (1995). *How good people make tough choices.* New York: William Morrow.

Lickona, T. (1993). The return of character education. *Educational Leadership, 51*(3), 6–11.

McKerrow, K. (1997). Ethical administration: An oxymoron? *Journal of School Leadership, 7*(2), 210–225.

Mijares, A. (1996). Escaping the malaise: First-hand guidance for ethical behavior. *The School Administrator,* 9(54), 26–29.

Noddings, N. (1988). An ethic of caring and its implications for instructional arrangements. *American Journal of Education,* 96(3), 215–230.

Parks, S. D. (1993). Is it too late? Young adults and the formation of professional ethics. In T. R. Piper, M. C. Gentile, & S. D. Parks (Eds.), *Can ethics be taught?* (pp. 13–72). Boston: Harvard Business School.

Paul, J. L., Berger, N. H., & Osnes, P. G. (1997). Ethics, research, and school-based decision making. In J. L. Paul, N. H. Berger, P. G. Osnes, Y. G. Martinez, & W. C. Morse (Eds.), *Ethics and decision making in local schools.* Baltimore: Paul H. Brookes Publishing.

Piper, T. R. (1993). Rediscovery of purpose: The genesis of the leadership, ethics, and corporate responsibility initiative. In T. R. Piper, M. C. Gentile, & S. D. Parks (Eds.), *Can ethics be taught?* (pp. 1–12). Boston: Harvard Business School.

Raywid, M. A. (1986). Some moral dimensions of administrative theory and practice. *Issues in Education,* 4(2), 151–166.

Sergiovanni, T. J. (1992). *Moral leadership: Getting to the heart of school improvement.* San Francisco: Jossey-Bass.

Sergiovanni, T. J. (1996). *Leadership for the schoolhouse: How is it different? Why is it important?* San Francisco: Jossey-Bass.

Sergiovanni, T. J. (2001). *The principalship: A reflective practice perspective* (4th ed.). Needham Heights, MA: Allyn and Bacon.

Sichel, B. A. (1993). Ethics committees and teacher ethics. In K. Strike & P. L. Ternasky (Eds.), *Ethics for professionals in education: perspectives for preparation and practice* (pp. 162–175). New York: Teachers College Press.

Starratt, R. J. (1991). Building an ethical school: A theory for practice in educational leadership. *Educational Administration Quarterly,* 27, 185–202.

Strike, K. A., Haller, E. J., & Soltis, J. F. (1998). *The ethics of school administration* (2nd ed.). New York: Teachers College Press.

7

LEADING SCHOOLS IN CONTEXT

Standard 6: A school administrator is an educational leader who promotes the success of all students by understanding, responding to, and influencing the larger political, social, economic, legal, and cultural context.

INTRODUCTION

Understanding how schools are immersed in and linked to a large array of external forces is essential to being an effective educational leader. Public schools and school systems are extensions of the local communities within which they are located. As such, these educational institutions are influenced greatly by the political, economic, and cultural contexts of these communities. The communities, in turn, are part of the larger social and governmental structures as defined by local, state, and federal legislation.

This chapter will review various issues relative to the governance of schools and school systems, including the political processes that are used to bring the social and cultural contexts of the community to bear upon educational decision-making and programming. The legal foundation for public school systems, and the economic issues intrinsically involved in these systems, also are discussed as further extensions of larger governance questions. The chapter concludes with a focus on the global issues of schools related to technology, equity, and diversity. All of these various contexts are included in an understanding of ISLLC Standard 6.

LEADING COMPLEX ORGANIZATIONS

Administrators struggle daily with the challenges of managing and leading schools and school systems. Educational institutions are complex organizations, and school leaders need multiple tools to effectively facilitate their development into learning organizations. As the field of educational administration has evolved, organizational theorists have advanced varying views of schools as social systems, in an effort to provide a better understanding of how school organizations function.

Noting that there are numerous effective ways to solve organizational problems, Bolman and Deal (1991) have consolidated these organizational theories into four categories, which they call *frames.* "Frames are both windows on the world and lenses that bring the world into focus," note Bolman and Deal (1991, p. 11). Skilled leaders can wisely match the appropriate frame to each problem situation, in effect using "their artistry to articulate and communicate their vision so that others are also able to see things differently (Bolman & Deal, 1991, p. 11). These four organizational frames are as follows:

1. *Structural.* Drawing from the field of sociology, this frame emphasizes the importance of formal roles and relationships. Organizational charts, policies, and procedures are crafted to provide clear understanding of roles and responsibilities within the system.

2. *Human Resource.* Building upon the ideas of organizational social psychologists, this frame recognizes that organizations consist of individuals with needs, feelings, and prejudices. This perspective encourages leaders to craft the organization in such a way that people can accomplish their goals while being satisfied with what they are accomplishing.

3. *Political.* Coming from the field of political science, this frame recognizes that conflict often emerges from within the organization, as different interest groups compete for both power and scarce resources. The adept leader uses political skill and acumen to disperse power in such a way that the organizational goals can be accomplished.

4. *Symbolic.* Drawing upon social and cultural anthropology, this perspective views organizations as cultural entities, propelled by ceremonies, symbols, myths, and traditions. Problems can occur when traditions are ignored, abandoned, or altered, causing the individuals to feel a deep sense of loss for the organization's historical roots and purposes. (Bolman & Deal, 1991, pp. 15–16)

An inexperienced school leader primarily may make use of one or two preferred frames, seeing the others as inappropriate and superficial. However, effective leaders must possess the capacity to integrate all four frames and must be able to match the appropriate frame to each unique problem. As noted in Figure 7.1, any situation can serve numerous purposes, and individuals within the organization simultaneously may view this situation from competing frames. The intuitive, skilled administrator possesses the skills to view the situation through each individual's lens, in the process being able to speak to and integrate the issue across the varying frames.

This basic understanding of schools and school systems through Bolman and Deal's four frames helps to provide the foundation for the sixth ISSLC standard.

Process	Structural Frame	Human Resource Frame	Political Frame	Symbolic Frame
Planning	Strategies to set objectives and coordinate resources	Gatherings to promote participation	Arenas to air conflicts and realign power	Ritual to signal responsibility, produce symbols, negotiate meanings
Decision Making	Rational sequence to produce right decision	Open process to produce commitment	Opportunity to gain or exercise power	Ritual to provide comfort and support until desicion happens
Reorganizing	Realign roles and responsibilities to fit tasks and environment	Maintain a balance between human needs and formal roles	Redistribute power and form new coalitions	Maintain an image of accountability and responsiveness; negotiate new social order
Evaluating	Way to distribute rewards or penalties and control performance	Process for helping individuals grow and improve	Opportunity to exercise power	Occasion to play roles in shared ritual
Approaching conflict	Maintain organizational goals by having authorities resolve conflict	Develop relationships by having individual confront conflict	Develop power by bargaining, forcing, or manipulating others to win	Develop shared values and use conflict to negotiate meaning

Process				
Goal setting	Keep organization headed in the right direction	Keep people involved and communication open	Provide opportunity for individuals and groups to make interests known	Develop symbols and shared values
Communication	Transmit facts and information	Exchange information, needs, and feelings	Vehicles for influencing or manipulating others	Telling stories
Meetings	Formal occasions for making decisions	Informal occasions for involvement, sharing feelings	Competitive occasions to win points	Sacred occasions to celebrate and transform the culture
Motivation	Economic incentives	Growth and self-actualization	Coercion, manipulation, and seduction	Symbols and celebrations

Figure 7.1 Four Interpretations of Organizational Processes. *Source:* Bolman, L. G., & Deal, T. E. (1991). *Reframing organizations: Artistry, choice, and leadership.* San Francisco: Jossey-Bass, p. 323. Copyright 1991 Jossey-Bass. Reprinted by permission.

GOVERNANCE AND SCHOOLS

The governance of public schools in the United States in the 21st century is much like the picture of a family member who is several generations removed from the original founding father of the group. The modern person will show some identifiable family resemblances and characteristics, but really appearing to be a unique, contemporary person. American public education is a product of the representative government that gave it "life," so to speak, but it shows the very noticeable impact of the societal evolution that has shaped changes in American culture. Various issues and critical events have caused the consideration and reconsideration of what is important to people, and of how they address those important concerns.

That the American society is unique among global entities is well recognized. Eastin (1999) states, "The historian Theodore White once observed that the United States is the only multiracial, multiethnic, multireligious society on earth where people live in relative peace and harmony" (p. 24). Public schools in the United States, and their governance, are also unique.

Public school leaders must recognize and work within this unique governance framework if they are to succeed in leading and managing these schools. They must have "a systematic method of scanning, monitoring, and interpreting events, in concert with a simultaneous past, present, and future orientation" (Patterson, Purkey, & Parker, 1986, p. 116). Key within this method is the recognition that, while the Reserve Clause of the Tenth Amendment to the United States Constitution designates the responsibility for education to the states, federal regulation of education has increased in the last several decades as more federal revenue has been allocated to public schools. Although education is not mentioned in the U.S. Constitution, the federal government has justified this intervention into the education arena by virtue of its implied powers coming from the "general welfare" clause. The mix of local, state, and federal dollars involved in typical public school programming has created a sometimes confusing, sometimes conflicting, and sometimes seemingly impossible, set of expectations for school systems. These conflicting demands require the school leader to have a high tolerance for ambiguity and to know how to coordinate these multiple elements.

PUBLIC EDUCATION IN A DEMOCRATIC SOCIETY

Leaders of public schools in a democratic society must call upon a wide variety of human, conceptual, and technical skills to successfully address the political, social, cultural, legal, and economic realities that are involved in leadership. This is especially true of the building principal, whose venue is the closest to the people who constitute that democratic society.

Political Processes

Spring (1993) notes, "As major disseminators of knowledge, public schools are targets for a variety of groups trying to influence the values, ideas, and information distributed to students" (p. 25). Schools are charged with addressing both conservative and liberal functions of the community that they serve. Thus, the public expects the schools to teach children the elements of their culture so as to ensure its continuance (conservative function), but the public also expects schools to give their children more than what they had and thus improve the culture (liberal function). Embedded with those major purposes are multiple issues and opinions about how best, and to what degree, the schools ought to go about accomplishing these tasks. The result is a constant flow of information aimed at influencing the actions of leaders and shaping the policies of public schools.

With this political backdrop in mind, superintendents and principals must cultivate an awareness of and sensitivity to the various influences within the community they serve. This requires that they spend time listening and gathering information from all segments of the community, that they look for areas of common concern and understanding among what appear to be disparate points of view, and that they cultivate collaboration among a complex set of constituents who appear to operate solely out of self-interest.

One of the essential tools in the leader's political skills' repertoire is that of constructive dialogue. It is a skill that begins with the solid belief that all parties involved in the issue have legitimate and valid points of view, based on their own values and experiences. It is a skill that only works with the goal of "win-win" in place rather than the traditional "selling" a plan of action approach. Yankelovich (1991) states:

> This alternative does not seek to sell the public anything. It does not manipulate. It does not propagandize or seduce. It advances two-way communication and dialogue rather than unidirectional informing. It is a resource to assist the public to make its own choices and to reach public judgment. (p. 249)

Constructive dialogue is a skill that builds collective decision-making into a plan of action in which everyone has a sense of legitimate ownership.

Multiple methods are useful in resolving issues and taking action. Sergiovanni, Burlingame, Coombs, and Thurston (1999) cite four methods of reconciling differences:

1. *Consensual Decision-Making.* All parties engage in dialogue with the aim of agreeing on the best possible choice.
2. *Institutional Authority.* The legitimate authority of the government or institution, as vested by election or appointment, is used to resolve the situation.
3. *Majority Rule.* All parties involved vote to express their collective wisdom.
4. *Bargaining.* This process assumes that there is a common ground that benefits all parties to some extent. (pp. 229–230)

The effective administrator needs to know the relative advantages of each of these and be able to use all of them. Consensual decision-making results in the strongest decisions, but is very time-consuming. In addition, working for consensus can mean that a small, determined minority can bring any process of change to a deliberate halt. The use of institutional authority works best for issues in which policies are clearly stated, but is risky if perceived as autocratic and arbitrary. Majority rule is best used after all appropriate information relative to the issue is known and shared, while use of the bargaining process is enhanced to the degree that the "common ground" is more basic and fundamental, resulting in stronger support for the resolution. Approached in the appropriate way, conflict over issues and concerns in the school result in stronger commitment to the goals of public education.

The organizational extension of this political decision-making in schools is the formulation and promulgation of policies that shape expectations for teachers and students, parents, and staff. Here, again, it is the superintendent and principal who are the primary focus, in the eyes of the educational consumer, in enacting these policies. As such, the leader must have a clear knowledge of the process by which policies are formulated, the scope and intent of these policies, and the likely response of various constituencies when they are put into effect. By thinking proactively, educational leaders will avoid unintended consequences and subversive responses that undermine the organization and siphon resources away from students and their education.

Social Systems

The school district is a subsystem within the overall system of the community, locally, regionally, and nationally. As such, it is directly influenced by the forces for change flowing throughout those systems. "Societal needs, pushed along by technological changes in transportation and communication, have probably

affected the governance of education more than most people realize" (Pipho, 2000, p. 10).

To be truly effective in educational programming, schools must
address societal needs, and when the schools are perceived as not
adequately addressing those needs, however they are defined, it is
the building principal who should be among the first to decipher
the early signals of these concerns. The principal and superintendent must take special care to create and maintain close ties and
strong communication with the grassroots community served by
the school or school district. "Schools that analyze and utilize information about their school communities make better decisions
about not only what to change, but how to institutionalize systemic
change" (Bernhardt, 1998, p. 1). These improved decisions occur
as a result of regular interactions with parent groups and with
business and government leaders in the community. Membership
in community service groups also offers a forum for the educational leader to monitor the concerns of the community, and also
to continually represent and interpret the programming of the
school to the wider community. In this way, the administrator provides one of the best vehicles for public schools to maintain their
openness and enhance their relevance within the community.

Cultural Values

Just as the school district is one of the primary connections to
the social system of the community, it is also the primary connection to the community's cultural values. Values "are consciously or
unconsciously held priorities that are expressed in all human activity" (Razik & Swanson, 2001, p. 361), and community values represent the context within which the school district must function.
These values, especially those related to schools, have undergone
major shifts in the last several decades as society has moved from
the manufacturing age to the information age. What is expected
from schools, and what is appropriate on the part of teachers and

learners, has changed and continues to change in fundamental ways. As a result, the way schools are organized and led must be constantly reexamined and monitored for "fit" with the community's prevailing beliefs about them.

Through proximity and regular interaction with parents and students, the administrator has the unique opportunity and responsibility to continuously scan the local school's environment for indicators of these beliefs and values. The administrator must ask regularly, "Is this school system and the way it interacts with students and parents contextually appropriate for this community and its cultural values?" To respond to this question adequately, the leader must have keen insight in detecting the attitudes and belief systems generating community sentiment. This must be coupled with the ability to analyze seemingly separate behaviors and synthesize these elements into an understanding of the community's cultural makeup as a multidimensional reality. Further, the educational leader has the obligation to assist school staff members in their understanding of how to best provide contextually relevant educational services for the community.

At the building level, the principal also must represent the community's unique cultural values within the larger organization of the school district, which may contain a number of different subcommunities and ethnic cultures. Organizational decision-making processes and policies must be applied with an understanding of how the community served by the school will respond, based upon understanding its values and beliefs. The reality of a culturally pluralistic society served by the school district thus guides the principal's judgments and actions within the school organization as well as with the local school community.

Legal Context

Basic to maintaining a representative form of government is universal public education, which is an American ideal embedded within the early quest for freedom in this country. Central to this ideal is the notion that "nothing is more effective in countering political oppression than the diffusion of knowledge." To achieve this goal of universal public education, the colonists of this country had to overcome their orientation to the class system of English education in exchange for a commitment to a more broadly based access to educational opportunity. Though great public debate formed around the issue of public education for many years, educational leaders such as Horace Mann planted the seeds for the free, public, common, universal education that exists in this country today (Alexander & Alexander, 2001).

A direct outgrowth of these early efforts by public school advocates in this country is that most individual state constitutions share principles undergirding their educational systems. These principles outline the clear foundations for publicly supported schools to which all had access. Specific elements of these principles delineate that:

1. The legislature is required to bear responsibility for enactment of laws to govern the public or common schools.
2. The public schools, by and large, are considered to be a cohesive unit: one organization or organic whole whose particular organizational patterns and subparts are within the prerogative of the legislature.
3. The schools as public entities are to be of the body politic of the state, controlled by the public and governed by the people.
4. The nature of the public school is that it be free and common to all, with no charges to limit access.
5. The concept of public common schools as a state government enterprise requires that tax resources be allocated throughout the state in a manner that will ensure that the quality of a child's education will not depend on private or personal influence or wealth nor on the financial capabilities of the lo-

cality or political subdivision of the state. (Alexander &
Alexander, 2001, pp. 30–31)

Awareness of the legal context and foundation from which the
American public school has evolved provides school district leaders with a basis for understanding current law and court decisions
about public education. However, a great deal of opportunity for
state and local interpretation of these principles exists. Issues related to areas such as equity, uniformity, and access are challenged
regularly in the courts and, therefore, are continually undergoing
legal refinement and redefinition by the states.

The federal government also exercises legal influence on public
education through supplementary financial support within the
states and enforcement of constitutional provisions protecting individual rights and freedoms. Financial support is extended primarily through the distribution of categorical revenue grants that,
when accepted by individual states, require these states to meet
the restrictions and regulations embedded in the legislation supporting the revenue. Cunningham and Cordeiro (2000) note that
federal involvement in education has been justified through the
following major responsibilities: (a) land grant, (b) public relief and
welfare, (c) national defense, (d) equal opportunity, and (e) economic competitiveness and school safety (pp. 33–34). Federal legislation, of course, reflects the political agenda and aims of those
who shaped and voted it into existence. Thus, the relationship between the federal and state government in matters of education
and schooling continues to be debated. School leaders must be
cognizant of the obvious as well as subtle influence of the federal
government on public policy and local educational programming.

State legislatures and the United States Congress use state and
federal agencies to implement and administer legislation for education programs, policies, and procedures. At the local level, the school
board carries out this function. Though this delegation of power is
highly scrutinized, it remains the predominant theory of authority

distribution and regulation of education. The important factor for school leaders here is that "legal standards do not necessarily define best educational practice" (Sergiovanni et al., 1999, p. 305). It behooves school administrators to know the law and its source, the scope of its application in schools, and how it impinges upon educational practice. All of this, however, must be accomplished within the overall context of the school system's values and beliefs.

Local community members and educational leaders have access to the framework of policies, laws, and regulations enacted by local, state, and federal authorities through the structure of representative government. A basic understanding of this structure enables school leaders to participate actively in this process to improve educational opportunity and protecting the rights of those being served by the educational system. "Legal knowledge is important in understanding how to work within the system to accomplish desired educational objectives, but it is not a substitute for an educational philosophy" (Sergiovanni et al., 1999, p. 305).

Economic Issues

In recent years the economic arena has become very familiar to educators. Razik and Swanson (2001) note:

It is not possible to understand why public schools have acquired the nature they possess or how to change that nature without understanding how decisions about schooling are made and how public and private resources are transformed into the realization of societal and individual aspirations for education. (p. 258)

Educational institutions generate both public and private good, and thus both politics and economics interact in shaping schools. Communities are concerned about two major economic questions: how much schools cost them and how much schools benefit them.

School leaders must be sensitive to this cost/benefit ratio being used to measure the school's relative success in delivering educational services. They must take every opportunity to inform their constituents of the merits of the school's programs and of the many positive results of investments made in the public schools. Obviously, strong communication skills are necessary here, as are excellent public relations strategies. Because the majority of members of the typical school community do not have children attending public schools, the principal needs the vision to be creative in working with the school staff in developing programs that extend the curriculum into the community. These programs might include family members, such as grandparent and senior citizen initiatives, or linking schools with local businesses, such as school-business partnerships and career shadowing experiences for students. In this way the local school becomes a "community-school," closely linked with and supported by many community elements.

Closely tied with the cost/benefit issue for school leaders is that parents and children now have an increasing number of choices for schooling. Pipho (2000) notes, "Public schools will increasingly have to accommodate these changes by forming alliances with private and for-profit providers" (p. 17). This changing educational landscape will require school leaders to "think outside the box" in terms of what kinds of educational programming can and should be available for students, and how these programs can and should be delivered to them. They will need skills in proactive planning and in bringing the best minds together to set goals and allocate resources to meet the challenges that the economics of education present.

GLOBAL ISSUES

Technology and Schooling

One of the newest and most fundamental global issues currently affecting public schools and their services, as they have been structured traditionally, is that of distance learning and the entire array of burgeoning opportunities for education arising from the development and rapid proliferation of the Internet. No longer is education perceived as a process that takes place in given locations during specific times. With the Internet's access to countless sources of information and databases around the world, the classroom becomes literally global and learning can place 24 hours a day, 7 days a week.

What does this mean for public schools and school leaders? First of all, principals and superintendents need to see their role as leaders and facilitators of educational services, not just as managers of facilities and personnel. As such, they must pay attention to new areas of professional development for staff, so that the Internet and all its possibilities are included in the delivery of the curriculum. Simply making technological advances available within the district is not sufficient because "[t]echnology is not the key to radical change—teachers are the key" (Girod & Cavanaugh, 2001, p. 46). Further, the curriculum itself must be reviewed constantly to include new information, insights, and skills made possible by the use of World Wide Web technology. Teachers need professional assistance to "shift their thinking from boldfaced words and questions at the end of the chapter to situated activities and subject matter ideas, real-world tasks, and authentic performance tests" (Girod & Cavanaugh, 2001, p. 40).

Anywhere, anytime, learning also is forcing schools to reexamine the standard practices of issuing credits and Carnegie units based merely upon seat-time and "teacher-directed" learning methods. School leaders must have the vision, and help their staff members to understand, that "schooling" can and must be directed by professional staff, but these same individuals may not be the immediate delivery agents of the teaching-learning process. Bureaucratic structures and procedures will have to be rethought in light of these new paradigms. The principal is in the best position to move this agenda forward.

Equity and Diversity

Also prominent among global issues for school leaders is the challenge of making sure that schools are addressing the educational needs of a diverse student population in ways that are characterized by both equity and excellence. Williams (1999) notes: "Populations continue to move and grow, and opportunities to adjust learning experiences to more successfully educate increasingly diverse populations continue to be ignored and resisted" (p. 110). Although the makeup of the professional educational staff in the United States continues to be mostly a white, majority population, the demographic composition of students in the country's public schools grows steadily more and more diverse in race, ethnicity, and culture. Banks (2000) cautions, "Increased diversification in the school population has produced serious academic and social problems needing urgent and thoughtful attention" (p. 27).

Key to meeting this challenge is understanding the cultural context of the diverse student body. The principal is in the primary position for seizing the opportunities available for building positive relationships among students and between staff and students because "[s]chool-based reforms are needed to help students learn how to live together in civic, moral, and just communities that respect and value all students' rights and cultural characteristics" (Banks, 2000, p. 27). Events that expand awareness of the values of diverse populations for school staff, and curriculum experiences that use the resources of the local diverse community provide avenues for more authentic learning experiences for students from all backgrounds. Leaders of schools and school systems with diverse student populations must have strong human relations skills and excellent planning and goal-setting abilities to effectively organize site-based programs in such buildings.

SUMMARY

Political decisions, global concerns, societal changes, community values, governance questions, diverse students, policy development, the legal system, democratic processes—these are but a few of the major issues facing the contemporary public school leader. Groups and individuals who just a few years ago were relatively rare in educational forums increasingly are visible and vocal today. Educational leaders must possess a wide array of skills in the curricular knowledge base of the school and in the practical arena of working effectively with internal and external groups.

Pipho (2000) challenges, "If anything can be learned from studying the history of public school governance changes, it is that the public has a low tolerance for the status quo if it isn't serving their needs" (p. 19). The essence of effective school leadership in the democratic context is the constant monitoring of school community needs and appropriate deployment of resources to address these needs, as stated in ISLLC Standard 6.

SUGGESTED INTERNSHIP ACTIVITIES RELATED TO STANDARD 6

Review the current skill levels you noted on your ISLLC Standards Self-Assessment under Standard 6. Note areas in which you wish to improve your skills and, working with your mentor and supervisor, identify activities that you can complete during your internship experience. The following listing of activities related to Standard 6 is provided to help you identify projects that may be appropriate for your clinical experience:

1. Select an existing school board or building-level policy that is outdated. Research the topic and prepare proposed new language for consideration. Participate in the process of revision through the implementation phase.
2. Attend a local board meeting and arrange an interview with a board member to discover how they perceive the challenges and rewards of representing the community as a school board member.

3. Identify a specific social, political, or cultural tension that is present in the school district. Participate on an action committee to address the issue. Provide research and a plan to address the issue(s).

4. Identify the community agencies that routinely support the students and/or the families in the school district. Identify avenues for access, cooperative efforts, and challenges to serving this constituency.

5. Take the budget for a specific program or activity, such as athletics, and determine a per-pupil expenditure. Determine whether the resources are expended equitably across the program.

6. Investigate the vehicles that district administrators use to remain current regarding legal issues. Select a specific issue and collect the most recent rulings and information related to the issue. Share this information with other district administrators.

7. Review board of education meeting minutes to identify a recently enacted school policy. Trace the policy development process beginning with the issue to the formulation of the policy.

8. Identify a state or federally funded school program that your district/building would like to apply for. Review the legislation that funds the program, the goals put forth for the program, qualifications to apply for funding, and expected outcomes. Make a recommendation on the feasibility of applying for the program to your mentor and participate in the process of securing the funding.

9. Visit two site-based governed schools in other districts. Observe the processes used to lead change at the building level. Discuss these observations with your mentor, emphasizing the leadership implications.

10. Participate in a legislative forum with local and/or state political leaders to discuss school-related issues.

11. Meet with local government and social agency representatives who advocate for at-risk children and their families. Visit several collaborative programs operated by these entities to develop an awareness of the programs provided for youth outside of the traditional school-day program.
12. Enroll in an on-line course and focus on the leadership implications of anytime, anywhere learning faced by local school districts.
13. Based on your ISLLC Standards Self-Assessment under Standard 6, select one or two books from the suggested readings that will help expand your knowledge on topics related to this standard. Also, select one of the Web site resources listed, review the information available, and identify how this resource can assist you in your professional development.

SUGGESTED READINGS

Blase, J., & Blase, J. (1997). *The fire is back! Principals sharing school governance.* Thousand Oaks, CA: Corwin Press.

Bolman, L. G., & Deal, T. E. (1991). *Reframing organizations: Artistry, choice, and leadership.* San Francisco: Jossey-Bass.

Bracey, G. W. (2002). *The war against America's public schools: Privatizing schools, commercializing education.* Boston, MA: Allyn and Bacon.

Education Commission of the States. (1999). *The changing landscape of education governance* (ECS publication SI-99-4). Denver, CO: Author.

Fu, V. R., & Stremmel, A. J. (1999). *Affirming diversity through democratic conversations.* Upper Saddle River, NJ: Prentice-Hall.

Johnson, S. M. (1996). *Leading to change: The challenge of the new superintendency.* San Francisco: Jossey-Bass.

Paris, D. C. (1995). *Ideology and educational reform: Themes and theories in public education.* Boulder, CO: Westview Press.

Sarason, S. B. (1999). *Political leadership and educational failure.* San Francisco: Jossey-Bass.

Soder, R. (1995). *Democracy, education, and the schools.* San Francisco: Jossey-Bass.

Spring, J. (1993). *Conflict of interests: The politics of American education* (2nd ed.). New York: Longman.

Spring, J. (1994). *Wheels in the head: Educational philosophies of authority, freedom, and culture from Socrates to Paulo Freire.* New York: McGraw-Hill.

WEB SITE RESOURCES

Institute for Educational Leadership (IEL)
www.iel.org

U.S. Department of Education
www.ed.gov

U.S. House of Representatives
www.house.gov

U.S. Senate
www.senate.gov

White House
www.whitehouse.gov

National Center for Educational Studies
www.nces.ed.gov

Education Law Association (formerly National Organization on Legal Problems in Education)
www.educationlaw.org

National School Boards Association
www.nsba.org

AACTE Education Policy Clearinghouse
www.edpolicy.org

The Council of Chief State School Officers
www.ccsso.org

REFERENCES

Alexander, K., & Alexander, M. D. (2001). *American public school law* (5th ed.). Belmont, CA: Wadsworth.

Banks, J. A. (2000). The social construction of difference and the quest for educational equity. In R. S. Brandt (Ed.), *2000 ASCD yearbook: Education in a new era* (pp. 21–45). Alexandria, VA: Association for Supervision and Curriculum Development.

Bernhardt, V. L. (1998). *Data analysis for comprehensive schoolwide improvement.* Larchmont, NY: Eye on Education.

Bolman, L. G., & Deal, T. E. (1991). *Reframing organizations: Artistry, choice, and leadership.* San Francisco: Jossey-Bass.

Cunningham, W. G., & Cordeiro, P. A. (2000). *Educational administration: A problem-based approach.* Needham Heights, MA: Allyn and Bacon.

Eastin, D. (1999). Getting to the heart of the matter: Education in the 21st century. In D. D. Marsh (Ed.), *1999 ASCD yearbook: Preparing our schools for the 21st century* (pp. 13–24). Alexandria, VA: Association for Supervision and Curriculum Development.

Girod, M., & Cavanaugh, S. (2001). Technology as an agent of change in teacher practice. *Technical Horizons in Education Journal, 28*(9), 40–47.

Patterson, J. L., Purkey, S. C., & Parker, J. V. (1986). *Productive school systems for a nonrational world.* Alexandria, VA: Association for Supervision and Curriculum Development.

Pipho, C. (2000). Governing the American dream of universal public education. In R. S. Brandt (Ed.), *2000 ASCD yearbook: Education in a new era* (pp. 5–19). Alexandria, VA: Association for Supervision and Curriculum Development.

Razik, T. A., & Swanson, A. D. (2001). *Fundamental concepts of educational leadership* (2nd ed.). Upper Saddle River, NJ: Merrill Prentice-Hall.

Sergiovanni, T. J., Burlingame, M., Coombs, F. S., & Thurston, P. W. (1999). *Educational governance and administration* (4th ed.). Boston, MA: Allyn and Bacon.

Sperry, D. J. (1999). *Working in a legal and regulatory environment: A handbook for school leaders.* Larchmont, NY: Eye on Education.

Spring, J. (1993). *Conflict of interests: The politics of American education* (2nd ed.). New York: Longman.

Williams, B. (1999). Diversity and education for the 21st century. In D. D. Marsh (Ed.), *1999 ASCD yearbook: Preparing our schools for the 21st century* (pp. 89–114). Alexandria, VA: Association for Supervision and Curriculum Development.

Yankelovich, D. (1991). *Coming to public judgment: Making democracy work in a complex world.* Syracuse, NY: Syracuse University Press.

8

CONCLUDING AND ASSESSING THE INTERNSHIP EXPERIENCE

The preceding chapters have provided the framework for the administrative field experience, crafted around the six ISLLC standards. As the intern and mentor collaborate throughout the clinical activities, they undoubtedly will recognize that relatively few administrative responsibilities can be categorized and packaged neatly into only one standard. Leadership is a complex, multifaceted endeavor, and each administrative task likely will involve multiple standards. The purpose of this book, however, has been to provide both veteran and aspiring leaders with a more complete understanding of knowledge and skills encompassing each standard, and so it was necessary to address each standard individually. Participating in shared experiences framed around this ISSLC structure provides a common language and foundation on which the university supervisor, intern, and mentor can build comprehensive, complete, and authentic clinical activities.

CONCLUDING THE CLINICAL EXPERIENCE

As recommended in Chapter 1, as the intern engages in the field experiences, she or he should build a portfolio that documents successful attainment of the ISSLC standards and mastery of the Personalized Internship Plans (PIPs). Many educational administration preparation programs, and an increasing number of states, now require or are considering the use of portfolios to document initial administrative competence for aspiring administrators and continuous professional development as veteran administrators apply for license renewal. In addition, portfolios can be useful when interviewing for administrative positions because they give potential employers concrete examples of the candidate's skills. In addition to the initial self-assessment, PIPs, artifacts collected during the internship and through course activities, field experience log, and reflective papers, the portfolio also should include an ISLLC self-assessment completed at the conclusion of the clinical experience (see Appendix B). This culminating self-assessment affords the intern one final opportunity to reflect on the quality of his or her performance during the field experiences and to self-evaluate progress against each standard. This assessment can help the potential school leader to identify areas in which continued growth is desired.

The university supervisor will complete a summative evaluation of the intern's experience and will rely heavily on information from the following sources: (a) materials contained in the portfolio, (b) on-site observations by the supervisor, and (c) the mentor's assessment of the intern's performance. To assist the mentor in providing a written evaluation, a sample assessment form is provided in Appendix C. This form closely parallels the ISLLC standards, so that written feedback is aligned with the ISLLC model.

The importance of providing continuous, open, and honest feedback—by both the mentor(s) and university supervisor—cannot be overstated. Certainly these individuals have a responsibility to provide candid assessments to interns so that they will gain a clear understanding of their areas of greatest strength as well as areas in which they need to improve. This evaluative feedback will assist the intern in making a personal assessment regarding whether or not she/he is sufficiently prepared to become a successful leader.

The mentor and supervisor also should recognize that their responsibilities extend beyond the intern to the educational administration profession as a whole. Therefore, if they believe the intern is not adequately prepared for administrative success, they have a professional obligation to provide this feedback. In this event, the aspiring administrator may continue to work with the educational administration program faculty, engaging in additional course and field experiences to remediate any areas of deficiency, or alternatively may decide against pursuit of an administrative career.

So that the quality of the administrative internship experiences can continue to be maintained at the highest level, it is recommended that the mentor also complete an assessment of the university's internship format. (See Appendix C.) Administrator preparation programs are dedicated to the development of educational leaders as lifelong learners and reflective practitioners. As such, university supervisors must model this expectation, and they potentially have much to gain by asking the mentors to provide this feedback. Since the administrator preparation program's reputation hinges on the quality of its graduates, this information can be an invaluable tool in aiding professors with restructuring course expectations and improving program quality.

BEYOND THE INTERNSHIP

It is important to reassert that the ISSLC standards have been designed to apply to the broad spectrum of preK–12 administration because the developers "were unanimous in their belief that the central aspects of the role are the same for all school leadership positions" (ISLLC, 1996, p. 7). Consequently, this content provides an excellent framework as the administrator candidate accepts her/his first administrative position (likely at the building level), engages in continuous professional development, and prepares for future opportunities to advance in the field of educational administration, at the district level.

When the aspiring leader concludes the internship experiences and successfully completes the university's graduation requirements, he or she should understand that professional development does not end upon receiving administrative licensure. Attaining one's initial administrative appointment is actually only another step along the long journey to becoming an effective educational leader. As any veteran educational leader will attest, no preparation program—no matter how outstanding—can offer the opportunity to experience every administrative challenge that will be faced by the novice principal or superintendent. The ISSLC standards—and the most recent self-assessment—can be used to assess entry-level competence and to identify areas in which the new administrator wishes to broaden knowledge and skills.

The following suggestions are intended to help the novice in making the transition into this new administrative assignment.

1. *Develop a support network.* Novice administrators immediately will realize that they do not have all the answers to every problem they encounter (and, of course, they are not expected to). Consequently, they will find it beneficial to consult with others who may have experienced similar situations, or they may simply need to blow off steam with a sympathetic ear—someone who understands the challenges of administrative life. For a variety of reasons, the novice administrator may be unwilling to discuss school-related issues with peers within the same district, or actually may have no peers within the district, as in the case of a superintendent or building-level administrator in a small district.

Individuals new to educational leadership should seek to establish a network of practitioners who can be supportive, valued colleagues. These individuals certainly may include the novice's mentoring administrator and university supervisor, but the novice also should look both within the school system and to neighboring districts for experienced administrators who share similar educational beliefs. Many state administrator organizations have regional associations; athletic conferences frequently have monthly administrator meetings; and intermediate school districts also may have administrators meetings geared to each level within the school system (superintendency, secondary, middle, and elementary). These formal and informal channels provide ample opportunity for novice administrators to network and form close relationships with like-minded educational leaders.

2. *Create a Professional Development Plan, noting activities to expand the novice administrator's knowledge and skills.* As a lifelong learner, the new administrator should continue to identify areas to enrich and extend his/her professional skills. For example, the new principal may decide to expand his or her knowledge of curriculum and instructional methods or special education regulations, areas that may not have been extensively developed within the educational administration program. The new principal may decide to enroll in additional graduate coursework, to work toward superintendent licensure, or simply to continue to learn new skills. Local and intermediate school districts also may have workshops, and state and national conferences offer excellent ways for the leader to remain current on the latest educational trends.

3. *Be a reflective practitioner* (Schön, 1983). Leaders are called upon to make countless decisions each day and rarely are provided the luxury of taking the time to revisit these judgment calls. However, when routine practices go unexamined, the school leader's behaviors may not be consistent with school policy and/or with personal values and beliefs. Reflective practitioners continually examine their actions, assessing the effects of their decisions on

others. Effective leaders model reflective behaviors, so that others within the school organization also will engage in self-analysis of their actions. School systems should be learning communities; consequently, all educators should be continually engaged in the process of learning.

4. *When the time is right, give back to the profession by being an administrative mentor.* After having served several years in a leadership position, and upon having gained a more comprehensive understanding of the demands of administration, the now-experienced school leader should consider serving as a mentor. A high-quality internship experience cannot be achieved without the willingness of exemplary leaders to guide and nurture aspiring administrators. Effective school leaders understand that assuming this responsibility provides a service to the educational administration profession, and they are simply returning the favor bestowed upon them earlier when their mentor volunteered to supervise their clinical experiences.

SUMMARY

As the clinical experiences draw to a close, administrator candidates should take time to reflect on the quality of the learning activities used to prepare them to be effective instructional leaders and change agents. The ISLLC standards, which have served as the basis for this internship guide, are the framework around which these clinical experiences are based.

Upon assuming the initial administrative appointment, the administrative novice should identify areas of personal strength and areas in which ongoing professional improvement is desired. As the "Head Learner" of the school or school system, the school leader has an obligation to model lifelong learning for all staff, students, and constituents, as he or she strives to transform the institution into a learning community.

SUGGESTED READINGS

Capper, C. A. (Ed.). (1993). *Educational administration in a pluralistic society.* New York: State University of New York Press.

Carter, G. R., & Cunningham, W. G. (1997). *The American school superintendent: Leading in an age of pressure.* San Francisco: Jossey-Bass.

Crow, G. M., & Matthews, J. J. (1997). *Finding one's way: How mentoring can lead to dynamic leadership.* Thousand Oaks, CA: Corwin Press.

Daresh, J. C. (2001). *Beginning the principalship* (2nd ed.). Thousand Oaks, CA: Corwin Press.

Darling-Hammond, L. (2001). *The right to learn: A blueprint for creating schools that work.* San Francisco: Jossey-Bass.

Murphy, J., & Louis, K. S. (1999). *Handbook of research on educational administration* (2nd ed.). San Francisco: Jossey-Bass.

Sanders, E. T. W. (1999). *Urban school leadership: Issues and strategies.* Larchmont, NY: Eye on Education.

Schlechty, P. (1997). *Inventing better schools: An action plan for educational reform.* San Francisco: Jossey-Bass.

REFERENCES

Interstate School Leaders Licensure Consortium. (1996). *Standards for school leaders.* Washington, DC: Council of Chief State School Officers.

Schön, D. A. (1983). *The reflective practitioner: How professionals think in action.* New York: Basic Books.

APPENDIX A

ISLLC Standards for School Leaders

STANDARD I

A school administrator is an educational leader who promotes the success of all students by facilitating the development, articulation, implementation, and stewardship of a vision of learning that is shared and supported by the school community.

Knowledge

The administrator has knowledge and understanding of:

- learning goals in a pluralistic society
- the principles of developing and implementing strategic plans
- systems theory
- information sources, data collection, and data analysis strategies
- effective communication
- effective consensus-building and negotiation skills

Dispositions

The administrator believes in, values, and is committed to:

- the educability of all
- a school vision of high standards of learning
- continuous school improvement
- the inclusion of all members of the school community
- ensuring that students have the knowledge, skills, and values needed to become successful adults
- a willingness to continuously examine one's own assumptions, beliefs, and practices
- doing the work required for high levels of personal and organization performance

Performances

The administrator facilitates processes and engages in activities ensuring that:

- the vision and mission of the school are effectively communicated to staff, parents, students, and community members
- the vision and mission are communicated through the use of symbols, ceremonies, stories, and similar activities
- the core beliefs of the school vision are modeled for all stakeholders
- the vision is developed with and among stakeholders
- the contributions of school community members to the realization of the vision are recognized and celebrated
- progress toward the vision and mission is communicated to all stakeholders
- the school community is involved in school improvement efforts
- the vision shapes the educational programs, plans, and actions
- an implementation plan is developed in which objectives and strategies to achieve the vision

and goals are clearly articulated

- assessment data related to student learning are used to develop the school vision and goals
- relevant demographic data pertaining to students and their families are used in developing the school mission and goals
- barriers to achieving the vision are identified, clarified, and addressed

- needed resources are sought and obtained to support the implementation of the school mission and goals
- existing resources are used in support of the school vision and goals
- the vision, mission, and implementation plans are regularly monitored, evaluated, and revised

STANDARD 2

A school administrator is an educational leader who promotes the success of all students by advocating, nurturing, and sustaining a school culture and instructional program conducive to student learning and staff professional growth.

Knowledge

The administrator has knowledge and understanding of:

- student growth and development
- applied learning theories
- applied motivational theories
- curriculum design, implementation, evaluation, and refinement

- principles of effective instruction
- measurement, evaluation, and assessment strategies
- diversity and its meaning for educational programs

- adult learning and professional development models
- the change process for systems, organizations, and individuals

- the role of technology in promoting student learning and professional growth
- school cultures

Dispositions

The administrator believes in, values, and is committed to:

- student learning as the fundamental purpose of schooling
- the proposition that all students can learn
- the variety of ways in which students can learn
- lifelong learning for self and others
- professional development as an integral part of school improvement

- the benefits that diversity brings to the school community
- a safe and supportive learning environment
- preparing students to be contributing members of society

Performances

The administrator facilitates processes and engages in activities ensuring that:

- all individuals are treated with fairness, dignity, and respect
- professional development promotes a focus on

  student learning consistent with the school vision and goals
- students and staff feel valued and important

- the responsibilities and contributions of each individual are acknowledged
- barriers to student learning are identified, clarified, and addressed
- diversity is considered in developing learning experiences
- lifelong learning is encouraged and modeled
- there is a culture of high expectations for self, student, and staff performance
- technologies are used in teaching and learning
- student and staff accomplishments are recognized and celebrated
- multiple opportunities to learn are available to all students
- the school is organized and aligned for success
- curricular, cocurricular, and extracurricular programs are designed, implemented, evaluated, and refined
- curriculum decisions are based on research, expertise of teachers, and the recommendations of learned societies
- the school culture and climate are assessed on a regular basis
- a variety of sources of information is used to make decisions
- student learning is assessed using a variety of techniques
- multiple sources of information regarding performance are used by staff and students
- a variety of supervisory and evaluation models is employed
- pupil personnel programs are developed to meet the needs of students and their families

STANDARD 3

A school administrator is an educational leader who promotes the success of all students by ensuring management of the organization, operations, and resources for a safe, efficient, and effective learning environment.

Knowledge

The administrator has knowledge and understanding of:

- theories and models of organizations and the principles of organizational development
- operational procedures at the school and district level
- principles and issues relating to school safety and security
- human resources management and development

- principles and issues relating to fiscal operations of school management
- principles and issues relating to school facilities and use of space
- legal issues impacting school operations
- current technologies that support management functions

Dispositions

The administrator believes in, values, and is committed to:

- making management decisions to enhance learning and teaching
- taking risks to improve schools
- trusting people and their judgments

- accepting responsibility
- high-quality standards, expectations, and performances
- involving stakeholders in management processes
- a safe environment

Performances

The administrator facilitates processes and engages in activities ensuring that:

- knowledge of learning, teaching, and student development is used to inform management decisions

- operational procedures are designed and managed to maximize opportunities for successful learning
- emerging trends are recognized, studied, and applied as appropriate
- operational plans and procedures to achieve the vision and goals of the school are in place
- collective bargaining and other contractual agreements related to the school are effectively managed
- the school plant, equipment, and support systems operate safely, efficiently, and effectively
- time is managed to maximize attainment of organizational goals
- potential problems and opportunities are identified
- problems are confronted and resolved in a timely manner
- financial, human, and material resources are aligned to the goals of schools

- the school acts entrepreneurially to support continuous improvement
- organizational systems are regularly monitored and modified as needed
- stakeholders are involved in decisions affecting schools
- responsibility is shared to maximize ownership and accountability
- effective problem-framing and problem-solving skills are used
- effective conflict resolution skills are used
- effective group-process and consensus-building skills are used
- effective communication skills are used
- a safe, clean, and aesthetically pleasing school environment is created and maintained
- human resource functions support the attainment of school goals
- confidentiality and privacy of school records are maintained

STANDARD 4

A school administrator is an educational leader who promotes the success of all students by collaborating with families and community members, responding to diverse community interests and needs, and mobilizing community resources.

Knowledge

The administrator has knowledge and understanding of:

- emerging issues and trends that potentially impact the school community
- the conditions and dynamics of the diverse school community
- community resources

- community relations and marketing strategies and processes
- successful models of school, family, business, community, government, and higher education partnerships

Dispositions

The administrator believes in, values, and is committed to:

- schools operating as an integral part of the larger community
- collaboration and communication with families
- involvement of families and other stakeholders in school decision-making processes
- the proposition that diversity enriches the school

- families as partners in the education of their children
- the proposition that families have the best interests of their children in mind
- resources of the family and community needing to be brought to bear on the education of students
- an informed public

Performances

The administrator facilitates processes and engages in activities ensuring that:

- high visibility, active involvement, and communication with the larger community is a priority
- relationships with community leaders are identified and nurtured
- information about family and community concerns, expectations, and needs is used regularly
- there is outreach to different business, religious, political, and service agencies and organizations
- credence is given to individuals and groups whose values and opinions may conflict
- the school and community serve one another as resources
- available community resources are secured to help the school solve problems and achieve goals

- partnerships are established with area businesses, institutions of higher education, and community groups to strengthen programs and support school goals
- community youth family services are integrated with school programs
- community stakeholders are treated equitably
- diversity is recognized and valued
- effective media relations are developed and maintained
- a comprehensive program of community relations is established
- public resources and funds are used appropriately and wisely
- community collaboration is modeled for staff
- opportunities for staff to develop collaborative skills are provided

STANDARD 5

A school administrator is an educational leader who promotes the success of all students by acting with integrity, fairness, and in an ethical manner.

Knowledge

The administrator has knowledge and understanding of:

- the purpose of education and the role of leadership in modern society
- various ethical frameworks and perspectives on ethics
- the values of the diverse school community
- professional codes of ethics
- the philosophy and history of education

Dispositions

The administrator believes in, values, and is committed to:

- the ideal of the common good
- the principles in the Bill of Rights
- the right of every student to a free, quality education
- bringing ethical principles to the decision-making process
- subordinating one's own interest to the good of the school community
- accepting the consequences for upholding one's principles and actions
- using the influence of one's office constructively and productively in the service of all students and their families
- development of a caring school community

Performances

The administrator:

- examines personal and professional values
- demonstrates a personal and professional code of ethics
- demonstrates values, beliefs, and attitudes that inspire others to higher levels of performance
- serves as a role model

- accepts responsibility for school operations
- considers the impact of one's administrative practices on others
- uses the influence of the office to enhance the educational program rather than for personal gain
- treats people fairly, equitably, and with dignity and respect
- protects the rights and confidentiality of students and staff
- demonstrates appreciation for and sensitivity to the diversity in the school community

- recognizes and respects the legitimate authority of others
- examines and considers the prevailing values of the diverse school community
- expects that others in the school community will demonstrate integrity and exercise ethical behavior
- opens the school to public scrutiny
- fulfills legal and contractual obligations
- applies laws and procedures fairly, wisely, and considerately

STANDARD 6

A school administrator is an educational leader who promotes the success of all students by understanding, responding to, and influencing the larger political, social, economic, legal, and cultural context.

Knowledge

The administrator has knowledge and understanding of:

- principles of representative governance that undergird the system of American schools

- the role of public education in developing and renewing a democratic society and an

economically productive nation
- the law as related to education and schooling
- the political, social, cultural, and economic systems and processes that impact schools
- models and strategies of change and conflict resolution as applied to the larger political, social,

cultural, and economic contexts of schooling
- global issues and forces affecting teaching and learning
- the dynamics of policy development and advocacy under our democratic political system
- the importance of diversity and equity in a democratic society

Dispositions

The administrator believes in, values, and is committed to:

- education as a key to opportunity and social mobility
- recognizing a variety of ideas, values, and cultures
- importance of a continuing dialogue with other decision makers affecting education

- actively participating in the political and policy-making context in the service of education
- using legal systems to protect student rights and improve student opportunities

Performances

The administrator facilitates processes and engages in activities ensuring that:

- the environment in which schools operate is influenced on behalf of students and their families

- communication occurs among the school community concerning trends, issues, and potential changes in the

environment in which schools operate
- there is ongoing dialogue with representatives of diverse community groups
- the school community works within the framework of policies, laws, and regulations enacted by local,

state, and federal authorities
- public policy is shaped to provide quality education for students
- lines of communication are developed with decision makers outside the school community

Source: Interstate School Leaders Licensure Consortium. (1996). *Standards for school leaders*. Washington, DC: Council of Chief State School Officers.

APPENDIX B

ISLLC Self-Assessment

Intern Name _____ Date _____

On the left side of the indicator, note how important you believe this statement is to the effective functioning of a school leader. Use the following scale:

5 = Extremely important
4 = Important
3 = Somewhat important
2 = Marginally important
1 = Not important

On the right side of the indicator, note your present level in effectively performing tasks related to this statement. Use the following scale:

5 = Highly skilled
4 = Skilled
3 = Somewhat skilled
2 = Marginal skills
1 = Few skills at the present time

Standard 1: A school administrator is an educational leader who promotes the success of all students by facilitating the development, articulation, implementation, and stewardship of a vision of learning that is shared and supported by the school community.

5	4	3	2	1	Knowledge/Dispositions/Performances	5	4	3	2	1
					The administrator has knowledge and understanding of: 1K.1 learning goals in a pluralistic society					
					1K.2 the principles of developing and implementing strategic plans					
					1K.3 systems theory					
					1K.4 information sources, data collection, and data analysis strategies					
					1K.5 effective communication					
					1K.6 effective consensus-building and negotiation skills					
					The administrator believes in, values, and is committed to: 1D.1 the educability of all					
					1D.2 a school vision of high standards of learning					
					1D.3 continuous school improvement					
					1D.4 the inclusion of all members of the school community					
					1D.5 ensuring that students have the knowledge, skills, and values needed to become successful adults					
					1D.6 a willingness to continuously examine one's own assumptions, beliefs, and practices					
					1D.7 doing the work required for high levels of personal and organization performance					
					The administrator facilitates processes and engages in activities ensuring that: 1P.1 the vision and mission of the school are effectively communicated to staff, parents, students, and community members					
					1P.2 the vision and mission are communicated through the use of symbols, ceremonies, stories, and similar activities					
					1P.3 the core beliefs of the school vision are modeled for all stakeholders					
					1P.4 the vision is developed with and among stakeholders					
					1P.5 the contributions of school community members to the realization of the vision are recognized and celebrated					

5	4	3	2	1	Knowledge/Dispositions/Performances	5	4	3	2	1
					1P.6 progress toward the vision and mission is communicated to all stakeholders					
					1P.7 the school community is involved in school improvement efforts					
					1P.8 the vision shapes the educational programs, plans, and actions					
					1P.9 an implementation plan is developed in which objectives and strategies to achieve the vision and goals are clearly articulated					
					1P.10 assessment data related to student learning are used to develop the school vision and goals					
					1P.11 relevant demographic data pertaining to students and their families are used in developing the school mission and goals					
					1P.12 barriers to achieving the vision are identified, clarified, and addressed					
					1P.13 needed resources are sought and obtained to support the implementation of the school mission and goals					
					1P.14 existing resources are used in support of the school vision and goals					
					1P.15 the vision, mission, and implementation plans are regularly monitored, evaluated, and revised					

Standard 2: A school administrator is an educational leader who promotes the success of all students by advocating, nurturing, and sustaining a school culture and instructional program conducive to student learning and staff professional growth.

5	4	3	2	1	Knowledge/Dispositions/Performances	5	4	3	2	1
					The administrator has knowledge and understanding of: 2K.1 student growth and development					
					2K.2 applied learning theories					
					2K.3 applied motivational theories					
					2K.4 curriculum design, implementation, evaluation, and refinement					

5	4	3	2	1	Knowledge/Dispositions/Performances	5	4	3	2	1
					2K.5 principles of effective instruction					
					2K.6 measurement, evaluation, and assessment strategies					
					2K.7 diversity and its meaning for educational programs					
					2K.8 adult learning and professional development models					
					2K.9 the change process for systems, organizations, and individuals					
					2K.10 the role of technology in promoting student learning and professional growth					
					2K.11 school cultures					
					The administrator believes in, values, and is committed to: 2D.1 student learning as the fundamental purpose of schooling					
					2D.2 the proposition that all students can learn					
					2D.3 the variety of ways in which students can learn					
					2D.4 lifelong learning for self and others					
					2D.5 professional development as an integral part of school improvement					
					2D.6 the benefits that diversity brings to the school community					
					2D.7 a safe and supportive learning environment					
					2D.8 preparing students to be contributing members of society					
					The administrator facilitates processes and engages in activities ensuring that: 2P.1 all individuals are treated with fairness, dignity, and respect					
					2P.2 professional development promotes a focus on student learning consistent with the school vision and goals					
					2P.3 students and staff feel valued and important					
					2P.4 the responsibilities and contributions of each individual are acknowledged					
					2P.5 barriers to student learning are identified, clarified, and addressed					

5	4	3	2	1	Knowledge/Dispositions/Performances	5	4	3	2	1
					2P.6 diversity is considered in developing learning experiences					
					2P.7 lifelong learning is encouraged and modeled					
					2P.8 there is a culture of high expectations for self, student, and staff performance					
					2P.9 technologies are used in teaching and learning					
					2P.10 student and staff accomplishments are recognized and celebrated					
					2P.11 multiple opportunities to learn are available to all students					
					2P.12 the school is organized and aligned for success					
					2P.13 curricular, cocurricular, and extracurricular programs are designed, implemented, evaluated, and refined					
					2P.14 curriculum decisions are based on research, expertise of teachers, and the recommendations of learned societies					
					2P.15 the school culture and climate are assessed on a regular basis					
					2P.16 a variety of sources of information is used to make decisions					
					2P.17 student learning is assessed using a variety of techniques					
					2P.18 multiple sources of information regarding performance are used by staff and students					
					2P.19 a variety of supervisory and evaluation models is employed					
					2P.20 pupil personnel programs are developed to meet the needs of students and their families					

Standard 3: A school administrator is an educational leader who promotes the success of all students by ensuring management of the organization, operations, and resources for a safe, efficient, and effective learning environment.

5	4	3	2	1	Knowledge/Dispositions/Performances	5	4	3	2	1
					The administrator has knowledge and understanding of: 3K.1 theories and models of organizations and the principles of organizational development					
					3K.2 operational procedures at the school and district level					
					3K.3 principles and issues relating to school safety and security					
					3K.4 human resources management and development					
					3K.5 principles and issues relating to fiscal operations of school management					
					3K.6 principles and issues relating to school facilities and use of space					
					3K.7 legal issues impacting school operations					
					3K.8 current technologies that support management functions					
					The administrator believes in, values, and is committed to: 3D.1 making management decisions to enhance learning and teaching					
					3D.2 taking risks to improve schools					
					3D.3 trusting people and their judgments					
					3D.4 accepting responsibility					
					3D.5 high-quality standards, expectations, and performances					
					3D.6 involving stakeholders in management processes					
					3D.7 a safe environment					
					The administrator facilitates processes and engages in activities ensuring that: 3P.1 knowledge of learning, teaching, and student development is used to inform management decisions					
					3P.2 operational procedures are designed and managed to maximize opportunities for successful learning					
					3P.3 emerging trends are recognized, studied, and applied as appropriate					

5	4	3	2	1	Knowledge/Dispositions/Performances	5	4	3	2	1
					3P.4 operational plans and procedures to achieve the vision and goals of the school are in place					
					3P.5 collective bargaining and other contractual agreements related to the school are effectively managed					
					3P.6 the school plant, equipment, and support systems operate safely, efficiently, and effectively					
					3P.7 time is managed to maximize attainment of organizational goals					
					3P.8 potential problems and opportunities are identified					
					3P.9 problems are confronted and resolved in a timely manner					
					3P.10 financial, human, and material resources are aligned to the goals of schools					
					3P.11 the school acts entrepreneurially to support continuous improvement					
					3P.12 organizational systems are regularly monitored and modified as needed					
					3P.13 stakeholders are involved in decisions affecting schools					
					3P.14 responsibility is shared to maximize ownership and accountability					
					3P.15 effective problem-framing and problem-solving skills are used					
					3P.16 effective conflict resolution skills are used					
					3P.17 effective group-process and consensus-building skills are used					
					3P.18 effective communication skills are used					
					3P.19 a safe, clean, and aesthetically pleasing school environment is created and maintained					
					3P.20 human resource functions support the attainment of school goals					
					3P.21 confidentiality and privacy of school records are maintained					

Standard 4: A school administrator is an educational leader who promotes the success of all students by collaborating with families and community members, responding to diverse community interests and needs, and mobilizing community resources.

5	4	3	2	1	Knowledge/Dispositions/Performances	5	4	3	2	1
					The administrator has knowledge and understanding of: 4K.1 emerging issues and trends that potentially impact the school community					
					4K.2 the conditions and dynamics of the diverse school community					
					4K.3 community resources					
					4K.4 community relations and marketing strategies and processes					
					4K.5 successful models of school, family, business, community, government, and higher education partnerships					
					The administrator believes in, values, and is committed to: 4D.1 schools operating as an integral part of the larger community					
					4D.2 collaboration and communication with families					
					4D.3 involvement of families and other stakeholders in school decision-making processes					
					4D.4 the proposition that diversity enriches the school					
					4D.5 families as partners in the education of their children					
					4D.6 the proposition that families have the best interests of their children in mind					
					4D.7 resources of the family and community needing to be brought to bear on the education of students					
					4D.8 an informed public					
					The administrator facilitates processes and engages in activities ensuring that: 4P.1 high visibility, active involvement, and communication with the larger community is a priority					
					4P.2 relationships with community leaders are identified and nurtured					

5	4	3	2	1	Knowledge/Dispositions/Performances	5	4	3	2	1
					4P.3 information about family and community concerns, expectations, and needs is used regularly					
					4P.4 there is outreach to different business, religious, political, and service agencies and organizations					
					4P.5 credence is given to individuals and groups whose values and opinions may conflict					
					4P.6 the school and community serve one another as resources					
					4P.7 available community resources are secured to help the school solve problems and achieve goals					
					4P.8 partnerships are established with area businesses, institutions of higher education, and community groups to strengthen programs and support school goals					
					4P.9 community youth family services are integrated with school programs					
					4P.10 community stakeholders are treated equitably					
					4P.11 diversity is recognized and valued					
					4P.12 effective media relations are developed and maintained					
					4P.13 a comprehensive program of community relations is established					
					4P.14 public resources and funds are used appropriately and wisely					
					4P.15 community collaboration is modeled for staff					
					4P.16 opportunities for staff to develop collaborative skills are provided					

Standard 5: A school administrator is an educational leader who promotes the success of all students by acting with integrity, fairness, and in an ethical manner.

5	4	3	2	1	Knowledge/Dispositions/Performances	5	4	3	2	1
					The administrator has knowledge and understanding of: 5K.1 the purpose of education and the role of leadership in modern society					

5	4	3	2	1	Knowledge/Dispositions/Performances	5	4	3	2	1
					5K.2 various ethical frameworks and perspectives on ethics					
					5K.3 the values of the diverse school community					
					5K.4 professional codes of ethics					
					5K.5 the philosophy and history of education					
					The administrator believes in, values, and is committed to: 5D.1 the ideal of the common good					
					5D.2 the principles in the Bill of Rights					
					5D.3 the right of every student to a free, quality education					
					5D.4 bringing ethical principles to the decision-making process					
					5D.5 subordinating one's own interest to the good of the school community					
					5D.6 accepting the consequences for upholding one's principles and actions					
					5D.7 using the influence of one's office constructively and productively in the service of all students and their families					
					5D.8 development of a caring school community					
					The administrator: 5P.1 examines personal and professional values					
					5P.2 demonstrates a personal and professional code of ethics					
					5P.3 demonstrates values, beliefs, and attitudes that inspire others to higher levels of performance					
					5P.4 serves as a role model					
					5P.5 accepts responsibility for school operations					
					5P.6 considers the impact of one's administrative practices on others					
					5P.7 uses the influence of the office to enhance the educational program rather than for personal gain					
					5P.8 treats people fairly, equitably, and with dignity and respect					

5	4	3	2	1	Knowledge/Dispositions/Performances	5	4	3	2	1
					5P.9 protects the rights and confidentiality of students and staff					
					5P.10 demonstrates appreciation for and sensitivity to the diversity in the school community					
					5P.11 recognizes and respects the legitimate authority of others					
					5P.12 examines and considers the prevailing values of the diverse school community					
					5P.13 expects that others in the school community will demonstrate integrity and exercise ethical behavior					
					5P.14 opens the school to public scrutiny					
					5P.15 fulfills legal and contractual obligations					
					5P.16 applies laws and procedures fairly, wisely, and considerately					

Standard 6: A school administrator is an educational leader who promotes the success of all students by understanding, responding to, and influencing the larger political, social, economic, legal, and cultural context.

5	4	3	2	1	Knowledge/Dispositions/Performances	5	4	3	2	1
					The administrator has knowledge and understanding of: 6K.1 principles of representative governance that undergird the system of American schools					
					6K.2 the role of public education in developing and renewing a democratic society and an economically productive nation					
					6K.3 the law as related to education and schooling					
					6K.4 the political, social, cultural, and economic systems and processes that impact schools					
					6K.5 models and strategies of change and conflict resolution as applied to the larger political, social, cultural, and economic contexts of schooling					
					6K.6 global issues and forces affecting teaching and learning					

5	4	3	2	1	Knowledge/Dispositions/Performances	5	4	3	2	1
					6K.7 the dynamics of policy development and advocacy under our democratic political system					
					6K.8 the importance of diversity and equity in a democratic society					
					The administrator believes in, values, and is committed to: 6D.1 education as a key to opportunity and social mobility					
					6D.2 recognizing a variety of ideas, values, and cultures					
					6D.3 importance of a continuing dialogue with other decision makers affecting education					
					6D.4 actively participating in the political and policy-making context in the service of education					
					6D.5 using legal systems to protect student rights and improve student opportunities					
					The administrator facilitates processes and engages in activities ensuring that: 6P.1 the environment in which schools operate is influenced on behalf of students and their families					
					6P.2 communication occurs among the school community concerning trends, issues, and potential changes in the environment in which schools operate					
					6P.3 there is ongoing dialogue with representatives of diverse community groups					
					6P.4 the school community works within the framework of policies, laws, and regulations enacted by local, state, and federal authorities					
					6P.5 public policy is shaped to provide quality education for students					
					6P.6 lines of communication are developed with decision makers outside the school community					

Adapted from: Interstate School Leaders Licensure Consortium. (1996). *Standards for school leaders*. Washington, DC: Council of Chief State School Officers.

APPENDIX C

Additional Internship Forms

Personalized Internship Plan (PIP)

Name of Intern _____

Name of Mentor(s) _____

Name of Supervisor _____ Date _____

Internship Goal #____ (Complete a separate sheet for each goal.)
(Goal should address an area of improvement identified through the ISLLC self-assessment and three-way conference with intern, mentor, and supervisor. Goals should be stated in broad terms, and several activities will need to be completed over a sustained period of time in order to document successful goal completion. For example, an activity that can be completed in a few days is not of sufficient magnitude to be considered a long-term goal.)

ISLLC Standard(s) Addressed:
(Note all ISLLC standards, and any specific indicators within standards, that address this clinical goal.)

Learning Activities to Address Internship Goal:
   (List all activities that are necessary to practice and refine this skill. In addition to clinical experiences, it also is appropriate to identify course activities, conference attendance, or professional readings to assist the intern in achieving this goal.)

Evidence to Document Attainment of Goal:
   (List any artifacts to be included in the intern's portfolio, documenting successful goal attainment. In addition to artifacts, the intern also should include a paper in the portfolio, reflecting on what she/he has learned and how personal skills have been refined as a result of engaging in this learning goal.)
Target Date for Completion of Goal: _____

_____

Goal Attainment: This goal has been successfully completed.

                                                        Date _____

_____   _____
            Intern   Supervisor

_____   _____
           Mentor   Mentor

Administrative Internship Log

Intern Name _____

Date	Time	Location	Mentor	Intern Activity	ISLLC Standard(s) Addressed	Total Hours
Example: August 21, 2001	7:00–3:30	West Middle School	J. T. Adamson	Seventh-Grade Student-Parent Orientation	2, 3, 4	8 hours
1.						
2.						
3.						
4.						
5.						
6.						
7.						
8.						
9.						
10.						
11.						
12.						
13.						
14.						
15.						
16.						
17.						
18.						
19.						
20.						

Sample Field Experience Log

Intern Name: <u>Dave Jackson</u>   Date: <u>   09/22/01   </u>

Mentor School: <u>ABC Middle School</u>   ISLLC Standard(s) Addressed: <u>3</u>

OBSERVATION:

The past two days I have served as the substitute assistant principal, since Mr. Smith was attending an all-day conference. The majority of my days have been filled with handling student discipline referrals. Yesterday, after the passing period at the end of first period, Mr. Williams, an African American teacher, brought two boys to the office for fighting, Anthony and Tommy. Anthony is an eighth-grade African American student who has a husky build. Although Anthony tends to be rather vocal around the building, he generally obeys school rules and makes average grades. Tommy is a seventh-grade Caucasian student who is small in stature. Tommy is a student in the EMH classroom, and he is usually very quiet and well-mannered.

I separated the boys and spoke with Anthony first. Anthony said he was walking through the narrow hallways and accidentally bumped into Tommy. Tommy pushed him, so Anthony hit him several times. According to Anthony, Tommy tried to push him away but did not fight back. When I spoke with Tommy, he confirmed Anthony's version of the situation. He thought Anthony had pushed him on purpose and, as a result, pushed him back. Tommy did not intend to fight Anthony, but he did say he knew pushing was not the appropriate way to handle the situation. Both boys admitted to me they should not have used physical means to resolve the conflict.

Just to check my facts, I went to Mr. Williams' classroom to hear his eyewitness account. His version was similar to the boys. He said there really was no reason for Tommy to push Anthony. However, he also said that Anthony was overly aggressive, and Mr. Williams had a difficult time getting Anthony to stop.

After considering the situation and consulting with Mrs. Adams, my mentor principal, I decided to assign Tommy a two-day in-school suspension and Anthony a three-day in-school suspension (ISS). According to the school handbook, ISS is assigned when students are in a physical altercation. I spoke with both boys, and both boys generally were accepting of their consequence. Anthony was a bit concerned that he had received one more ISS day than Tommy, but I explained it was due to his aggressive response to the situation. (I also took Tommy's special education placement into consideration, but I did not explain that to Anthony.) I then called their parents, who were accepting of the punishment.

At 7:30 this morning, Anthony's mother, Mrs. James, arrived in the office to speak with me. She seemed to be very concerned about Anthony's progress in school and wanted to discuss the fight with me. Mrs. James explained that Anthony was upset last night, since he felt he and Tommy should have received identical punishments. She then said, "I have to be blunt with you. Is this because my son is Black and the other boy isn't?" I must admit that I was taken aback by this comment, because I had not even taken race into consideration when determining the consequence. However, I did not show my surprise (and, inside I was also a bit angry at this comment).

I explained that the teacher who witnessed the altercation is African American, and he reported that Anthony was the aggressor in the situation. As we continued the discussion, Mrs. James seemed quite satisfied with my explanation. She concluded by saying, "I just had to ask that question, because Anthony felt he was mistreated because of his race." We ended the conference with the understanding that I would call Anthony into the office and provide a more detailed explanation of why his consequence was more severe than Tommy's.

REFLECTION:

The most important lesson I learned today was that, even when race seemingly is not a factor in a given situation, it still needs to be considered. As a Caucasian adult, I simply viewed this situation as a physical altercation between two boys. However, Anthony saw it as a fight between a Black and a White student, and he noticed that he was being disciplined by a White male. I assumed there would be no problem in Anthony's acceptance of his punishment. Actually, Anthony accepted his punishment, but he also felt that Tommy should have received exactly the same consequence. In his mind, the differing punishments were due to his race. Anthony further felt justified in being aggressive, since "Tommy started the fight," even though Tommy had only given him a shove.

My second meeting with Anthony went relatively well, although I suspect that he will continue to believe that he was mistreated in this situation. I don't think I convinced him that the differing consequences were proper.

RECOMMENDATIONS:

After the school day was over, Mrs. Adams and I reviewed the situation and discussed alternative ways of handling the situation. We both agreed that race should be considered when handling disciplinary situations. This does not mean, of course, that differing punishments will be given because of race, but when conflicts occur between students of different races, it is wise to ask the students if any racial issues contributed to the conflict.

This incident pointed out to me that I need to gain additional experiences in working in a diverse setting. In addition to seeking out additional field experiences in urban schools, I also intend to explore possible reading materials and conferences that address diversity and the differing needs of people of color.

Assessment of Intern's Performance
(To be completed by mentor at end of field experiences)

Intern Name _____   Date:_____

Mentor Name _____

Listed below are several questions related to your intern's performance during the field placement in your school or school district. Please use the following scale to rate the intern, according to
the behaviors you observed during this experience. In addition,
please include comments to provide a more detailed description of
his/her performance.

5	4	3	2	1	N/O
Outstanding	Above Average	Average	Below Average	Seriously Lacking	Not Observed

1. How reliable and efficient was the   5   4   3   2   1   N/O
   intern in meeting her/his field
   experience responsibilities?

   Comments:

2. How effective was the intern in   5   4   3   2   1   N/O
   fulfilling the goals identified in
   the Personalized Internship
   Plans (PIPs)?

   Comments:

3. Listed below are the six ISLLC
   standards on which the intern
   must demonstrate his/her
   competency in preparation for
   an administrative career. Please
   note the intern's current
   competence in each of these areas.

Standard 1: A school administrator   5   4   3   2   1   N/O
   is an educational leader who
   promotes the success of all
   students *by facilitating the
   development, articulation,
   implementation, and stewardship
   of a vision of learning that is
   shared and supported by the
   school community.*

   Comments:

Standard 2: A school administrator   5   4   3   2   1   N/O
   is an educational leader who
   promotes the success of all
   students *by advocating, nurturing,
   and sustaining a school culture
   and instructional program
   conducive to student learning
   and staff professional growth.*

   Comments:

Standard 3: A school administrator
   is an educational leader who
   promotes the success of all
   students *by ensuring management*
   of the organization, operations,
   and resources for a safe, efficient,
   and effective learning environment.

   5 4 3 2 1 N/O

   Comments:

Standard 4: A school administrator
   is an educational leader who
   promotes the success of all students
   by collaborating with families and
   community members, responding to
   diverse community interests and
   needs, and mobilizing community
   resources.

   5 4 3 2 1 N/O

   Comments:

Standard 5: A school administrator
   is an educational leader who
   promotes the success of all students
   by acting with integrity, fairness,
   and in an ethical manner.

   5 4 3 2 1 N/O

   Comments:

Standard 6: A school administrator   5   4   3   2   1   N/O
    is an educational leader who
    promotes the success of all
    students *by understanding,*
    responding to, and influencing
    the larger political, social,
    economic, legal, and cultural
    context.

    Comments:

4. Please provide your overall   5   4   3   2   1   N/O
    rating of the intern's leadership
    potential and capability to be
    an effective administrator.

    Comments:

5. Please provide your overall   5   4   3   2   1   N/O
    assessment of the intern's
    performance during this
    internship experience.

    Comments:

6. List at least three significant strengths of the intern, which will
    positively affect her/his ability to be an effective administrator.

7. To assist the intern in developing a continuing professional development plan, please identify at least three growth areas in which improvement is recommended.

8. Please provide any additional information that would assist the university supervisor in assessing the intern's readiness to assume an administrative position.

Mentor Signature _____   Date _____

(Please complete and return this form to the university field supervisor at the end of the internship experience. Although this information is confidential, mentors are encouraged to hold a conference at the conclusion of the internship, in which candid feedback is provided concerning the intern's performance.)

Assessment of Administrative Internship Program

On behalf of our educational administration program and university, we wish to <u>THANK YOU</u> for volunteering to mentor one of our students. Our faculty is continually assessing the quality of the clinical experiences, to ensure that aspiring school leaders are well prepared for their first administrative post. To assist us in this endeavor, we ask you to complete this form and return it to the university field supervisor at the end of your mentee's internship experience.

1. From your experiences supervising interns placed through our program, what knowledge and skills do they bring to this experience that you can attribute to their course experiences in the administrator preparation program?

2. After working with our intern(s), please identify any programmatic areas of deficiency. What administrative knowledge and skills SHOULD the interns be provided through formal coursework that they currently are not learning?

3. Please comment on the number of clinical hours required throughout this program (400 hours). Do you feel this expectation is excessive, about right, or insufficient in providing the intern with the appropriate preparation to assume an administrative position? Why?

4. Would you be willing to supervise another intern for our program in the future? Why or why not?

5. Please list any additional feedback that you wish to provide our educational administration faculty, which will assist us in improving program quality.

Mentor Signature _____   Date _____

REFERENCE LIST

ABC News. (1999, April 29). Violence in U.S. schools [On-line]. Available Internet: http://abcnews.go.com/sections/us/DailyNews/schoolshootings990420.html.

Achilles, C. M., Keedy, J. L., & High, R. M. (1999). The workaday world of the principal: How principals get things done. In L. W. Hughes (Ed.), *The principal as leader* (2nd ed.) (pp. 25–57). Upper Saddle River, NJ: Prentice-Hall.

Achilles, C. M., Reynolds, J. S., & Achilles, S. H. (1997). *Problem analysis: Responding to school complexity.* Larchmont, NY: Eye on Education.

Alexander, K., & Alexander, M. D. (2001). *American public school law* (5th ed.). Belmont, CA: Wadsworth.

Alexander, W. F., & Serfass R. W. (1999). *Futuring tools for strategic quality planning in education.* Milwaukee, WI: ASQ Quality Press.

Allen, M. (2000). Effective induction programs. *The Progress of Education Reform 1999–2001* (Report of the Education Commission of the States), 2(3), 5.

Azzara, J. R. (2000–01). The heart of school leadership. *Educational Leadership, 58*(4), 62–64.

Bagby, R., Bailey, G., Bodensteiner, D., & Lumley, D. (2000). *Plans & policies for technology in education: A compendium* (2nd ed.). Alexandria, VA: National School Boards Association.

Banks, J. A. (2000). The social construction of difference and the quest for educational equity. In R. S. Brandt (Ed.), *2000 ASCD yearbook: Education in a new era* (pp. 21–45). Alexandria, VA: Association for Supervision and Curriculum Development.

Barge, K. J. (1994). *Leadership: Communication skills for organizations and groups.* New York: St. Martin's Press.

Beane, J. A. (1995). Introduction: What is a coherent curriculum? In J. A. Beane (Ed.), *Toward a coherent curriculum* (pp. 1–14). Alexandria, VA: Association for Supervision and Curriculum Development.

Beck, L. G. (1992). Meeting the challenge of the future: The place of a caring ethic in educational administration. *American Journal of Education, 100,* 454–496.

Beck, L. G. (1996). Why ethics? Why now? Thoughts on the moral challenges facing educational leaders. *The School Administrator,* 9(54), 8–11.

Beck, L. W. (1970). Professions, ethics, and professional ethics. In G. L. Immegart & J. M. Burroughs (Eds.), *Ethics and the school administrator* (pp. 43–56). Danville, IL: The Interstate Printers and Publishers.

Bernhardt, V. L. (1998). *Data analysis for comprehensive schoolwide improvement.* Larchmont, NY: Eye on Education.

Blanchard, K., & Peale, N. V. (1988). *The power of ethical management.* New York: William Morrow.

Block, P. (1993). *Stewardship: Choosing service over self-interest.* San Francisco: Berrett-Koehler Publishers.

Bolman, L., & Deal, T. (1991). *Reframing organizations: Artistry, choice, and leadership.* San Francisco: Jossey-Bass.

Bonstingl, J. J. (2001). *Schools of quality: An introduction to Total Quality Management in education* (3rd ed.). Alexandria, VA: Association for Supervision and Curriculum Development.

Boyd, V. (1992). *School context: Bridge or barrier to change?* Austin, TX: Southwest Educational Development Laboratory.

Bracey, G. W. (2000). Tenth annual Bracey report on the condition of public education. *Phi Delta Kappan, 82,* 133–144.

Bradley, M. K., Kallick, B. O., & Regan, H. B. (1991). *The staff development manager: A guide to professional growth.* Needham Heights, MA: Allyn and Bacon.

Bradshaw, L. (1989). Making links. In D. Warwick (Ed.), *Linking schools and industry* (pp. 63–78). Oxford, England: Basil Blackwell.

Brogan, P. (2000). Educating the digital generation. *Educational Leadership, 58*(2), 57–59.

Brooks, J. G., & Brooks, M. G. (1993). *In search for understanding: The case for constructivist classrooms.* Alexandria, VA: Association for Supervision and Curriculum Development.

Brouillette, L. (1999). Instructional improvement. In L. W. Hughes (ed). *The principal as leader* (p. 164). Upper Saddle River, NJ: Prentice Hall, Inc.

Bull, B. L., & McCarthy, M. M. (1995). Reflections on the knowledge base in law and ethics for educational leaders. *Educational Administration Quarterly, 31,* 613–631.

Caine, R. N., & Caine, G. (1991). *Making connections: Teaching and the human brain.* Alexandria, VA: Association for Supervision and Curriculum Development.

Caine, R. N., & Caine, G. (1997). *Unleashing the power of perceptual change.* Alexandria, VA: Association for Supervision and Curriculum Development.

Carr, J. F., & Harris, D. E. (2001). *Succeeding with standards: Linking curriculum, assessment, and action planning.* Alexandria, VA: Association of Supervision and Curriculum Development.

Castallo, R. T., Fletcher, M. R., Rossetti, A. D., & Sekowski, R. W. (Eds.). (1992). *School personnel administration: A practitioner's guide.* Needham Heights, MA: Allyn and Bacon.

Clark, D. C., & Clark, S. N. (1996). Better preparation of educational leaders. *Educational Researcher, 25*(8), 18–20.

Combs, A., Miser, A., & Whitaker, K. (1999). *On becoming a school leader: A person-centered challenge.* Alexandria, VA: Association for Supervision and Curriculum Development.

Cook, W. J. (1995). *Strategic planning for America's schools* (Rev. ed.). Arlington, VA: American Association of School Administrators.

Cordeiro, P. A., Krueger, J. A., Parks, D., Restine, N., & Wilton, P. T. (1993). Taking stock: Learnings gleaned from universities participating in the Danforth program. In M. M. Milstein & associates (Eds.), *Changing the way we prepare educational leaders* (pp. 17–38). Newbury Park, CA: Corwin.

Cordeiro, P., & Smith-Sloan, E. (1995, April). *Apprenticeships for administrative interns: Learning to talk like a principal.* Paper presented at the annual meeting of the American Educational Research Association, San Francisco. (ERIC Document Reproduction Service No. ED 385 014).

Costa, A. L., & Kallick, B. (Eds.). (2000). *Discovering and exploring habits of mind.* Alexandria, VA: Association for Supervision and Curriculum Development.

Cuban, L. (1996). Reforming the practice of educational administration through managing dilemmas. In S. L. Jacobson, E. S. Hickcox, and R. B. Stevenson (Eds.), *School administration: Persistent dilemmas in preparation and practice* (pp. 3–17). Westport, CT: Praeger.

Cunningham, W. C., & Gresso, D. W. (1993). *Cultural leadership: The culture of excellence in education.* Needham Heights, MA: Allyn and Bacon.

Cunningham, W. G., & Cordeiro, P. A. (2000). *Educational administration: A problem-based approach.* Needham Heights, MA: Allyn and Bacon.

Dalaker, J., & Naifeh, M. (1998). *Poverty in the United States: 1997* (U.S. Bureau of the Census, Current Population Reports, series P60-201). Washington, DC: U.S. Government Printing Office.

Danielson, C. (1996). *Enhancing professional practice: A framework for teaching.* Alexandria, VA: Association for Supervision and Curriculum Development.

Danielson, C., & McGreal, T. (2000). *Teacher evaluation to enhance professional practice.* Alexandria, VA: Association for Supervision and Curriculum Development.

Daresh, J. C., & Playko, M. A. (1992). *The professional development of school administrators: Preservice, induction, and inservice applications.* Needham Heights, MA: Allyn and Bacon.

Darling-Hammond, L. (1997). *The right to learn: A blueprint for creating schools that work.* San Francisco: Jossey-Bass.

Davis, M., Hawley, P., McMullan, B., & Spilka, G. (1997). *Design as a catalyst for learning.* Alexandria, VA: Association for Supervision and Curriculum Development.

Day, C. W. (2001). Rethinking school design. *Learning by Design, 10,* 4–6.

Deal, T. E., & Peterson, K. D. (1999). *Shaping school culture: The heart of leadership.* San Francisco: Jossey-Bass.

Dembowski, F., with Ekstrom, C. D. (1999). *Effective school district management: A self-review instrument and guide.* Arlington, VA: American Association of School Administrators.

Deming, W. E. (1986). *Out of Crisis.* Cambridge, MA: MIT Center for Advanced Engineering Studies.

Doud, J. L., & Keller, E. P. (1998). *A ten-year study: The K–8 principal in 1998.* Alexandria, VA: National Association of Elementary School Principals.

Drake, T. L., & Roe, W. H. (1999). *The principalship* (5th ed.). Upper Saddle River, NJ: Prentice-Hall.

Dryfoos, J. G. (1994). *Full-service schools: A revolution in health and social services for children, youth, and families.* San Francisco: Jossey-Bass.

DuFour, R., & Eaker, R. (1998). *Professional learning communities at work: Best practices for enhancing student achievement.* Bloomington, IN: National Educational Service.

Dunklee, D. R. (2000). *If you want to lead, not just manage: A primer for principals.* Thousand Oaks, CA: Corwin.

Eastin, D. (1999). Getting to the heart of the matter: Education in the 21st century. In D. D. Marsh (Ed.), *1999 ASCD yearbook: Preparing our schools for the 21st century* (pp. 13–24). Alexandria, VA: Association for Supervision and Curriculum Development.

Edmonds, R. (1979). Effective schools for the urban poor. *Educational Leadership, 37*(1), 15–18, 20–24.

Elias, M., Zins, J., Weissberg, R., Frey, K., Greenberg, M., Haynes, N., Kessler, R., Schwab-Stone, M., & Shriver, T. (1997). *Promoting social and emotional learning: Guidelines for educators.* Alexandria, VA: Association for Supervision and Curriculum Development.

Elmore, R. (2000). *Building a new structure for school leadership.* Washington, DC: Albert Shanker Institute.

English, F. W. (2000). *Deciding what to teach and test: Developing, aligning, and auditing the curriculum* (Millenium ed.). Newbury Park, CA: Corwin.

English, F. W., & Larson, R. L. (1996). *Curriculum management for educational and social service organizations* (2nd ed.). Springfield, IL: Charles C. Thomas.

English, F. W., & Steffy, B. E. (1997). Using film to teach leadership in educational administration. *Educational Administration Quarterly, 33,* 107–115.

Enomoto, E. K. (1997). Negotiating the ethics of care and justice. *Educational Administration Quarterly, 33*, 351–370.

Epstein, J. L. (1995). School/family/community partnerships: Caring for the children we share. *Phi Delta Kappan 76*, 701–12.

Epstein, J. L., Coates, L., Salina, K. C., Sanders, M. G., & Simon, B. S. (1997). *School, family, and community partnerships: Your handbook for action.* Thousand Oaks, CA: Corwin.

Fenstermaker, W. C. (1996). The ethical dimension of superintendent decision making: A study of AASA members finds a lack of awareness of association's code of ethics. *The School Administrator, 9*(54), 16–24.

Fenwick, T., & Parsons, J. (2000). *The art of evaluation.* Toronto: Tompson Educational Publishing.

Ferrandino, V. L. (2001). Challenges for 21st-century elementary school principals. *Phi Delta Kappan, 82*, 440–442.

Fink, E., & Resnick, L. (2001). Developing principals as instructional leaders. *Phi Delta Kappan, 82*, 598–606.

Fisher, R., Ury, W., & Patton, B. (1991). *Getting to yes: Negotiating agreement without giving in.* New York: Penguin Books.

French, P. A. (1997). Moral principles, rules, and policies. In J. L. Paul, N. H. Berger, P. G. Osnes, Y. G. Martinez, & W. C. Morse (Eds.), *Ethics and decision making in local schools* (pp. 85–97). Baltimore: Paul H. Brookes.

Gallagher, D. R., Bagin, D., & Kindred, L. W. (1997). *The school and community relations* (6th ed.). Needham Heights, MA: Allyn and Bacon.

Gardner, H. (1991). *The unschooled mind: How children think and how schools should teach.* New York: Basic Books.

Gardner, H. (1999). *Intelligence reframed: Multiple intelligences for the 21st century.* New York: Basic Books.

Girod, M., & Cavanaugh, S. (2001). Technology as an agent of change in teacher practice. *Technical Horizons in Education Journal, 28*(9), 40–47.

Glatthorn, A. A. (1994). Constructivism: Implications for curriculum. *International Journal of Educational Reform, 3*, 449–455.

Glickman, C. D. (2000–01). Holding sacred ground: The impact of standardization. *Educational Leadership, 58*(4), 46–51.

Goens, G. A. (1996). Shared decisions, empowerment, and ethics: A mission impossible for district leaders? *The School Administrator, 9*(54), 12–14.

Goleman, D. (1995). *Emotional intelligence.* New York: Bantam.

Goodlad, J. (1990). *Teachers for our nation's schools.* San Francisco: Jossey-Bass.

Goodstein, L., Nolan, T., & Pfeiffer, J. W. (1992). *Applied strategic planning: How to develop a plan that really works.* New York: McGraw-Hill.

Greer, J. T., & Short, P. M. (1999). Restructured schools. In L. W. Hughes (Ed.), *The principal as leader* (2nd ed.) (pp. 89–104). Upper Saddle River, NJ: Prentice-Hall.

Griffiths, D. E., Stout, R. T., & Forsyth, P. B. (Eds.). (1988a). *Leaders for America's schools: The report and papers of the National Commission on Excellence in Educational Administration.* Berkeley, CA: McCutchan.

Griffiths, D. E., Stout, R. T., & Forsyth, P. B. (1988b). The preparation of educational administrators. In D. E. Griffiths, R. T. Stout, P. B. Forsyth (Eds.), *Leaders for America's schools: The report and papers of the National Commission on Excellence in Educational Administration* (pp. 284–304). Berkeley, CA: McCutchan.

Grobe, T., Curnan, S. P., & Melchior, A. (1993). *Synthesis of existing knowledge and practice in the field of educational partnerships* Washington, DC. U.S. Department of Education, Office of Educational Research and Improvement.

Guskey, T. R. (2000). *Evaluating professional development.* Thousand Oaks, CA: Corwin.

Hackmann, D. G., & English, F. W. (2001, Spring). About straw horses and administrator shortages: Confronting the pragmatics of the administrative internship. *UCEA Review, 50*(2), 12–15.

Hackmann, D. G., Russell, F. S., & Elliott, R. J. (1999). Making administrative internships meaningful. *Planning and Changing, 30,* 2–14.

Hackmann, D. G., Tack, M. W., & Pokay, P. A. (1999). Results-oriented school improvement: Lessons from practice. *International Journal of Educational Reform, 8*(1), 8–14.

Hart, A. W., & Pounder, D. G. (1999). Reinventing preparation programs: A decade of activity. In J. Murphy and P. B. Forsyth (Eds.), *Educational administration: A decade of reform* (pp. 115–151). Thousand Oaks, CA: Corwin.

Henry, M. E. (1996). *Parent-school collaboration: Feminist organizational structures and school leadership.* Albany, NY: State University of New York Press.

Hickman, C. R., & Silva, M. A. (1984). *Creating excellence: Managing corporate culture, strategy, and change in a new age.* New York: New America Library.

Hodgkinson, H. (1991). Reform versus reality. *Phi Delta Kappan, 73*, 8–16.

Holloway, J. H. (2000). Healthy buildings: Successful students. *Educational Leadership, 57*(6), p. 88–89.

The Holmes Group. (1990). *Tomorrow's schools: Principles for the design of professional development schools.* East Lansing, MI: Author.

Hoyle, J. R. (1995). *Leadership and futuring: Making visions happen.* Thousand Oaks, CA: Corwin.

Hughes, L. (1999). *The principal as leader* (2nd ed.). Upper Saddle River, NJ: Prentice-Hall.

Hunter, M. C. (1982). *Mastery teaching.* Thousand Oaks, CA: Corwin.

Immegart, G. L., & Burroughs, J. M. (1970). *Ethics and the school administrator.* Danville, IL: The Interstate Printers and Publishers.

Interstate School Leaders Licensure Consortium. (1996). *Standards for school leaders.* Washington, DC: Council of Chief State School Officers.

Jackson, A. W., & Davis, G. A. (2000). *Turning points 2000: Educating adolescents in the 21st century.* New York: Teachers College Press.

Jacobs, H. H. (1997). *Mapping the big picture: Integrating curriculum and assessment K–12.* Alexandria, VA: Association for Supervision and Curriculum Development.

Jacobson, S. L. (1996). School leadership in an age of reform: New directions in principal preparation. *International Journal of Educational Reform, 5*(3), 271–277.

Jensen, E. (1998). *Teaching with the brain in mind.* Alexandria, VA: Association for Supervision and Curriculum Development.

Jensen, M. C. (1987). *How to recruit, select, and retain the very best teachers.* Eugene, OR: ERIC Clearinghouse on Educational Management.

Jones, J. J., & Walters, D. L. (1994). *Human resource management in education.* Lancaster, PA: Technomic.

Jung, C. (1923). *Psychological types* (H. G. Baynes, Trans.). New York: Harcourt Brace.

Kaufmann, F. X., Majone, G., & Ostrom, V. (1986). *Guidance, control, and evaluation in the public sector.* Berlin: deGruyter.

Keefe, J., & Jenkins, J. (1997). *Instruction and the learning environment.* Larchmont, NY: Eye on Education.

Kidder, R. M. (1995). *How good people make tough choices.* New York: William Morrow.

Kirst, M. W. (1991). Improving children's services: Overcoming barriers, creating new opportunities. *Phi Delta Kappan, 72,* 615–618.

Kouzes, J., & Posner, B. (1993). *Credibility: How leaders gain it and lose it, why people demand it.* San Francisco: Jossey-Bass.

Krueger, J. A., & Milstein, M. M. (1995). Promoting excellence in educational leadership: What really matters? *Planning and Changing, 26,* 148–167.

Lam, S. F. (1997). *How the family influences children's academic achievement.* New York: Garland Publishing.

Lambert, L. (1998). *Building leadership capacity in schools.* Alexandria, VA: Association for Supervision and Curriculum Development.

Larabee, D. F. (2000). Resisting educational standards. *Phi Delta Kappan, 82,* 28–33.

Lecos, M. A. (1997). The promise of professional development schools. *Principal, 77*(1), 14, 16, 18–19.

Leithwood, K., Jantzi, D., Coffin, G., & Wilson, P. (1996). Preparing school leaders: What works? *Journal of School Leadership, 6,* 316–342.

Levine, S. L. (1989). *Promoting adult growth in schools.* Needham Heights, MA: Allyn and Bacon.

Levinson, E., & Grohe, B. (2001). Funding: It's time to be sufficient. *Converge, 4*(4), 54–59.

Lezotte, L. (1997). *Learning for all.* Okemos, MI: Effective School Products.

Lickona, T. (1993). The return of character education. *Educational Leadership, 51*(3), 6–11.

Lieberman, A. (1992). School/university collaboration: A view from the inside. *Phi Delta Kappan, 74,* 147–156.

Lugaila, T. A. (1998). *Marital status and living arrangements: March 1998* (update). (U.S. Department of Commerce Publication No. P20-514). Washington, DC: U.S. Census Bureau.

Lumley, D., & Bailey, G. D. (1997). *Planning for technology: A guidebook for teachers, technology leaders, and school administrators.* Bloomington, IN: National Educational Service.

McDonald, R. (1980). *The problems of beginning teachers: A crisis in training.* Princeton, NJ: Educational Testing Service.

McKerrow, K. (1997). Ethical administration: An oxymoron? *Journal of School Leadership, 7*(2), 210–225.

Means, B. (2000). Technology in America's schools: Before and after Y2K. In R. S. Brandt (Ed.). *Education in a new era* (pp. 185–210). Alexandria, VA: Association for Supervision and Curriculum Development.

Mijares, A. (1996). Escaping the malaise: First-hand guidance for ethical behavior. *The School Administrator, 9*(54), 26–29.

Miller, E. (1995, November/December). Shared decision-making by itself doesn't make for better decisions. *The Harvard Education Letter, 11*(6), 1–4.

Milstein, M. (1990). Rethinking the clinical aspects in administrative preparation: From theory to practice. In S. L. Jacobson & J. Conway (Eds.), *Educational leadership in an age of reform* (pp. 119–130). New York: Longman.

Milstein, M. M., and associates. (1993). *Changing the way we prepare educational leaders.* Newbury Park, CA: Corwin.

Milstein, M. M., Bobroff, B. M., & Restine, L. N. (1991). *Internship programs in educational administration: A guide to preparing educational leaders.* New York: Teachers College Press.

Milstein, M. M., & Krueger, J. A. (1997). Improving educational administration preparation programs: What we have learned over the past decade. *Peabody Journal of Education, 72*(2), 100–116.

Morgan, G. (1997). *Images of organization* (2nd ed.). Thousand Oaks, CA: Sage.

Murphy, J. (1992). *The landscape of leadership preparation: Reframing the education of school administrators.* Newbury Park, CA: Corwin.

Murphy, J. (1995). *School-based management.* Thousand Oaks, CA: Corwin.

Nanus, B. (1992). *Visionary leadership.* San Francisco: Jossey-Bass.

National Association of Secondary School Principals. (1996). *Breaking ranks: Changing an American institution.* Reston, VA: Author.

National Commission on Excellence in Education. (1983). *A nation at risk: The imperative for educational reform.* Washington, DC: U.S. Department of Education.

National Policy Board for Educational Administration. (1989). *Improving the preparation of school administrators: An agenda for reform.* Charlottesville, VA: University of Virginia.

National Policy Board for Educational Administration. (1993). *Principals for our changing schools: The knowledge and skill base.* Lancaster, PA: Technomic.

National Policy Board for Educational Administration. (2001). *New NCATE standards for educational administration.* [On-line]. Available Internet: http://www.npbea.org/projects/NCATE_materials.html.

National PTA. (1997). *National standards for parent/family involvement programs.* Chicago, IL: Author.

National Staff Development Council. (2000). *Learning to lead, leading to learn.* Oxford, OH: Author. [On-line]. Available Internet: www.nsdc.org.

National STW Learning and Information Center. (1999, May). *What is school-to-work?* Available Internet: http://stw.ed.gov/general/whatis.htm.

Neuman, M., & Simmons, W. (2000). Leadership for student learning. *Phi Delta Kappan, 82,* 8–12.

Newmann, F., & Wehlage, G. (1995). *Successful school restructuring: A report to the public and educators by the Center for Restructuring Schools.* Madison, WI: University of Wisconsin.

Newmann, F., Secada, W., & Wehlage, G. (1995). *A guide to authentic instruction and assessment: Vision, standards and scoring.* Madison, WI: Wisconsin Center for Education Research.

O'Hair, M. J., & Spaulding, A. M. (1997). Institutionalizing public relations through interpersonal communication: Listening, nonverbal, and conflict-resolution skills. In T. J. Kowalski (Ed.), *Public relations in educational organizations: Practice in an age of information and reform* (pp.157–185). Englewood Cliffs, NJ: Prentice-Hall.

Oliva, P., & Pawlas, G. (2001). *Supervision for today's schools* (6th ed.). New York: John Wiley & Sons.

Orlich, D. C. (1989). *Staff development: Enhancing human potential.* Needham Heights, MA: Allyn and Bacon.

Palestini, R. H. (1999). *Educational administration: Leading with mind and heart.* Lancaster, PA: Technomic.

Parks, S. D. (1993). Is it too late? Young adults and the formation of professional ethics. In T. R. Piper, M. C. Gentile, & S. D. Parks (Eds.), *Can ethics be taught?* (pp. 13–72). Boston: Harvard Business School.

Patterson, J. (1997). *Coming clean about organizational change: Leadership in the real world.* Arlington, VA: American Association of School Administrators.

Patterson, J. L. (1993). *Leadership for tomorrow's schools.* Alexandria, VA: Association for Supervision and Curriculum Development.

Patterson, J. L., Purkey, S. C., & Parker, J. V. (1986). *Productive school systems for a nonrational world.* Alexandria, VA: Association for Supervision and Curriculum Development.

Paul, J. L., Berger, N. H., & Osnes, P. G. (1997). Ethics, research, and school-based decision making. In J. L. Paul, N. H. Berger, P. G. Osnes, Y. G. Martinez, & W. C. Morse (Eds.), *Ethics and decision making in local schools.* Baltimore, MD: Paul H. Brookes Publishing.

Paulter, A. (1990). *A review of UCEA member institutions' clinical experiences/internships/field experiences for educational leaders.* Paper presented at the annual meeting of the University Council for Educational Administration, Pittsburgh, PA.

Peper, J. B. (1988). Clinical education for school superintendents and principals: The missing link. In D. E. Griffiths, R. T. Stout, P. B. Forsyth (Eds.), *Leaders for America's schools: The report and papers of the National Commission on Excellence in Educational Administration* (pp. 360–366). Berkeley, CA: McCutchan.

Phelan, P., Davidson, A. L., & Yu, H. C. (1993). Students' multiple words: Navigating the borders of family, peer, and school cultures. In P. Phelan & A. L. Davidson (Ed.), *Renegotiating cultural diversity in American schools* (pp. 52–88). New York: Teachers College Press.

Piper, T. R. (1993). Rediscovery of purpose: The genesis of the leadership, ethics, and corporate responsibility initiative. In T. R. Piper, M. C. Gentile, & S. D. Parks (Eds.), *Can ethics be taught?* (pp. 1–12). Boston: Harvard Business School.

Pipho, C. (2000). Governing the American dream of universal public education. In R. S. Brandt (Ed.), *2000 ASCD yearbook: Education in a new era* (pp. 5–19). Alexandria, VA: Association for Supervision and Curriculum Development.

Pounder, D. G. (1995). Theory to practice: A description and multidimensional evaluation of the University of Utah's educational administration Ed.D. program. (ERIC Document Reproduction Service No. ED 384 113).

Raywid, M. A. (1986). Some moral dimensions of administrative theory and practice. *Issues in Education, 4*(2), 151–166.

Razik, T. A., & Swanson, A. D. (2001). *Fundamental concepts of educational leadership* (2nd ed.). Upper Saddle River, NJ: Prentice-Hall.

Reynolds, J. C. (1997). Designing the internship for small and large schools. *Rural Educator, 18*(3), 12–15.

Rockman, S. (1998). *Leader's guide to education technology.* Alexandria, VA: National School Boards Association.

Rose, L. C. & Gallup, A. M. (2000). The 32nd annual Phi Delta Kappa/Gallup poll of the public's attitudes toward the public schools. *Phi Delta Kappan, 82,* 41–58.

Russell, J. F., & Flynn, R. B. (1992). *School-university collaboration.* Bloomington, IN: Phi Delta Kappa Educational Foundation.

Ryan, K. (1980). *Biting the apple: Account of first year teachers.* New York: Longman.

Sagor, R. (1992). *How to conduct collaborative action research.* Alexandria, VA: Association for Supervision and Curriculum Development.

Saint, S., & Lawson, J. R. (1994). *Rules for reaching consensus: A modern approach to the age-old process of making decisions.* San Diego, CA: Pfeiffer & Company.

Schein, E. H. (1984). *Organizational culture and leadership.* San Francisco: Jossey-Bass.

Schiffbauer, P. (2000). A checklist for safe schools. *Educational Leadership, 57*(6), 72–74.

Schmoker, M. (1999). *Results: The key to continuous school improvement* (2nd ed.). Alexandria, VA: Association for Supervision and Curriculum Development.

Schneider, T., Walker, H., & Sprague, J. (2000). *Building safety into schools.* Eugene, OR: ERIC Clearinghouse on Educational Management.

Schwahn, C., & Spady, W. (1998). *Total leaders: Applying the best future-focused change strategies to education.* Arlington, VA: American Association of School Administrators.

Schwartz, J. B. (1990). Will your school-business partnership stand the test of time? *NASSP Bulletin, 74*(529), 99–102.

Senge, P. M. (1990). *The fifth discipline: The art & practice of the learning organization.* New York: Doubleday.

Sergiovanni, T. J. (1992). *Moral leadership: Getting to the heart of school improvement.* San Francisco: Jossey-Bass.

Sergiovanni, T. J. (1994). *Building community in schools*. San Francisco: Jossey-Bass.

Sergiovanni, T. J. (1996). *Leadership for the schoolhouse: How is it different? Why is it important?* San Francisco: Jossey-Bass.

Sergiovanni, T. J. (2001). *The principalship: A reflective practice perspective* (4th ed.). Needham Heights, MA: Allyn and Bacon.

Sergiovanni, T. J., Burlingame, M., Coombs, F. S., & Thurston, P. W. (1999). *Educational governance and administration* (4th ed.). Boston, MA: Allyn and Bacon.

Seyfarth, J. T. (1999). *The principal: New leadership for new challenges.* Upper Saddle River, NJ: Prentice-Hall.

Sichel, B. A. (1993). Ethics committees and teacher ethics. In K. Strike & P. L. Ternasky (Eds.), *Ethics for professionals in education: Perspectives for preparation and practice* (pp. 162–175). New York: Teachers College Press.

Speck, M., & Knipe, C. (2000). *Why can't we get it right? Professional development in our schools.* Thousand Oaks, CA: Corwin Press

Sperry, D. J. (1999). *Working in a legal & regulatory environment: A handbook for school leaders.* Larchmont, NY: Eye on Education.

Spring, J. (1993*). Conflict of interests: The politics of American education* (2nd ed.). New York: Longman.

Starratt, R. J. (1991). Building an ethical school: A theory for practice in educational leadership. *Educational Administration Quarterly, 27*(2), 185–202.

Strike, K. A., Haller, E. J., & Soltis, J. F. (1998). *The ethics of school administration* (2nd ed.). New York: Teachers College Press.

Stringer, E. T. (1996). *Action research: A handbook for practitioners.* Thousand Oaks, CA: Sage Publications.

Sylwester, R. (2000). Unconscious emotions, conscious feelings. *Educational Leadership, 58*(3), 20–24.

Tenbusch, J. P. (1998, March). Teaching the teachers: Technology staff development that works. *Electronic School*, A16–A20.

Thompson, D. C., & Wood, R. C. (1998). *Money and schools: A handbook for practitioners.* Larchmont, NY: Eye on Education.

Thompson, S. (2001). The school leadership challenge. *Strategies for School System Leaders on District-Level Change* (An issues series by the Panasonic Foundation in cooperation with the American Association of School Administrators), 8(1), 1–2.

Tomlinson, C. A. (1999). *The differentiated classroom: Responding to the needs of all learners.* Alexandria, VA: Association for Supervision and Curriculum Development.

Ubben, G. C., Hughes, L. W., & Norris, C. J. (2001). *The principal: Creative leadership for effective schools* (4th ed.). Needham Heights, MA: Allyn and Bacon.

Uchida, D., Cetron, M., & McKenzie, F. (1996). *Preparing students for the 21st century.* Arlington, VA: American Association of School Administrators.

University Council for Educational Administration. (2001). *Policy governing membership in UCEA.* [On-line.] Available Internet: http://www.ucea.org.

Valentine, E. P. (1997). *Strategic management in education* (2nd ed.). Baltimore: The Pasteur Center for Strategic Management.

Weller, L. D., & Weller, S. (2000). *Quality human resources leadership: A principal's handbook.* Lanham, MD: Scarecrow Press.

Wilbur, F. P., & Lambert, L. M. (1995). *Linking America's Schools and colleges: Guide to partnerships and national directory* (2nd ed.). Washington, DC: America's Association for Higher Education.

Williams, B. (1999). Diversity and education for the 21st century. In D. D. Marsh (Ed.), *1999 ASCD yearbook: Preparing our schools for the 21st century* (pp. 89–114). Alexandria, VA: Association for Supervision and Curriculum Development.

Williams, R. B. (1993). *More than 50 ways to build team consensus.* Palatine, IL: IRI/Skylight Publishing.

Wiseman, D. L. & Nason, P. L. (1995). The nature of interactions in a field-based teacher education experience. *Action in Teacher Education, 17*(3), 1–12.

Wyman, W. (2001). Teaching quality: School and teacher leadership. *The Progress of Education Reform 1999–2001* (Report of the Education Commission of the States), 2(4), 3.

Yankelovich, D. (1991). *Coming to public judgment: Making democracy work in a complex world.* Syracuse, NY: Syracuse University Press.

Zepeda, S. J. (1999). *Staff development: Practices that promote leadership in learning communities.* Larchmont, NY: Eye on Education.

AUTHOR INDEX

SUBJECT INDEX

accountability, 50–51
achievement. *See* student
    achievement
action plan, 51–52
action research, 52–53, 73, 80
administrative mentor, 206
administrator preparation programs:
    decline of, 2; recommendations
    for improving, 2–3
ambiguity, tolerance for, 183
assessing instruction and learning,
    68–70
assessment, 66–67; authentic, 67;
    formative, 67; student, 69;
    summative, 67
attendance. *See* student
    attendance
authentic performance, 192

bargaining. *See* reconciling
    differences

basic needs, 144
benchmarks, 37–38, 48, 51
benefit maximization, principle of,
    159
beyond the internship, 203–6
brain research, 74
budget process 113

celebrate success, 54
change: leading, 48–50;
    organizational, 49; process 61;
    reactions to, 48
classroom: climate, 68;
    environment, positive, 67–68;
    management, 111
clinical activities, 201; draft
    internship plan, 29; final
    personalized internship plan,
    30; portfolio development, 30;
    reflective logs, 30; self
    assessment, 28–29; supervisor

ABOUT THE AUTHORS

Donald G. Hackmann is currently associate professor and program coordinator of educational administration in the Department of Educational Leadership and Policy Studies at Iowa State University. He has more than fifteen years of experience in public schools in Missouri and Illinois, having served as a middle-level teacher and middle/junior high school and secondary school administrator. He earned a Doctor of Education degree in General School Administration from the University of Missouri–Columbia.

Donna M. Schmitt-Oliver is professor emeritus of educational leadership at Eastern Michigan University, where she served for more than twenty-five years as both a professor and administrator at the College of Education. She has taught in public schools in Michigan and Wisconsin, and is currently the assistant superintendent for curriculum and instruction with the Monroe County (Michigan) Intermediate School District. Her Doctor of Education degree in educational leadership is from Western Michigan University.

Jaclynn C. Tracy earned her Ph.D. in adult and continuing education from Michigan State University. She is currently professor of educational leadership and interim head of the Department of Leadership and Counseling at Eastern Michigan University. She has served as internship director for the past eight years and the coordinator of off-campus programming for the EMU College of Education. Dr. Tracy has taught in the public schools and served in central office administration for fifteen years.